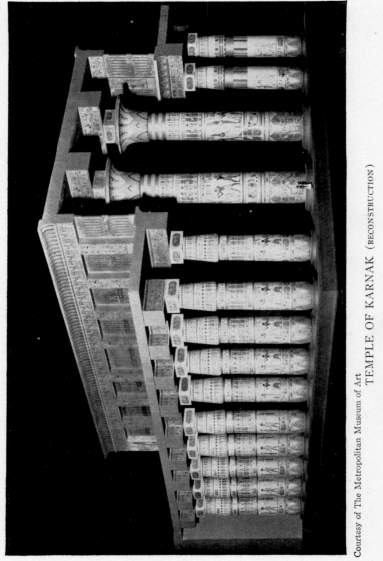

TEMPLE OF KARNAK (RECONSTRUCTION)

THE
HEBREW HERITAGE

A Study of Israel's Cultural and Spiritual Origins

CHARLES W. HARRIS
Professor of Religion, Lafayette College

THE ABINGDON PRESS

NEW YORK   CINCINNATI   CHICAGO

HARRIS
THE HEBREW HERITAGE

Copyright, 1935, by
CHARLES W. HARRIS

Printed in the United States of America

CONTENTS

PART I

THE GENESIS AND DEVELOPMENT OF EARLY CULTURES

PART II

THE RISE AND GROWTH OF THE HEBREW NATION

CONTENTS

PART III

RELIGIOUS AND MORAL VALUES IN HEBREW PROPHECY

PART IV

RELIGIOUS THOUGHT IN NEIGHBORING STATES

PART V

THE CONQUEST OF IDEAS

ILLUSTRATIONS AND MAPS

ABBREVIATIONS

A. V.—Authorized Version.

Cf.—Compare.

Circa (c)—About.

Cit.—Citation.

C. of T.—*Corridors of Time.*

et al—And others.

f. (ff.)—Following.

Ibid.—The same.

I. C. C.—*International Critical Commentary.*

New Tr.—New Translation.

O. I. C.—*Oriental Institute Communications.*

O. T.—Old Testament.

O. T. Amer. Tr.—*The Old Testament An American Translation.*

R. V.—Revised Version (English edition).

Supra—Above.

Tr.—Translated.

Author's Note: The biblical citations are chiefly from the Revised
Version, English edition. In some instances the author has followed
The Old Testament An American Translation, edited by J. M. P.
Smith, by courtesy of the University of Chicago Press. More rarely he
has used his own translatión.

The usage of the divine name "Yahweh" is followed in the text, while
the citations contain the word "Lord."

SUMMARY OF CONTENTS

CHAPTER I

EARLY CULTURE OF MANKIND

Antiquity of man traced through the weapons and tools he fashioned—Found in river valleys and in caves—These implements can be arranged in cultural groups indicating their sequence—Names borrowed from the locality where first important finds were made—Early types of man from the beginning of the Pleistocene Period—Neanderthal man associated with the Mousterian culture surviving until the true man arrives—Upper Paleolithic men distinguished by implements of improved type—The hunters of the period were artists—Was early man religious?—The Neolithic age—The development of religion.

CHAPTER II

THE RELIGION OF THE NOMAD

The present-day Arab, nomadic by instinct and necessity although stationary in habits of thought and customs, represents the race which from ancient times has occupied his peninsular home—"The Semitic world"—Evidence in the Old Testament of a Hebrew nomadic stage—Sacred trees thought to be the abode of divine beings—Not at first condemned as idolatrous shrines but reformers in the eighth century decree their destruction—Sacred fountains—Origin of the belief—Biblical examples—Sacred stones—Belief of the supernatural resident in inanimate objects is called animism—The most ancient sanctuaries—Worship of ancestors.

CHAPTER III

SEMITIC ORIGINS

The Semitic world peopled with gods designated as local deities, as demons and spirits of the field—Day of Atonement bore witness to ancient belief in a field deity—Prevalence and meaning of totemism—Did the early Semite pass through a totemic stage?—A religion with elements of sacrifice, magic, ritual—Circumcision, its origin, its meaning, upon whom practiced—The ritual Decalogue of Exodus 34, its commands and taboos—The law of blood revenge, devolving upon the clan—Hospitality, its extent and limitations.

CHAPTER IV

THE SUMERIANS

Influence of Babylonia and Egypt in neighboring states and upon posterity—Sumerians first to attain civilization in Babylonia—Limited area of their state—Two political entities, Sumer and Akkad, giving their name to the country—Later designations are Shinar, Babylonia, Mesopotamia, or Land of the Two Rivers, and the modern Irak—Staple products—Who were the Sumerians? Political history—Third dynasty of Ur—Rise of Babylon—Hammurabi—Sumerian state comes to an end in 1720 B. C.—Gods of Sumer and Akkad, temples and ritual.

CHAPTER V

THE STORY OF EXCAVATION AND DECIPHERMENT

The oblivion in which Sumerian civilization was buried—Sumer and Akkad completely absorbed by the Babylonian state, as it in turn was eclipsed by Assyria—Excavations were begun in the vicinity of Nineveh by Botta—Discoveries in Khorsabad—Layard uncovered on the site of Nineveh the remains of a royal library of 30,000 tablets—What cuneiform is—Rawlinson works independently in Persia at Behistun—Systematic excavation was begun in 1872 by societies—Work of translation continued—A Chaldean genesis—Importance of the epoch.

CHAPTER VI

SUMERIAN MYTHS AND CULTS

Assyrian literary finds prove to be transcripts of Babylonian writings—But we must look for their originals among early Sumerians—Origin of nature myths—How kept alive—Similarity of myths and ritual in the Near East suggest a "pattern myth" from which the rest borrowed—Babylonians had two accounts of creation—Their version of the Flood—Attitude toward the future life—The seasonal gods Tammuz and Ishtar—The ritual by which they were served—Recent excavations of sites of Sumerian cities—Amazing discoveries in predynastic cemeteries of Ur—Evi-

date of the Exodus are problematical—Moses, the founder of the
nation, born and bred in Egypt, his Egyptian name, his learning,
his exile, and marriage are well known—His call to deliver his
people coexistent with the revelation of God as Yahweh—The
Passover—The Passage of the Red Sea—The stay at Sinai and
what transpired there—Yahweh becomes the God of Israel—The
Covenant is ratified, the moral Decalogue is made known—The
wilderness wanderings—Summary.

CHAPTER XII

ISRAEL'S CULTURAL HERITAGE

Egypt a dominating influence in Hebrew affairs before and
after the Exodus—Egyptians governed Palestine between 1600
and 1200 B. C.—After 1200 B. C. there were occasional examples
of Egyptian political influence in Palestine, the contact of travelers to and from Egypt, the constant stream of trade—Nature of
the influence religious, moral, artistic, and political—Examples
deduced are Serpent and Bull worship—The Cult of the Ark
which in appearance resembled the Egyptian shrine; the religious
processions strikingly similar—The Temple of Egyptian design;
its furniture recalling that belonging to Egyptian temples—The
rite of circumcision—The Cult of the Dead—Hebrew view of
the future alternated between the Babylonian despair and Egyptian hope—Diffusion of Egyptian culture in Palestine shown by
recent excavations in Samaria, Megiddo, and Bethshan.

CHAPTER XIII

THE LAND OF PROMISE

Palestine's limited area—The protective barriers of sea and
desert—The natural features from west to east are the Maritime
Plain; the Shepelah, or hill country; the Central Mountain Range,
the Jordan and the Dead Sea, the Eastern Tableland—Characteristics of each—Climate, soil, and products, environmental
factors determining the development of the peoples of the land—
The roads were arteries of trade or highways for armies, and
made the country accessible to cultural and religious influences
—Races of Palestine, Paleolithic and Neolithic followed in historic times by successive migrations, namely, the Amorites, the
Canaanites, and the Aramaeans—Outsiders are Philistines, Hittites, and governing races of which the earliest are Babylonian

and Egyptian—Babylonian influence most continuous and therefore highly influential.

CHAPTER XIV

THE CULTURE AND CULTS OF CANAAN

The Canaanites, like the Hebrews, were nomadic in origin— They apparently settled in Canaan following the Amorites but preceding by a century or so the Aramaean invasion—Rapidly assimilated culture, which was chiefly of Babylonian source— While less virile than the Hebrews they maintained themselves in Palestine until about 1000 B. C.—Excavations on Canaanite levels of Palestinian cities such as Jericho and Megiddo indicate that their civilization was that of the Bronze Age—Phoenician tablets found at Ras Shamra give us a literary source of great value, a poem of 800 lines—Phoenician myth and cult transitional between Babylonian or Egyptian prototype and the Greek form —Canaanite agricultural festivals, their origin and times of celebration—How observed and why objected to by Hebrew moralists—Origin and spread of the alphabet—Seirites of Mount Sinai credited with the origin while the Phoenicians, Aramaean traders and later on biblical writers are factors in the diffusion of letters —Tablets at Ras Shamra written in Phoenician tongue using the cuneiform characters which are reduced to twenty-eight alphabetic signs.

CHAPTER XV

THE CULTURAL AND RELIGIOUS ADVANCE IN A TRANSITIONAL AGE

Excavation of ancient Jericho apparently confirms the biblical narrative of the destruction of the city by invading Hebrew tribes—Source material for the period the books of Joshua and Judges—Writers have a different viewpoint, one stressing a conquest compressed within a generation, the other holding the view of initial victories followed by a gradual settlement—The surprising contents of the book of Judges—The Samson stories— The period, although marked by violence, gives promise of development, marking an advance over life in the desert—Lack of cohesion among the tribes, some of them disappearing—However, there was a race consciousness—The language of the Hebrews— Canaanite festivals taken over for which the Hebrew designations were the Passover, a spring festival; the Feast of Weeks, midsummer; the Feast of Ingathering, fall—The festivals were

observed somewhat after the Canaanitish manner and eventually
led to license—Productive of good in so far as they were central
gathering places and unified the people.

CHAPTER XVI

EARLY KINGS OF ISRAEL

No indication in the book of Judges of Egyptian government
in Palestine; nor a direct statement in First Samuel of Philistine
rule, although the latter is implied—Philistia aspired to take
Egypt's place when the Egyptian army was withdrawn—Israel
resents the presence of the Philistines in the hill country—Need
of a national leader—Saul champions the cause of Jabesh Gilead
and is hailed as a deliverer—Later has the title of king—His warfare in the nature of skirmishes—Seat of the kingdom at Gibeah
—Valor of Jonathan—Saul's achievements—Suffers by comparison with David—Disastrous effect upon his mind caused by the
break with Samuel—Trafficking with the dead—Last battle—
Eulogy for Saul. David overpraised as to character, underrated
in achievement—Material for the study of his life abundant—
Early days in Bethlehem and in the court of Saul—Experiences
as an outlaw—His seven-year reign in Hebron—King in Jerusalem over united Israel—Military success abroad, capture of
Jerusalem—Character of David—Solomon lived in reflected glory
—Save for his building achievements little to his credit—His
wisdom was shrewdness, a trader, not a statesman—Ruinous
extravagance and senseless folly marked the close of his reign.

CHAPTER XVII

SOLOMON'S ACHIEVEMENTS IN ANCIENT MEGIDDO

A store-city, the Solomonic level of which has been recently
uncovered—Its situation guarding the Plain of Megiddo strategic
—Its connection with ancient and modern history—Nature of a
mound or *Tell*—Schumacher first to explore the site—Expedition of the University of Chicago now at work—What the fourth
stratum or Solomonic level has revealed—Housing objects of
value in near-by museum.

CHAPTER XVIII

INDUSTRY AND VOCATIONS

Transition from nomadic to agricultural and town life may

be regarded as now complete—The staple products of agriculture —A momentous question, Who would bless the crops?—General advance in industry, trade, arts, and letters—Building activity begins with David and Solomon, who summon the Phoenicians to their aid—Examples of engineering still existing are tunnels for water conduits in Jerusalem, Megiddo, and elsewhere—Fine Arts: Sculpture and painting barred as violating the second Commandment, music encouraged, variety of musical instruments— Letters: Canaanitish language spoken and written—Alphabetic signs employed—Writing a professional activity of the scribes —Traders and the working class had no voice in the government. This retarded economic development, but democracy persisted because of the conception of the brotherhood of Israel.

CHAPTER XIX
HEBREW FAMILY LIFE

Importance assigned the home by the biblical writers—Hebrews from early times set high value upon family life—The household in patriarchal times was often large—Desert dwellings were tents of goats' skins, placed close together for protection—When they became a settled people, the villages they built resembled the tent encampments and were as unprotected—They had, however, walled towns and caves easily defended—Pretentious homes were built in prosperous periods of stone or brick or wood—Head of the household was the father, known in early times as patriarch —He was, in fact, the ruler, his word was law and he was responsible for the conduct of affairs in the household and without— Plural marriages and slave girls permitted—Adultery uncommon —Women usually held in high esteem—Many love marriages— Negotiations leading to marriage—Who comprised the household?

CHAPTER XX
THE SOURCES OF HEBREW LITERATURE

The Hebrews by the middle of the eleventh century were proficient in writing—A preparatory stage before narrative writing during which books were produced, no longer in existence but referred to in the Old Testament—The first narrative extant, writing contained in the Second Book of Samuel and the opening chapters of First Kings—Biographic, concerning David, his family, friends, and various interests—The writer a contemporary and probably an eyewitness; journalistic style—His successful attempt led him or others to push back the narrative to the early life of David, to Saul and Samuel, and later to add the stories of tribal heroes, an original draft of the book of Judges—By the ninth century time was ripe for a history which would embody the sagas of the nation—The knowledge of Hebrew writers practical rather than theoretical—Importance of their writings— Source writers of the Pentateuch are known as the Jahvist, the Elohist, the Deuteronomists, and the Priestly Writer—In the fourth century a compilation of the four writings form the present Hexateuch known thereafter as "The Law"—Other writings produced during the period by Prophets, Poets, Sages, and Historians—The nature of inspiration—A parallel to the growth of the Old Testament afforded by the development of the New Testament—Importance of recognizing documentary sources— Literary value of the oral tradition.

CHAPTER XXI

THE ORACLES OF ISRAEL

The shrines once places of oracular response became at a later period of development sanctuaries with an organized priesthood and ritual, the knowledge of futurity being gained by other means—Magical practices like divination, sorcery, and astrology forbidden in Israel: see Deuteronomy, chapter 18—Legitimate sources by which knowledge of future events was obtained were dreams, the sacred lot, and the prophets' word—Two movements in Israel through which we trace the lineage of the writing prophets: (a) the communal group known as ecstatics with a highly emotional cult. The members of these societies lived a restricted social life and were narrowly influential; (b) the individual prophet or seer distinguished from his successors in that his messages were unrecorded—Characteristics: democratic, fearless, widely influential—The two streams meet in Elijah and Elisha, later in the eighth-century prophets.

CHAPTER XXII

THE REFORMER

Amos was the pioneer of eighth-century prophets and their successors—First to record oral discourses, first to see Israel in relation to a world power, first to insist upon the moral character of God who acts in accordance with his nature—Little known of his

early life and environment—His literary powers, his grasp of
world events, his allusions to past and present history, his knowledge of "the far and near" are criteria by which we may estimate
his intellectual preparation for his prophetic office—Difficult to
account for his ability—His discourses addressed to the Northern
Kingdom where he disturbed ritualists like Amaziah—An era of
material prosperity which was characterized by moral corruption, namely, extravagance, licentiousness, corruption of the
courts, luxurious living on the part of the rich, while the poor
were oppressed and native-born Israelites were sold into slavery
—No hope in the religious leaders, who stressed cult and sacrifice
but neglected moral reforms—Nomadic religion too far removed
from common interests to be of any avail—Amos' singular detachment gave him a perspective, nor was he without sympathy—
Misunderstood, unheeded, finally banished from Samaria—The
fulfillment of his predictions—Permanent value of his message
on social reform—Quality of his writing evidenced by effective
use of metaphor, pure diction, parallelism of his verse—How the
book was written—Analysis of its contents.

CHAPTER XXIII

The Prophet of Divine Compassion

Hosea a prophet of the Northern Kingdom, but, unlike Amos,
a resident of the land—The occasion of Hosea's call to become a
prophet was a tragic misfortune in his household—The probable
interpretation of the enigmatical language of chapters one and
three—Why Hosea chose this mode of presenting his prophetic
call—The prophet's experience not uncommon in Israel where
fertility cults flourished and promoted prostitution—The identification of Yahweh with Baal—The unique feature of Hosea's
view of God and his intimate relation to Israel—The construction of the book: oral discourses, fragments of which are in
chapters four to fourteen, put in written form and versified, to
which he prefixed the prose material in chapters one and three.
The second chapter is verse and regarded as parenthetical—
Hosea, like his contemporary Amos, was essentially a reformer,
but his methods of approach influenced by his misfortune were
different—Contrast between the two prophets—Hosea has only
a faint hope for the salvation of Israel although he proclaims its
certainty conditioned by the repentance of the nation—The dialogue in chapter fourteen—An analysis of the book—Was Hosea
a priest?—Fulfillment of his predictions in the anarchy that fol-

lowed Jeroboam's death (743)—Hosea involved in the disaster
that overtook the nation.

CHAPTER XXIV

THE PROPHET AS A COUNSELOR

A critical examination of the book of Isaiah shows it to be a
work of composite authorship, in four distinct parts which are
varied in content and belong to widely separated periods—First
part, chapters 1-35, in the main assigned to Isaiah, a prophet of
the eighth century—Second part, chapters 36-39, an excerpt from
2 Kings, related to events at close of Isaiah's ministry—Third
part, chapters 40-55, dated at the close of the exile 538 B. C.
by an unknown author—Fourth part, chapters 56-66, added about
a century later, authorship unknown—Source material for present
study Isaiah 1-39, 2 Kings and contemporary prophets—First
section contains some material later than Isaiah, arrangement of
chapters indicating editorial supervision—Isaiah's ministry between 740 and 701 B. C.   Place, Jerusalem—Perhaps a noble,
in any case has access to the court—Inaugural vision which determined his call in chapter 6—Elements in the vision—The prophet
at first a reformer denouncing social evils—Later his work constructive, the keynote of his message being "Believe and ye shall
be established"—Three crises during his ministry: 1. The coalition of two states (Samaria and Syria) threatening Judah; 2.
the fall of Samaria; 3. the siege of Jerusalem by the Assyrians.
Isaiah, alive to the situation and possible disasters, counsels faith,
raises the morale of king and people—Tradition concerning the
manner of his death.   Micah a contemporary prophet—A countryman coming to Jerusalem and prophesying its destruction—
To him we owe a conception of religion suited to his day and
ours.

CHAPTER XXV

IN THE DAYS OF JEREMIAH

Life and times of the prophet told in the book which bears his
name—His writings reveal his character and his reaction to
political events, to social injustice, to the disloyalty of Israel to
Yahweh—Stirring events in Jeremiah's time—Threat of a
Scythian invasion the occasion of the prophet's early utterances,
disaster averted and Jeremiah discredited—From Anathoth, his
early home, and later from Jerusalem, he watched the procession
of events, the reforms of Josiah's reign, and the tragic death of

CHAPTER XXVI

The Visions of Ezekiel

CHAPTER XXVII

The Unknown Prophet

reflections upon Cyrus' military successes led him to regard the Persian as the deliverer of the Jews—His call to become a prophet implied rather than directly related, chapter 40, verses 3-8—The difficult task which confronted him in persuading the exiles to return to their own land—His argument in chapters 40-48—Comfort is extended to Israel by a compassionate and forgiving God; the might of Babylon is as ephemeral as the flowers of the field, the Word of God alone endures; in an imaginative flight he sees the returning exiles already in Jerusalem and populating the cities of Judah; God wills their return because of his goodness; his omnipotence will make the return possible—He ridicules the worship of images and declares the unity of God; he prophesies the fall of Babylon and sees their gods led into captivity; Cyrus is to be the unconscious agent effecting their deliverance—The most remarkable feature of the poem is seen in the four poems on "The Servant of Jehovah"— Did the prophet refer to Israel or to an elect group or to a Messiah?—His contribution to religious thought is the conception of a universal God and a universal religion.

CHAPTER XXVIII

ZOROASTER AND HIS FOLLOWERS

The home of the prophet was Iran, a vast territory divided among tribes of which the Medes and Persians were chief, allied to peoples of India and Europe as shown by their linguistic affinity—Theories as to the early Aryan or Indo-European home —Zoroaster gave his name to the religion he founded—His period and the scene of his activity disputed but the traditional date 660-583 B. C. quite generally accepted—Traditions of his youth, conversion, and career—Three stages in Iranic religion: 1. Pre-Zoroastrianism, or the ancient Iranian cult; 2. The religion of Zoroaster as taught by the prophet; 3. The development of Zoroastrianism—The Old Iranian faith was a nature religion, polytheistic, with elements of fear, crude superstitions and practices; important feature fire worship—The elements of Zoroaster's teaching were: (1) dualism, or the opposition of good to evil; (2) noble conception of Deity; (3) advanced ethical system; (4) immortality including rewards and punishments— Zoroastrianism a living faith, having today 100,000 adherents most of whom are in India and known as Parsi; the remainder, ten thousand, are in Persia—Influenced late Judaistic thought.

CHAPTER XXIX

HOMERIC RELIGION

Historical basis for the epic poems—Consensus of opinion concerning their authorship—*The Iliad* and the *Odyssey,* while in no sense sacred books, reflect the religious thought of the Greeks and were influential in preserving myths—Homer treats the gods as if they were both human and divine. On the human side they are jealous, partisan, have love affairs, and enact comic rôles; on the divine side, they express moral sentiments, hear the prayer of suppliants, and aid them in distress—They are seldom cruel—The religion of the Greeks, generally speaking, was a worship of beauty and goodness without debasing rites—The Homeric pantheon small.

Hesiod belongs to the century succeeding Homer—Meter of his verse like the *Iliad*—Pessimistic outlook upon life influenced by his environment—Critical of traditional religion—His shrewd observations upon life and conduct—His chief works were the *Theogony* and the *Work of Days.*

CHAPTER XXX

DEVELOPMENT OF GREEK RELIGION

During the two centuries following the Homeric period, Greek religion may be observed under four aspects: (*a*) the state religion, including the cultic practices of the harvest festivals; the ceremonial procession to the temples, the celebration of myths, extension of the priesthood, and multiplication of temples. (*b*) The mystery cults: Eleusinian in honor of Demeter at Eleusis; Dionysian, which at first was characterized by its emotional frenzied rites but afterward was purified of its extravagances while its ethical content was enlarged; Orphism, which stressed survival after death and rewards and punishment. (*c*) The religious influence of the poets of this period indicated by their didactic verse, which abounded in moral maxims, while the lyric poets celebrated the joys of the senses. The emphasis of the Greeks upon sensuous beauty. (*d*) Philosophy, at first occupied with questions relative to the physical world, its origin and structure, turned later to the inquiry of the nature of God—It was speculative and destructive until the Eleatics of a Greek colony in southern Italy laid the foundations for a rational belief. Parmenides and Xenophanes are the outstanding thinkers of the school. While their philosophy was open to strictures, its immediate effect was beneficial in that it destroyed superstition. It also paved the way for Platonic thought.

CHAPTER XXXI

THE GREAT FIFTH CENTURY IN GREECE

The fifth century witnesses the flowering of genius in many fields: architecture, sculpture, poetry, drama, and philosophy—Difficult to make a satisfactory evaluation in religion and morals when there are striking contrasts in habits of thought and in behavior—The contribution of poets in the field of morals and religion: Pindar strikes a deeply religious note in the odes with which he celebrates the victors and the gods in the Pythian Olympian and Isthmian games—Aeschylus, Sophocles, and Euripides reach the height of their attainments in successive periods—Their governing ideas inculcate reverence for the good and stress the punishment which follows the transgression of law —Philosophy and Religion: the teaching of the Sophists was destructive not only of religion and morals but of philosophy, but it paved the way for the reconstruction of thought on a more rational basis and sounder ethic—Socrates a philosopher and a teacher of morals—Without pretension—His method of teaching—His enemies cause his arrest—Makes his own defense —His last hours.

CHAPTER XXXII

THE HYMN BOOK OF THE SECOND TEMPLE

Returning exiles rebuilt their temple on an enlarged scale, dedicating it in 516 B. C.—Persian administration of Jewish state—The function of the high priest—The development of the Temple service led to a collection of songs already written and to the preparation of additional hymns—Collectively they were known as the Psalter, or Praise Songs—The five groups as they appear in our translation follow to some degree a historical and doctrinal development, but there are many exceptions—Psalms are poetry and observe the rules of form and accent peculiar to Hebrew verse, the most striking feature of which is parallelism or thought rhythm—Psalms are most frequently lyrical, expressing emotion, but many are didactic—Authorship—The origin and form of Hebrew poetry—Psalms are of universal interest, used in the services of the synagogue, the Christian Church, and privately—Variously classified—Psalms have played a large part in the history of the Christian Church and human experience.

CHAPTER XXXIII

THE BOOK OF JOB: A DRAMATIC POEM

Probable date about 400 B. C., belongs to the Wisdom literature of the Old Testament—A poem beginning and ending with prose narrative—The prologue has for its subject the patience of Job, a well-known character whose unexampled sufferings are met with fortitude—Two scenes are laid in heaven and two upon the earth—In the prologue, but nowhere in the poem, we have the character of Satan, who is pictured as a servant of God but cynical—The prologue thus furnishes us a reason for the suffering of Job. It is to be noted, however, that the speakers of the poem entirely ignore this factor—The poem may be regarded as a symposium in which four speakers take part: Job, Eliphaz, Bildad, and Zophar—Job's friends become protagonists debating with him the ancient problem, "Why should the innocent suffer?"—The key chapters of the poem are nine and ten, which reflect the extreme pessimism of Job. This section falls into cycles of speeches totaling nineteen—The book originally closed with chapter 31, the final sentence of which reads, "The words of Job are ended." Inasmuch as the problem had not been solved, but only stated, there were added at a later time the addresses of Elihu, the beautiful nature poem in chapters 38-41 and the epilogue—These added portions are designed to justify the ways of God to men.

CHAPTER XXXIV

A SKEPTIC DISCUSSES THE MEANING OF LIFE

The popularity of the book—How it differs from other Old-Testament writings—The authorship—The late date (c. 200 B. C.)—The title; the author refers to himself as Koheleth, which Luther regarded as a common noun meaning "the preacher," or it may be a proper noun and left untranslated—Reason for using a nom de plume in the first two chapters—Influence of Greek thought evident in the writing—Skepticism concerning the future life widespread; shared by the author, who denies immortality—His denial provoked by the tenets of Zoroastrianism or

the Greek mystery cults or Egyptian belief in survival after death
—His so-called cynicism due to misunderstanding—His philosophy of life challenges the reader at three points, namely, (a)
denial of immortality, (b) his insistence upon pleasure as a present good, (c) denial that life has meaning or purpose—Positive
values in Koheleth's attitude—1. He finds beauty in life (3. 16)
—2. He emphasized the value of work, although the end in view
is the dividend it immediately pays—3. He explodes the shams
prevalent in his day, the dicta of the Wisdom writers, the pretenses of philosophy, the hypocrisy in religion—Ecclesiastes
accepted by the Jewish council of Jamnia (90 A. D.) and later
by the Christian Church, influenced by its supposed Solomonic
authorship—Luther takes exception to the traditional view, and
so do most modern scholars.

CHAPTER XXXV

Hellenism and the Maccabean Uprising

At the beginning of the fourth century B. C., the Hellenic
period draws to a close leaving to posterity the names of Plato,
Aristotle, and Alexander—What is meant by Hellenism and the
Hellenistic age?—Achievements of the era—Alexander by his
Asiatic conquests gave a powerful impetus to Hellenism—Political changes after the Macedonian's death—The wisdom of
Ptolemy's choice—The Seleucids govern Syria and states farther
east—Palestine for a hundred years pays tribute to the Ptolemies,
who govern them tolerantly—In 198 B. C. the country falls to
Antiochus III—A successor, Antiochus Epiphanes, is actively
opposed by the Jews—Estimate of the character and aims of the
king—The Maccabean uprising; the career of Judas Maccabeus
and his brothers—Religious independence secured for the Jews
under Judas, political freedom by Simon—Period of independence brief on account of incompetence of later Maccabean rulers
—Rome interferes in the person of Pompey and again the Jews
change masters.

CHAPTER XXXVI

The Final Phase

Jews unable to achieve self-government—The Maccabean wars
devastated the country, and while recovery came the seeds of
bitter enmity had been sown—Continued opposition to Hellenism

on the part of a small but influential group. However, the spread
of Hellenism continued and its benefits were obvious to many,
notably the Sadducean group, Jewish youth and those of the
Dispersion. A survey of the period shows Greek influence in the
creation of Greek city-states, where many Jews resided; in social
changes effected by the gymnasium, the stadium, and the theater,
all powerful agents to spread the virus of Greek culture; in
Jewish literature notably Ecclesiastes, Greek translations of the
Bible, some Apochryphal books and some of the Pseudepigraphia
—The Book of Wisdom and the Greek idea of immortality—Two
types of mind among the Jews.

RETROSPECT

FOREWORD

FORMERLY it was thought that the unique place which Hebrew religion and biblical literature held precluded any comparison with the religion and sacred writings of other peoples. Today the value of comparative study is recognized and new emphasis given to the cultures and religions of the Near East.

The change in attitude may be traced to a recognition that "when alien races and diverse faiths confronted each other it might not always be the cause of war, but it was always the occasion of psychical conflict," which profoundly affected the cultures of the several national or racial groups involved in the contacts. Such comparative study has set into clearer light both the similarities and dissimilarities between Hebrew religion and civilization and the religions and civilizations of neighboring nations, which in turn has resulted in a more just appreciation of the unique elements in Hebrew religion.

In the earlier days of comparative study investigators concerned themselves chiefly with specific features revealing striking resemblances or striking contrasts. As a result it sometimes happened that on the basis of a limited number of carefully selected facts conclusions were reached which could not stand the test of unbiased study of all the relevant facts. With the remarkable increase in our knowledge of the literatures, religions, and general cultures of the nations in the ancient Near East with which the Hebrews came into more or less frequent contacts, it has become possible to make a much more comprehensive and scientific study of the genetic relationship which exists between the civilization of Israel and the civilizations of the Babylonians, Egyptians, Persians, Greeks, and other ancient peoples, and to reach more accurate and more reliable conclusions.

In the chapters which constitute this volume Professor Harris, out of a long and rich experience as a student and college teacher, is discussing in an interesting and suggestive manner the cultural contributions which in successive periods other nations made to the thought and life of the Hebrews. The title of the volume is significant: THE HEBREW HERITAGE—A STUDY OF ISRAEL'S CULTURAL AND SPIRITUAL ORIGINS. In the past the primary interest of Bible students has been in the cultural and spiritual contributions of Israel, to the beliefs and practices of later generations; which interest led to a close and intensive study of the literature, history, religion, and general culture of the Hebrews.

Chiefly as a result of archaeological discoveries it has become increasingly clear that Hebrew culture and civilization can be fully understood only as there is an adequate understanding and appreciation of the relationship which the Hebrew development sustains to the total historical and cultural background and atmosphere in which the former originated and flourished. It is the purpose of the author to picture this Oriental background from the earliest times to the close of the Old-Testament period and then to assist the reader in discovering the significant contributions made to Israel by each national or cultural group.

The writer of this Foreword has read the entire manuscript with much interest. Professor Harris has performed well what cannot have been an easy task. He gives every evidence of wide reading and a discriminating knowledge of the entire field of Oriental history and culture. With good judgment he has selected from an almost overwhelming mass of material the essential items, and he expresses himself so plainly that even the layman without technical knowledge should have no difficulty in catching his thought and acquiring a rather complete knowledge of the whole field.

It is hoped that the book will have a wide reading. The author is giving a vivid portrayal of successive cultures and civilizations and is outlining in more or less detail the incalculable debt which the leaders and teachers of Israel owe them. No one can read and study these pages without gaining a better understanding and a more convincing appreciation of the truth that throughout the ages God made himself known "in divers portions and in divers manners," not only to Israel, but also to spiritually sensitive souls among other nations.   F. C. EISELEN.

INTRODUCTION

THIS is not another book on Hebrew religion, nor is it a history of the Hebrew people, although the historical method is followed in the attempt of the author to show the extraneous influences which have affected the culture and religious history of the Hebrew people. What has frequently been termed the background of Israel's history is a very important part of the picture. It is possible, of course, to concentrate on Israel's contribution to religion and ethics, regarding them as isolated phenomena and their usefulness to mankind as unique, but this is to ignore important factors in the development of the Hebrews. As a matter of fact, they have never been an isolated social group. They have invariably lived in the midst of other peoples, even as they do today. That they have clung tenaciously to their traditions and had great pride of race is admitted, but how often they must have been conscious that they were living in somebody's world not their own! How transitory and unsuccessful their attempts at self-government!

Their success has not lain in their effort to win and achieve a place in the sun, but in their marvelous adjustment to adverse conditions. They·have extracted the sweet from the bitter. They have been tenants, but have contrived to charge the landlord interest.

No serious study of any early people can be made apart from the consideration of the external factors which contribute to their rise and growth. This is certainly true of the Hebrew. To begin with, he was a late comer, appearing on the pages of history long after other civilizations had attained maturity. He not only inherited the cities, the fields, and vineyards of the Canaanites, but their laws, their agricultural festivals and their religious cults. He kept his own race traditions, but in adapting himself to new conditions, he assimilated what he saw and felt, not always with fine discrimination.

29

Four hundred years after the Hebrew tribes entered Canaan they became a powerful state among the political groups in western Asia, but the period of their supremacy, even the length of their independence, was brief. They became the vassals of successive world powers, Assyria, Babylonia, Persia, Greece, and Rome. During this state of tutelage, with the exception of short periods of oppression, they were not slaves nor servilely treated. On the contrary, they had for the most part tolerant rulers who were satisfied with the tribute they exacted. A people like the Jews, naturally assimilative, would likely become the recipient of every cultural element which the governing power could furnish. This proved to be the case, even their religious opinions being modified.

The biblical writer alive to the danger of contact with a Canaanitish or Hellenistic civilization would naturally fail to stress the extraneous elements in the culture of Israel, even when these were helpful. It is otherwise with the modern historian. He is bound to set down all the facts. He can see a borrowing if the Hebrew writer does not. Among the students of Israel's religious and cultural advance no one is more aware of the significance of Hebrew contact with neighboring states than the archaeologist. He knows to a certainty the transitions which have taken place in the material condition of the Hebrews and is sensitive to changes or modifications in their outlook. He sees Solomon building in Jerusalem a Temple to Yahweh and a shrine in Megiddo for Astarte. He visualizes the first Temple as a Phoenician construction, modeled after an Egyptian edifice, and the third as the work of a Hellenistic king building for the Jews a Graeco-Roman shrine with Corinthian columns. Jewish remains lie buried in the midst of cultures, Egyptian, Canaanitish, Greek, and Roman. In seeking to decipher Israel's message, it is necessary to render intelligible all the writing on the palimpsest.

It may seem to some readers that an unusual amount of space has been devoted to Greek religion, discussed in Part IV. The reason for this is the importance of understanding the Hellenic period in its relationship to the Hellenistic age which followed and which may be regarded as a continuation of the former, under modified conditions. For three centuries the Jews lived in this new age, and were affected by it, the Jews in Palestine materially, the Jews of the Dispersion materially and spiritually. Moreover, Greek religious thought and philosophy in important respects were so far in advance of similar thought in contemporaneous states that they afford a standard of measurement. They offer not so much an antithesis to Hebraic thought as an interesting parallel and comparison. Who can read the stirring moral utterances of the great Greek poets without being reminded of the solemn words of the Hebrew prophets? The early Christian was not slow to realize the implications of Platonic thought, or the Socratic view of immortality. Can we believe that the Jews of the Hellenistic age were unmindful that Philo was the only Jew of the Dispersion to attempt a correlation of Greek and Hebrew thought?

Finally, the author expresses his hope that the reader will discern in this brief and incomplete survey of the cultures of the Near East the slowly developing, progressively revealed religion which contributed to Israel's advance and was forwarded through them to all mankind.

The author acknowledges the courtesy of the Oxford University Press for permission to copy the maps on pages 62 and 340, and the drawing on page 39. He is indebted to the Metropolitan Museum of Art for the use of reproductions of The Karnak Temple and The Scribe.

PART I

THE GENESIS AND DEVELOPMENT OF EARLY
CULTURES

CHAPTER I

EARLY CULTURE OF MANKIND[1]

WHOEVER studies the beginning of man's life on the planet and the preparation of the earth for human habitation will find himself wandering through vast corridors of time. He will need to accustom himself to the long hours of the geological clock, remembering that the earth is probably eighteen hundred million years old; that sometime during the last million mankind appeared; that the written record of his advance is comprised within the final five thousand years, a few ticks of the clock.

Of the prehistoric record—for record there is—we have a surprising amount of information. We are always running across it in the strata of the rocks, in gravel pits, in ancient river beds, and beneath the floor of caves. The early volumes are crumpled and, if they contain a record of life, the writing is illegible, but a later series with its thrilling tales of mountain building, sea transgression, submergence of continents, land and water prolific of life, ages of bitter cold, intervals between of tropic warmth, and finally man like ourselves appearing on the scene is a significant and intriguing story full of human interest, a serial by no means yet completed.[2]

TRACES OF EARLY MANKIND

The fossil remains of the earliest members of the human family are rarely found. This is not surprising, since their bones would be dissolved save in exceptional cases. But their weapons of flint and quartz were virtually indestructible and these have been scattered profusely about—in layers of earth beneath glacial drift, or in gravel terraces which

---

[1] "Culture" as employed in this volume denotes a particular stage of advancement in civilization or it describes the distinctive attainments which constitute the background of a racial or social group.
[2] See Peake and Fleure, *Corridors of Time*, Vol. I, p. 13. Oxford University Press.

35

marked the boundary of rivers when they were much higher
than they are today. Frequently with the implements of
chase are the bones of animals they hunted, identified as
arctic fauna or as beasts that crashed through forests of
tropical growth.

Since early man often sought shelter in caves, we find
there the traces of his occupancy, in mural decoration, in
implements buried at levels beneath the present floor, and
sometimes with these the skeleton remains of the hunter himself. We distinguish, therefore, two sources of deposit—
gravel drift and cave drift.

As early as 1869 it was perceived by Gabriel de Mortillet
that the collection of flints employed as tools or weapons
could be arranged in cultural assemblages and according to
periods, and when so arranged, they indicated a developing
technique. The early paleontologists gave names to their finds
borrowed from the localities which furnished them. Later
these denoted similar types found elsewhere and eventually
the industry of a period. Thus we have

1. Chellean, Chelles-sur-Marne
2. Acheulean, Saint Acheul near Amiens
3. Mousterian, Moustier near Les Eyzies
4. Solutrean, Solutre near Macon.
5. Magdalenian, Cave of La Madeleine near Dordogne.

The name given to the early period in which men worked
in stone was Paleolithic, in contrast to the more recent period,
Neolithic. But the former term is too general to denote
cultures which lasted not only through the Pleistocene period,
but preceded and followed it. So the terms "Lower" and
"Upper Paleolithic" came to be generally employed. It
happens that deposits of the lower Paleolithic are almost
invariably found in gravel drift, while those of the Upper
Paleolithic are in caves. The Lower Paleolithic industries,
Chellean, Acheulean, and Mousterian, are the work of men
who belong to the dawn of human life on the planet, while
the developed industry known as Aurignacian, Solutrean, and
Magdalenian belong to races of "true men," who lived, according to Peake and Fleure, in the post-Glacial period,

between 11500 and 6500 B. C. How long the previous Pleistocene period lasted we have no means of knowing. Conjecture places its beginning two hundred and fifty thousand years ago. That there was human industry contemporaneous to and probably preceding it, we need feel no doubt.

FORERUNNERS OF MAN

Both anthropoid apes and man have the same lemuroid or simian ancestry, but the ape left the line of descent in the Oligocene period, more than a million years ago. This meant a sifting, leaving a humanoid stock from which were derived the precursors of man and later man himself. Where the evolution took place we do not know. The opinion is widely held that Asia was the cradle of the human race.

HUMAN TYPES

Fossil remains of very early men have been found under circumstances which leave no doubt as to the correctness of the identification, although the evidence is meager—sometimes only a part of the skull, a jawbone, a few teeth, and a thigh-bone. These have been studied in connection with the locality where discovered. Reconstruction of the missing parts has been attempted and the results are tenable, if not absolutely proven. They have been recognized as types of human stock, variant and widely separated in time as well as place. They are enumerated in order of age, as the Java ape-man, the Heidelberg man, the Piltdown and the Neanderthal. Of the last named, we know considerable, since deposits have been found not only in the Neanderthal ravine near Bonn, but in Gibraltar, in sites of central and southern France, Rhodesia, and Palestine. Until Dorothy Garrod's discoveries in the Carmel Cemetery near Athlit, the best preserved specimen is that of La Chapelle-aux-Saints.

In general we may say of these types that they fashioned tools, knew the use of fire, and hunted game. They had larger brains than apes. They stood nearly erect. They had the power to communicate. The grave of a Neanderthal man indicates that the body had been buried with reverence. With the remains were implements of chase and the bones of an animal which had been prepared for food—preparation for the long journey before him. Did this not indicate a belief in survival after death?

However, none of these types are to be regarded as true men. They are the predecessors, not the ancestors, of man. They may be regarded as experiments in Nature's laboratory, to be succeeded by the *homo sapiens*.[3]

BEGINNING OF ART

Peake and Fleure believe that the Mousterian culture associated with the Neanderthal race began in Europe in the warm period preceding the Fourth Glacial Epoch and continued until post-glacial times, a period of not less than twenty-five or thirty thousand years. They suggest that the Neanderthal men came into Europe from Asia during a period when climatic conditions were favorable, that with the coming of the cold period they moved southward, some of them finding refuge in the caves of southern France and Italy, others moving across the land bridge that at that time connected Italy with Tunis.

The peculiarity of the Mousterian industry is the flaking on one side of the flint while the other remains flat. This was accomplished by chipping one surface of a square block of flint and then splitting it off with a sharp blow. Afterward the edge of the tool or weapon was "retouched" by striking off small flakes.

With the return of the milder climatic conditions of postglacial times, we find evidence of new races in Europe, employing a different technique and leaving traces of their culture in rock engravings, mural paintings, and sculpture. These first artists have been frequently called Paleolithic Greeks, but the name "Paleolithic" is unfortunate. It associates them with a past from which they were completely divorced and contrasts them with Neolithic man, where no contrast is perceived.

Another misnomer is "Cro-Magnon," a label based on the

---

[3] Cf. J. A. Thomson, *The Outline of Science*, Vol. I, p. 171. G. P. Putnam's Sons.

Mousterian implements showing both sides

conception that we have in Upper Paleolithic times a dominant race, whose industries termed Aurignacian, Solutrean,
Magdalenian, and Azilian are phases in their advancement.
On the contrary, we have several types and without entering
into the vexed question of race, we may distinguish these by
industries and periods rather than to employ "Cro-Magnon"
as a label for the whole.

The Aurignacian culture comes earliest, and passes through
several phases. Some of their flints indicate Mousterian influence and others Capsian. Bone implements now appear
for the first time, and a new kind of tool, the La Gravette
point, is developed.

The Solutrean industry which followed was characterized
by thin flakes, worked all over, and of the laurel-leaf type.
The high finish was obtained by pressure on the edge with a
bone tool rather than by chipping with another stone. These
hunters may have come from Turkestan or other Asiatic
steppes following their game, wild horses and cattle, westward. The Solutrean hunters seem to be for a time dominant, but later disappeared, perhaps following their game
eastward. Some of them, however, settled among the
Aurignacian people and were absorbed.

The cave deposits indicate clearly that the Magdalenian
culture followed the Solutrean. In this connection, it may be
stated that the successive layers of earth, sand, and gravel
below the cave floors form a storehouse of rich finds left by
the successive generations that have occupied the honeycombed hills and the rocky coasts of southern Europe. In
the early stages of the Magdalenian industry, contemporaneous to the Aurignacian, one sees the influence of the
latter culture. Later the advancement is rapid. Magdalenians worked with reindeer horn and afterward with red deer,
as the oak forests increased and arctic animals retreated.
Peake and Fleure distinguish six phases, which is not surprising, for the culture belongs to the greatest artists of
antiquity. Their implements are scattered widely over
Europe from Spain to Denmark, from Great Britain to
Austria. There is good reason for believing that the Magdalenian industry is developed Aurignacian, interrupted by

the Solutrean hunters, who for a time were dominant in Europe. We may, therefore, be dealing with the same race, when we consider the Aurignacian and Magdalenian periods. However, the period is very long—five thousand years, say the geologists—and with moderate climatic conditions prevailing in Europe, apart from the Alpine section, we must expect the infusion of races from the East and South.[4] Two skeletons found in the Grimaldi cave in southern France are apparently Negroid.

CAPSIAN CULTURE

A very important industry in the meantime was developing in north Africa known as Capsian from the finds at Gafsa. In its earliest stage it does not seem to be different from the Aurignacian; in its final development, it is associated with the Magdalenian in Spain. The inference drawn by Peake and Fleure is that the Aurignacians were a branch of the Capsian people, that the main stock remained in Africa; later, under pressure of drought conditions, they crossed over into Spain by a land bridge, and mingled with the Magdalenians; that the industry developed by the two peoples is to be identified with early Azilian culture.

TECHNICAL PERFECTION AND THE LOVE OF BEAUTY

Hitherto we have been dealing with ancient peoples as hunters. Their technique indicates a growing appreciation of beauty. The implements they fashioned were not for the purpose of whiling away a leisure hour but as weapons for the chase, for spearing fish, or as tools for boring, planing, and flaking. However, it was not enough to make an implement of utility and let it go at that. Even in Mousterian times men tried to excel in making their tools beautiful. They were hunters on their way to becoming artists.

With the Magdalenians, we find art in flower and full blown, whether in the making of small portable objects, like

[4] Peake and Fleure remark on the diversity of type of the hunters and artists of the Old Stone Age, and are inclined to believe this due to a response to conditions of growth. *C. of T.*, Vol. II, pp. 59-69. Oxford Press.

their beautifully engraved reindeer horn, or in mural surfaces, or in sculpture. As to the latter, a limitation is to be noted. They had not discovered the fact that clay must be baked in order to be preserved. This undoubtedly is the reason why the specimens are few and that there is no pottery. The better artists are never inaccurate in their drawing. Their rock engraving was remarkable, exhibiting a sense of form, and they had the ability to depict animals in motion. They learned to derive color from the red and yellow ocher of the soil and employed it freely. The reader will do well to examine the plates in any book dealing with prehistoric art. From this perusal he will rise with the question as to why modern artists have failed to attain the perfection of drawing which one discovers in the work of the Old Stone Age.

Were the Hunters Religious?

Were these people of the Old Stone Age religious? Many anthropologists say so. Much depends on the way one defines religion; much also on how one reads the evidence. That early man buried his dead with reverence must be conceded; that the implements of the chase were buried with him is to be noted; that the bodies were prepared for interment by being painted red is perhaps significant. It is argued that the presence of implements in the grave points to belief in survival after death, but it may be that the living feared to use the weapons once carried by the deceased. It is said that the red color so freely employed as pigment or powder was symbolical of blood and that its use was designed to give renewal in the after life. But the use of red pigment on the body of the living man may have been customary. Marett suggests that the dents in the rock within the engraved form of reindeer or bison were caused by hurling spears at the pictured object, that here we have an example of sympathetic magic, insuring success in the chase. This, of course, is possible but cannot be proved.

However, the supposition may be adopted tentatively that a people so highly developed artistically may have speculated concerning the future; may have feared, if they did not

worship, their dead ancestors; may have felt a sense of awe
in the presence of violent manifestations of nature. However
we may think about the origin of religion, we must grant
that the subject is still in its speculative stage.

THE NEOLITHIC PERIOD

The chronology adopted by Peake and Fleure, which terminates the Magdalenian period about 6500 B. C., enables them
to make an easy transition from Paleolithic to Neolithic times.

The spread of pine and oak forests over Europe had an
important bearing upon the occupations of early men, for
there were no longer the plains and steppes where the big
game was hunted. Moreover, the cold, damp period which
marked the Gschnitz phase was a deterrent to man's advance.
Speaking generally, civilization declined, or was stagnant, at
the close and following the final stage of the Azilian industry.
Two important innovations are to be noted at the dawn of
the Neolithic period: man had learned to fashion pottery,
and from becoming a food-collector he became a food-
producer.[5]

RELIGIOUS DEVELOPMENT

We shall not go far astray if we conclude that the religious
beliefs and cultic practices flourishing at the dawn of the
historic period had their rise and development in the Neolithic age or earlier. This is certainly true of the civilizations
of Egypt and Babylonia, as we shall show in subsequent
chapters. It is not less likely on the continent of Europe,
where the Neolithic stage came to an end nearly two millenniums later. If, as many scholars believe, there was an
early totemic stage in the religious development of the Egyptian, we must place it at the beginning of the Neolithic period.
MacAllister finds on prehistoric sites in Palestine evidence of
ancestor worship and sacrifice. The megalithic monuments
of France and Britain have a religious significance. If
Stonehenge was a sanctuary of the sun, as Clemen thinks
likely, we can see the reason why the horseshoe opening of
the inner circle of stones looked toward the rising of the

[5] Peake and Fleure, *C. of T.*, Vol. III, p. 29f. Oxford Press.

sun at the summer solstice. The monuments in France known as dolmens were often placed on the summit of hills, where they commanded a wide sweep of the horizon, leaving the impression that the locality may have been chosen by sun-worshipers.

If we could correctly read the evidence of the monuments, the graves, and the decorative work of Neolithic man, we should probably be certain of his religious status. As it is, we can only infer that man from the beginning was deeply sensible of Powers higher than himself, of survival after death, and the reality of spiritual life, however vaguely he felt about it.

SUPPLEMENTARY READING

Peake and Fleure, *Corridors of Time,* Vol. I, Apes and Men, Vol. II, Hunters and Artists.
H. F. Osborn, *Men of the Old Stone Age.*
J. Arthur Thomson, *The Outline of Science,* Vol. I, Part V.
R. R. Marett, *The Threshold of Religion,* Chapter VIII.
Cambridge Ancient History, Vol. I, Chapter I.

CHAPTER II

THE RELIGION OF THE NOMAD

FOREWORD: The nomad was the connecting link between prehistoric races and those who early attained civilization. He was retarded in development because of his unwillingness to live in a settled community. On the other hand, his occasional contacts either by conquest or trade with civilized states contributed to his advancement. Warlike nomads bent upon plunder must have added to their possessions, in the event of a successful raid, objects of beauty as well as utility and new examples of man's inventiveness. More peaceable tribes as carriers of goods from one trading center to another prospered and in time were weaned to the amenities of civilization. Some of the nomads occupied the grassy uplands of eastern and southeastern Europe, or moved along the same parallels as they penetrated Asia. They were of Aryan stock, and in the end their contribution to civilization was considerable. We shall have occasion to speak of them more than once in the course of these chapters. But our immediate and chief interest lies with the Semitic nomads of the south, who occupied the sparsely settled semiarid territory of Arabia. Before the period of desiccation had set in the peninsula must have been a fertile land capable of sustaining large numbers of people. But from historic times we are impressed by the migrations from its arid acres to the fertile crescent in the north. The movements were gradual, unequal, and at no time were great numbers concerned. While it would be rash to conjecture the order and dates of these tribal movements, we know roughly the periods of Semitic influx into the Euphratean valley and north. Later, when Semites are divided by their communal life into various centers, it is possible through their linguistic peculiarities to classify them. Of special interest to the student of the Bible is the Semitic origin of the Hebrew people, who in

45

remote times, whatever their nearer ancestry, must have come from Arabia, the cradle of all Semitic peoples.

ISRAEL'S DESERT ORIGIN

In our study of Israel's heritage it is necessary to fix firmly in our minds their desert ancestry. It was never forgotten. Jeroboam's rallying cry, "To thy tents, O Israel," was language that the revolutionists could understand. The great harvest festival, called "the feast of tents," kept alive the tradition of their wilderness wandering. The nomadic ideal of simplicity as opposed to the debasing and corrupt practices of Canaanite civilization was set forth by the prophets. The early writings reflect from their pages the pastoral joys and simplicities of patriarchal life. That there was idealization of the past is more than plausible, and it is the business of the historian to sift the evidence and separate the fancied from the real. In this he is aided by his knowledge of what the Arab nomad is in the present time. While his movements are migratory, he is stationary in his opinions and tenacious in his subscription to religious cults. He is today a Moslem, and probably the most conservative and fanatical among the followers of Islam. It is doubtful if he has changed religiously to any appreciable extent since Arabia surrendered to Mohammed in the seventh century. As a herdsman he follows the occupation of his ancestors who more than four thousand years ago trekked the wilderness. His communal life is the same. In character he is unchanged. He is the same implacable foe, generous to a fault in hospitality, emotional rather than reflective. He tells time by the sun; he neither reads nor writes but holds tenaciously to tradition. He is a poet, imaginative, sensuous. A study of the modern Arab, therefore, affords an interesting and fruitful comparison with those early Semitic peoples with whom we have most to do.

By the term "Semitic world" is meant Arabia and the arc of arable land in the north, to which Professor Breasted has given the felicitous title of "The Fertile Crescent." It stretches from the Persian Gulf to Egypt and includes the modern states of Irak, Syria, and Palestine. Between the

horns and southward is desert. To the north is a mountainous country which presents added protection to the agri-
culturalist. It is readily seen that the Crescent is topo-
graphically and climatically suited to meet the needs of men
and has from immemorial times been the object of their
covetous desire.

The principal divisions of the Semites are Babylonians and
Assyrians known as eastern Semitic stock; the Aramaeans,
or northern Semites; and the western Semites, including
the Phoenicians, the Canaanites, and Amorites. The last
named seem to be the same people, but represent successive
migrations from Arabia and are later differentiated by their
locality, the Canaanites preferring the low country and the
Amorites the hills. The southern Semites are the Arabs.
They, like the others, are descended from an early Arabic
stock. To these we must add the Hebrews, who were late
comers. They were of Aramaean ancestry and entered
Palestine from northern Mesopotamia. Later they were
amalgamated with other Semitic peoples, and from the fusion
was derived the race as we know it in historic times.

Practically the same language is spoken by all Semites.
The parent language seems to be old Arabic, and the differences between the branches of the Semitic people are not
more pronounced than among the Latin races in southern
Europe. In some instances the distinction seems to be purely
cultural, the language being the same.

That the Hebrews at an early date shared the superstitions
and followed the cultic practices of other Semitic peoples is
conclusive. Scattered all through the Old Testament are
references to early beliefs and practices which are clues to the
historian, as fossils in the rock to a geologist, and constitute
his chief source for nomadic religion among the Semites.

Sacred Trees

First of all we note the emphasis placed upon the sacred-
ness of certain trees. We are told that when Abraham[1] came
into the land of Canaan he worshiped at the oak of Moreh.

---
[1] Genesis 12. 6.

The reference seems to be to an oracular oak, that is, to a tree which was the dwelling place of deity. Here Abraham built an altar unto Jehovah. In Judges[2] there is an obscure reference to another of these whispering oaks. The passage[3] in which David hears "a whispering in the mulberry trees" is well known. The rustling of the leaves was to him the command of God urging him to attack the Philistines. Deborah, judge of the Hebrew tribes, gave her decisions under a palm tree which seemed to have marked a sacred locality and given authority to her utterances. When Jacob returned with his wives and kindred to Shechem, he took the foreign gods which were in possession of his family and buried them under the oak, probably the same tree underneath which Abraham had erected an altar. We may infer that Jacob thought the divinities who had inhabited the images would take up their residence in the tree.[4] When Jehovah appeared to Moses,[5] he was in the flaming bush, and later on he is spoken of as one "who dwells in the bush."[6]

The belief in trees as the haunts of gods is widespread among the Arabs. One could see a few years ago in the vicinity of Cairo a tree on every branch of which were hung rags, vestiges of clothing which the owners had placed there in order to come in close contact with the divine being who inhabited this place, and whose favor would be granted through this contact with something that they had worn.

To the prophets tree worship was idolatrous and hateful because of the license associated with the cult. We find Jeremiah complaining because the Israelites of his day were worshiping under every green tree.[7] While, of course, we may believe that the idolatry condemned by the prophet was borrowed from their heathen neighbors and represented an apostasy, we may just as reasonably conclude that tree worship was a traditional belief thousands of years old and persisting until Jeremiah's time.

The first act of reforming kings in Israel was to destroy the *Ashera* and *Asherim,* that is, the sacred tree and groves

---

[2] 9. 37.
[3] 2 Samuel 5. 24.
[4] Genesis 35. 4.
[5] Exodus 3. 2.
[6] Deuteronomy 33. 16.
[7] Jeremiah 3. 6.

which were frequented by the idolatry-loving Israelites. The *Ashera* was not a living tree but simply a stock. It had been stripped of its branches and was planted near an altar where sacrifice was offered. It was a symbol of a divine presence.[8] The plural *Asherim* designated the grove, which was often the scene of licentious practices utterly abhorrent to the prophets of Judah and Israel.

Not every tree was worshiped by the Semites. Among those thought sacred were pines, cedars, palms, and oaks and such as were in the vicinity of fountains or associated with some legend.

Tree worship was not confined to Semitic peoples. The Maypole and the fir tree employed at Christmas festivals are reminders of the idolatrous practices of Nordic ancestors who believed that such trees were sacred.

We are not to look intolerantly upon these early beliefs or judge of them as necessarily idolatrous. Considering Abraham to have been a man of faith, as the author of the book of Genesis asserts, we should expect him to seek God at the shrines where men felt he would be found. So men believe today and act accordingly. Richard W. Gilder, when camping with friends among the pine trees one summer, talked late into the night of the future of humanity and the way to know God, of the time when men face to face shall see God; and then as he turned to sleep with poetic imagination he conceived the pine branches above the tents to be whispering among themselves of what they had heard these men talking and saying each to the other:

"Heardest thou these wanderers dreaming of a time,
When man more near the eternal one shall climb?
How like the newborn babe that cannot tell,
The mother's arm that wraps it warm and well!"

SACRED FOUNTAINS

Everyone is familiar with the story of Hagar, Sarai's maid, who when she fled from her mistress[9] came to a fountain of water in the wilderness, where the angel of the Lord spoke

---

[8] Ashera was a goddess, the consort of Baal.
[9] Genesis 16. 7f.

to her.   It has been suggested that the story in its original
form indicated that the divinity of the fountain spoke to her.
Be that as it may, fountains were highly esteemed by the
thirsty dwellers of the desert and not infrequently the moving water seemed to them like the movement of the branches
of trees, and leaves, to be the action of a divine being.
Fountains fed by springs, waterbrooks, or any water having
movement is called living water.

The Hebrews during their sojourn in the wilderness spent
most of their time in the vicinity of a fountain in the north
of the Sinaitic peninsula.   The place was called Kadesh-
Barnea.   The term "Kadesh" means "sacred" and indicates
that the fountain was a haunt of a god or gods.   So the
inhabitants of the desert had always believed.   It is easy to
understand why the nomads who came to this oasis in the
wilderness should think of it as a shrine and accept the
legends associated with it.

Sacred Stones

The classic passage from which we understand that rocks
as well as trees and fountains were sacred is Genesis 28. 11f.,
where Jacob, after a dream in which God appears to him,
anoints a stone and says, "This is the house of God."   Near
the altars where sacrifices were offered there was always the
pillar, the symbol of the Divine Presence.   Moses' act of
smiting the rock in the wilderness in order that water might
gush out for the thirsty Israelites was thought of as an act
of impiety.[10]   Because of this he was barred from entrance
into the promised land.   Paul[11] alludes to the Jewish legend
that a rock followed the Israelites all through the days of
their wandering.

This belief of early man of powers or souls residing in
inanimate objects was widespread and persists unto the
present time.   In the South Sea Islands the term used for
the manifestation is *mana,* while in almost all books on
comparative religion and anthropology the term "animism"
is used.   The primitive mind discerns everywhere the pres-

[10] Numbers 20. 10f.
[11] 1 Corinthians 10. 4.

ence of the supernatural. He finds an "aliveness" in the
world about him. The inanimate world, as we call it, is to
him animated.

ANCESTOR WORSHIP

The oldest Phoenician shrines are caves. As the archaeologist has shown, the first inhabitants of Palestine were cave
dwellers, and doubtless their homes were occupied by the
Hebrews when they first entered the land. In the deep
recesses of these caves gods[12] were thought to dwell. Later,
when religion had reached a higher stage of development, the
gods of caves were thought to be unfriendly and no individual in private capacity could consult with them, for this
was to have commerce with evil. When Saul consulted the
witch of Endor, who was dwelling in a cave, he was trafficking according to the belief of the time with evil spirits.

THE FEAR OF THE THRESHOLD

One of the most curious beliefs of primitive times, which
still survives, is the fear of the threshold. It is common to
Aryan people from the highlands of Scotland to the Vedic
worshipers on the banks of the Ganges. It is quite as prevalent among Semitic peoples. To this day a Syrian bride is
carried in the arms of her husband across the threshold of
her future home. Livy, commenting upon a similar custom
in his day, expresses the opinion that the superstition dates
back to the days when brides were obtained by capture. He
was probably wrong.

In connection with Solomon's Temple, there were men
who held the office of "keepers of the threshold." Their
duty seems to have been to keep the worshiper from stepping
upon or stumbling over the threshold of the Temple. Now,
why this care or why the fear attached to the threshold?
The explanation seems to lie in the custom of early man in
burying his dead at the entrance of the cave, which was his
home, so that the spirit of the dead man might be as near as
possible to the place which he had frequented in his lifetime;
hence the fear or the awe associated with the threshold. It

---

[12] The spirits of ancestors.

throws an interesting light upon the incident recorded in
I Samuel 5, where the Philistine idol fell upon the threshold
and was destroyed, and on the verse in the Psalms which
is so often quoted, "The LORD shall keep thy going out and
thy coming in from this time forth and forevermore." He
was the keeper of the threshold.

SUPPLEMENTARY READING

Peake and Fleure, *Corridors of Time,* Vol. III, Chapter II.
John P. Peters, *Religion of the Hebrews,* Chapter III.
Henry P. Smith, *Religion of Israel,* Chapter II.
William Robertson Smith, *Religion of the Semites,* Lectures 4, 5.
Hastings, *Encyclopedia of Religion and Ethics,* article on
  animism.
Bible, Genesis 12. 6-7; 16. 1f.; 28. 10f.

CHAPTER III

SEMITIC ORIGINS

IN the preceding chapter attention was directed to the shrines of the early Semites. Many of them were in Canaan, and at their altars Abraham and his descendants worshiped. But we are not to conclude that they were the first to frequent these sanctuaries, or that ordinarily men worshiped one deity who appeared to them at different times and places.[1] On the contrary, Canaan, and, in fact, the entire Semitic world, was peopled with gods. These were known by the generic term *elim,* plural of *el,* and were differentiated by local designations. The supernatural embraced not only gods, but demons and the spirits of the field. It will be recalled that in Arabic literature the demons are called *jinn,* spirits which are not always bound on evil intent but frequently serve man's interest.

The Day of Atonement afforded an illustration of the persistence of the early feeling which men had for the spirits of the field. Two goats were chosen for the sacrificial offering, one was devoted to God, over the other the priest confessed the sins of the people and sent the goat bearing the guilt to the wilderness. The ultimate depository, we are told, was Azazel, a name given to a desert demon.[2] While the details are interesting, it is unnecessary to say more than this in explanation of an extraordinary rite. The late conception is clear. The guilt of the nation is confessed, it is transferred to the scapegoat which is led out of the community.[3] But the original idea was likely an offering to a patron spirit of the fields. The persistence of the name in historic times indicates that Azazel was still capable of receiving the offering, though both the character of the demon and the nature of the offering are changed.

[1] Genesis 12. 6-8 ; 13. 18.
[2] Leviticus 16. 8-10, 11, 21-22, R. V.
[3] And thrown over a precipice. Mishna Tractate Yoma 6.

Totemism

Did the early Semites emerge from a totemic stage? Robertson Smith thinks so, and has argued persuasively to that end in his epoch-making work, *The Religion of the Semites*.

Totemism, it may be remarked in passing, is prevalent over wide areas among Indian tribes in North America, where often the totem is merely a badge of the clan, in parts of Africa, and among non-Aryans in India. It is found also among Australian tribes, in Melanesia, and Polynesia.

Its dominant feature is the kinship between the clan and a totom animal, the name of which the clan bears. This promotes the solidarity of the clan and conserves some social values. While totemism is not a religion, it is coexistent with the cult of the dead and the worship of spirits. It invariably belongs to a low stage of culture and is left behind when a people attain civilization. There are excellent reasons for believing that Egypt passed through a totemic stage, but in that case it emerged from it long before the historic period.

While we cannot affirm that totemism prevailed among the early Semites, the view is congenial to many minds who find support for it, so they believe, in the Old Testament. It is true that some of its outstanding features give color to the theory, but it must be admitted that the reasons deduced rest on a slight foundation. Without going into arguments, pro or con, it is enough to say that Robertson Smith has envisaged an early Semitic society comprising demons and wild beasts on the one side and gods and men and some animals on the other. "The triumph of the gods over the demons was sealed and secure when the agricultural stage was reached." This may fairly represent the attitude of primitive man toward his environment, but it does not necessarily involve totemism. The gods, Professor Smith points out, are friendly. They dwell in the haunts of men, in the moving trees, the running water, and in the sheltering rock. This, in brief, is the hypothesis upon which he builds a religion of man's need rather than his fears. We shall see this in his view of sacrifice.

The Purpose of Sacrifice

How shall the gods be approached? There are two answers, by magical ceremonies and by sacrifice. Commonly, sacrifice took the form of a sacrificial feast in which a domesticated animal—a sheep, a goat, a heifer—was sacrificed. The blood was poured out as a drink offering to the deity, perhaps first upon the ground and later on a symbolic pillar. The roasted flesh was partaken of by the people and the rest of the animal was burned. As the cult advanced, considerable significance was attached to the smoking fat, its rising clouds like the odor of burning incense being acceptable to deity. The blood which, as we said, belonged to God was taboo to man. Even in New-Testament times the early Gentile converts were commanded to refrain from eating food which had been cooked with blood.

The sacrifice was a part, as has been stated, of the sacrificial feast in which there were two parties who entered by this act into a covenant of friendship. To eat together in early times was a token of kinship. It is to be observed in this connection that women did not eat with men because their kinship was outside of the clan and not within. The purpose of the sacrifice in some instances may have been to placate a god whom the worshiper had offended, but commonly it was a commerce with a friendly deity. Eventually other meanings were attached to sacrifice but this was the fundamental one.

In early times no member of a clan could sacrifice an animal for his own use apart from the sacrificial feast. The sacrifice of the animal was, therefore, a religious ceremony, which was thought to be no hardship for meat was only eaten at stated times; for example, on festive occasions. A spirit of gladness marked the sacrificial feast. It was not a time of mourning. There is truth in Marett's statement that early man danced his way rather than thought his way into religion.[4]

[4] R. R. Marett, *The Threshold of Religion.* There is, of course, another view of sacrifice in which the victim is regarded as a sin offering. Both views may have prevailed in early times.

MAGIC AND RELIGION

The reader should turn to Deuteronomy, chapter 18, verses 9-12, to see the part that magic played in Semitic life. While sternly condemned by their prophets, the Hebrews were familiar enough with the practice and potency of charms. Now, magic is not religion. The purpose of sacrifice at the lowest was to placate or appease the wrath of the gods. It was most frequently a sacrificial feast in which gods and men met on terms of friendship. It had an ethical element; it was capable of considerable significance. Sacrifice was a religious act; magic was not. Magic sought to coerce, not persuade the gods. It was without an ethical motive and not infrequently accompanied with subterfuge and trickery. It assumed that the gods were weaker or less subtle than men.

Frazer, in *The Golden Bough*,[5] argues that magic preceded religion and was the first means of approach to the unseen world which primitive man so dimly understood. But magic and religion were both familiar to the savage. They were as the back and palm of the hand stretched out to take what it could. Moreover, magic survived, outliving the prehistoric stage, and was so congenial to men's mind that we find it extensively practiced by Greek and Romans and not uncommon in our own midst.

CIRCUMCISION

Among the religious practices of the Hebrews great emphasis was placed upon circumcision. The institution was not peculiar to the Hebrews but was practiced by all Semitic peoples save only the Babylonians and the Assyrians. Circumcision was common among the Egyptians, and is a rite observed in modern times by nearly all the African tribes, by the Australians, and in some parts of North and South America. The rite is of great antiquity. When Abraham was commanded to circumcise Isaac, he was not to perform a rite which was unfamiliar to the patriarch but, rather, to give a new significance to a ceremony long practiced. Com-

---

[5] See Vol. I, Chap. I.
So A. T. Olmstead, *History of Palestine and Syria*, p. 15.

monly among primitive tribes, it is a rite of initiation performed at the age of puberty. The boys of the tribe were not thought to attain manhood until they had undergone this operation, which released them from the control of their mothers, admitted them to full membership in the tribe, and prepared them for marriage. Among the Hebrews, the ceremony is practiced in infancy and its purpose seems to be like that of baptism in the Christian Church to admit the child into the privileges of the religious community and to bring him into direct and intimate relation with God.

Many reasons have been assigned to explain the origin of circumcision. Some say it was hygienic; some state that it was a rite essential to the marriage relation; others that it was merely an initiation ceremony; but all these explanations are inadequate to explain the origin of a cult which probably at first was no more than an initiation ceremony wherein great stress was laid upon the potency of the blood as a charm. Afterward a new significance was read into the rite until it finally came to have the meaning which it has today.

RITUAL AND TABOOS

In Exodus, chapter 34,[6] we find a second decalogue differing in marked respects from the more familiar commands found in Exodus 20. The former is concerned with ritual, the latter with commands of moral import. One belongs to the beginning of the agricultural period in Canaan, the other is timeless. The first is of interest only to the Hebrew people, the latter is of universal significance.

A detailed examination of the ritual code shows that the first two commands relate to the worship of Israel's God. Foreign cults and molten images are prohibited. The injunctions which follow, bidding all males three times in the year to appear before God, enumerate the feasts which are to be observed, the Passover, the Feast of Weeks, the Feast of the Ingathering. Since these are applicable only to an agricultural people, they will be discussed later. There is one exception, the Passover, which at first seems to have been a

[6] Exodus 34. 14-26.

festival of the moon god. It was invariably observed at the
time of the full moon. Its celebration appealed to a nomadic
people whose nightly journeys were lighted by the moon and
whose calendar was determined by its phases. In historic
times, its origin was dismissed and it was celebrated as marking the deliverance of Israel from Egypt.

The commands which close the decalogue are prohibitory,
some of them betraying an ancient lineage. The last in the
enumeration[7] is curious, namely, the taboo against seething
a kid in its mother's milk. Frazer citing similar taboos
among present-day African tribes explains the prohibition as
due to the belief that boiling the milk would bring injury to
the mother, an example of sympathetic magic. An equally
satisfactory explanation is offered by those who see in the
taboo the prohibition of an idolatrous rite of neighboring
peoples.[8] That it was originally practiced by nomadic Israel
we may assume. Otherwise there would be no meaning to
the prohibition.

OTHER TABOOS

The familiar command not to eat swine's flesh has provoked much comment on the part of those who seek the
origin of the taboo, and several theories have been pro-
pounded only two of which call for mention: that the pig was
a totem animal and the taboo against eating it lingered after
the reasons assigned had long been forgotten; or that the
abhorrence on the part of Hebrews arose because it was a
cult practiced by their enemies. It is known from excavations in Palestine that at a very early date the pig was
sacrosanct, its bones being found in the vicinity of altars.[9]

Great significance was attached to the Sabbath day, which
originally was observed as a Babylonian institution occurring
monthly at the time of the new moon. The occasion was one
of great solemnity, and it was believed that the performance
of certain acts on that day would bring misfortune. To quote
again from the author of *The Golden Bough,* the incident

[7] Exodus 34. 26, also 23. 19, and Deuteronomy 14. 21.
[8] S. H. Hooke, *Myth and Ritual,* p. 71. The Clarendon Press, Oxford.
[9] See Stanley A. Cook, *The Religion of Ancient Palestine in the Light
of Archaeology,* p. 79. Oxford Press.

related in the book of Numbers[10] of a man gathering sticks on the Sabbath day and who was punished by death for so doing is explained by the belief that kindling a fire on the Sabbath would bring misfortune to the community.

In these and similar taboos we perceive how the long arm of custom reached over and seized in its iron grasp the children of a new day. Fortunately, the prohibitory element is not the only feature of Old-Testament legislation. It was on the whole the most humanitarian of all ancient codes, due to the influence not of early but of late legislators.[11]

This chapter should not be brought to a close without at least a passing reference to two features of nomadic life, customs so deeply ingrained in the social structure that they betray their ancient origin, and so universally followed that they have all the binding force of legal enactments, namely, blood revenge and hospitality. Both are characteristic of the modern Arab, who is an implacable foe to those he hates, and whose hospitality to the stranger is proverbial.

The earliest extant Hebrew poetry is a song of vengeance, the taunt of Lamech who sings to his wives:

> "Adah and Zillah, hear my voice . . .
> I have slain a man for wounding me,
> And a young man for bruising me;
> If Cain shall be avenged sevenfold,
> Truly Lamech seventy and sevenfold."[12]

The reference is to the blood penalty which will be exacted by the clan, one of whose members Lamech has slain. The law of blood revenge devolved upon the whole clan. It was their duty to exact justice, a life for a life; and if the murderer could not be found, to punish his tribal group.

No humanitarian codes of a later day succeeded in doing away with the *lex talionis*. A possible miscarriage of justice was avoided by the cities of refuge[13] to which the hunted man might flee for protection. Again there was the refuge

---

[10] Numbers 15. 32-36.
[11] The reference is to the Deuteronomists.
[12] Genesis 4. 23, 24.
[13] Numbers 35. 9f.

of his own clan, the members of which were bound to protect him.

The nomad has a strong sense of responsibility, and this is evinced not only toward the tribal members but toward strangers who as long as they are under the protecting tent roof of their host are safe in respect to person and property. Of course such hospitality cannot last forever. To be exact, it continues among modern Arabs just three days and four hours. After that the guest is on his own. He may stay on, but he must share in the expense and labor of the household to which he is attached. His stay might become permanent, leading, as Bertholet has remarked, to shifting numbers in the tribal census.[14]

The book of Genesis reflects on its pages the hospitality accorded to the stranger, but nowhere with such charm and restraint in the recountal as in the tale of Abraham, who received graciously three strangers and learned later that he had entertained "angels unaware."[15]

Supplementary Reading

Alfred Bertholet, *History of Hebrew Civilization*, Chapter III.
Morris Jastrow, Jr., *Hebrew and Babylonian Traditions*, Chapter III.
Solomon Reinach, *Orpheus*, Introductory chapter, Section II.
William Robertson Smith, *Religion of the Semites*, Lecture III.
Encyclopedia Britannica, articles on Totemism and Magic.
Encyclopedia of Religion and Ethics, article on "Totemism."
The Mishnah, tr. by Herbert Dandy, p. 169.

[14] See *History of Hebrew Civilization*, p. 120. Geo. Harrap & Co., London.
[15] Genesis 18. 1f.

CHAPTER IV

THE SUMERIANS

THE states which now claim our attention, Babylonia and Egypt, were contiguous to the territory occupied by the Semitic nomads. Due to their fertility, their unequaled situation, and the genius of the people who occupied them, these countries developed rapidly and became the seats of the earliest civilizations. Influential to the highest degree among states contemporary and contiguous to them and bequeathing to posterity a legacy of government, legislation, historic records, literature, art, and religion, they evoke the admiration of the modern world. It is essential that we pass in rapid review the facts relating to their geographical position, their rise to pre-eminence, and their place in history in order to estimate their contribution to ethics and religion.

We can properly begin with the Sumerians, who were the first people to attain civilization in Babylonia. The land which they occupied was small in area, being equivalent to the state of New Jersey. It was the lower part of that alluvial plain which stretches from the slopes of the Armenian plateau to the Persian gulf. The plain is watered by two great streams, the Euphrates and the Tigris, and their tributaries. The rivers bring a great amount of silt from the mountains and deposit it where they enter the gulf. Consequently, the sea has receded while the land area has constantly increased. At the present time, the deposit is equal to about ninety feet a year. Cities which six thousand years ago were on the sea are today ninety miles inland. The Sumerians called their country Sumer and the neighboring state on the north Akkad. In biblical records the plain was designated as Shinar (Genesis 11), and with the supremacy of Babylon, the name "Babylonia" was attached to the territory. Greeks knew it as Mesopotamia, and the name still clings, although some prefer the variant "Land of the Two Rivers." It is today a part of the Arabic state of Irak.

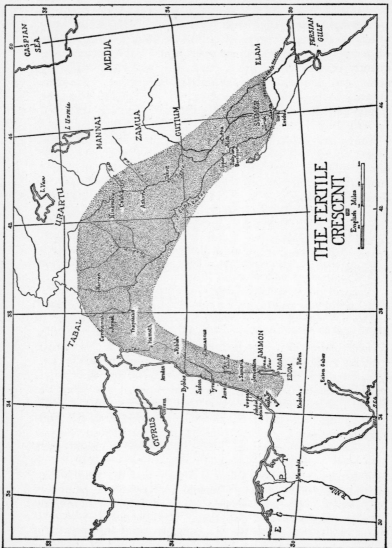

THE FERTILE
CRESCENT

English Miles

CASPIAN SEA
MEDIA
ELAM
PERSIAN GULF
MANNAI
ZAMUA
GUTIUM
SUMER
L. Urmia
L. Van
URARTU
Nineveh
Calah
Ashur
Arbela
Babylon
Cutha
Kish
Sippar
Nippur
Erech
Ur
Eridu
TABAL
Harran
Carchemish
Arpad
Thapsacus
HamatA
Riblah
Damascus
Orontes
Arvad
Byblos
Sidon
Tyre
Acre
Joppa
Samaria
Jerusalem
Bethel
Kedesh
Eziom Geber
Petra
AMMON
MOAB
EDOM
CYPRUS
Tarsus
Cilicia
Dead Sea
Memphis
EGYPT
Nile
RED SEA

Isothermal charts of Sumer and lower Mississippi, very nearly on the same degree of latitude, exhibit a similar range of temperature, although summer heat in the former frequently reaches 126 degrees Fahrenheit and runs ordinarily about 110 degrees in the shade from June to September. Wheat, barley, and the much-prized date palm were the staples produced in a land, the fertility of which was enhanced by irrigation.[1]

Sumer and Akkad were both agricultural states and possessed no mineral wealth. Since the predynastic tombs contained funerary articles of copper, silver, gold, and lapis lazuli, while other objects indicate the wide employment of limestone, diorite and alabaster, we must conclude that the Mesopotamian states from a very early period had an extensive commerce. Moreover, several of the metals named are found in widely separated parts of western Asia. In Hittite graves have been discovered cylinder seals of Sumerian workmanship, belonging to a period not later than 3000 B. C.

SUMERIAN ORIGIN

Who were the Sumerians? No one can answer with a great degree of certainty. They were not Semitic, nor were they of Mongolian extraction, as some have conjectured. A plausible suggestion makes them to be a Indo-European people, who not later than 4,000 B. C. entered the Tigris-Euphratean basin from the east and north. They gradually moved down the river until they came to the Delta.[2] Here they found settlements of people who had long preceded them.

Recent excavations at Al-Ubaid and elsewhere in the south indicate the early occupancy of the Delta by a race which one naturally associates with the later Semites. The country was at first a swamp and its occupants lived on islands. They were potters and excavations reveal superior workmanship, fine painted ware, saw-tooth flint sickles made of hard-baked clay. Model boats and fishhooks suggest another occupation.

---

[1] Samples of the superior wheat grown in Sumer have been found in jars; now exhibited in the Ashmolean Museum at Oxford.
[2] So C. L. Woolley in his book, *The Sumerians*.

For ornaments they had beads of shell and of carnelian, obsidian, and white quartz. Archaeology has shown that not one culture but several preceded the Sumerian.

The entrance of the Sumerians does not seem to have been contested. They soon showed themselves to be a dominant race, constructing canals, draining the marshes, cultivating the land, sowing crops, building towns and laying the foundations for a great and enduring civilization.

Considerable curiosity has been excited as to the probable home of the Sumerians before they came to the Delta. Apparently they had been a mountain people, for their principal deity was Enlil, a storm god, represented by a written character in which a mountain stands at the back. The zikkurat, or tower, which was a conspicuous feature of their temples, was built in such a way that it recalled the mountains where once they worshiped. The view that the Sumerians were Indian in origin is held by Hall, Frankfort, and others, but Peake and Fleure pertinently inquire, "Need we go so far?" To them it seems clear that they entered the country between 4000 and 3500 B. C., coming by sea from coasts on the Persian Gulf.[3]

The Semites, their neighbors, were also an alien people, having drifted into the fertile valley from Arabia. In their customs, habits of thought, backwardness in developing a civilization, they do not seem to have differed from their kinsmen of a later period. Eventually they were engulfed by the superior culture of the Sumerians who long remained the dominant race in southern Babylonia.

The monuments throw some light upon the physical characteristics of the two Delta races. We have on the one hand a round-headed people, smoothly shaven faces, prominent cheek bones; on the other, long-shaped heads, bearded faces and fleshy noses, unmistakably Semitic. Sir Arthur Keith writes of the former, "One can still trace the ancient Sumerian face eastward among the inhabitants of Afghanistan and Baluchistan until the valley of the Indus is reached some fifteen hundred miles from Mesopotamia."

[3] Peake and Fleure, *C. of T.*, Vol. III, p. 95. Oxford University Press.

The recent extensive exploration in Asiatic countries has brought to light a pottery of a very superior quality found in Russian Turkestan, in Elam, and in the cities of Sumer. The pottery was found at a low level, indicating its antiquity. It was made of a finely kneaded clay which had been turned on a wheel, with thin and delicate walls painted with geometrical designs in lustrous black paint. This superior quality of pottery, far better than that which followed, has been explained in various ways. The time sequence would indicate that it belonged to a period in the fifth millennium B. C. Stephen Langdon writes in commenting upon it: "A great prehistoric civilization spread from central Asia to the plateau of Iran, to Syria and to Egypt long before 4000 B. C., of which the pottery is an evidence."[4] He adds that the Sumerian people in his opinion are a later branch of this Central Asiatic race, and entered Mesopotamia about 5000 B. C. There is little to be said in favor of a view which recent discoveries do not support.

THE HISTORY OF SUMER

The early history of the Sumerians has been reconstructed, thanks to the excavator and the scholar. In this task they have been aided by the myths and legends preserved in later Babylonian literature, by the study of codes of laws, by the kings' lists, the inscribed monuments, the thousands of cylinder seals, and more recently by extensive discoveries in predynastic graves. The Sumerians had their own written records after 3100 B. C., as the tablets found in Lagash have shown,[5] but the knowledge of the prehistoric period must be learned in other ways.

The city-states of Sumer were independently governed and were frequently at war with one another over water rights, a disputed boundary line, or a strip of land. In addition to civil feuds, there were, of course, external foes against which they made common cause. Thus Sumer developed in time a powerful military organization. We can gain some knowl-

---

[4] This is disputed; see *Corridors of Time*, Vol. III, p. 92. Oxford University Press.
[5] From the first dynasty of Ur, c. 3500 B. C.

edge of this from sculptured reliefs which depict the phalanx, a compact and formidable unit, the use of the chariot driven by the king or commander of the troops and drawn by asses, the horse not being in general use before 2000 B. C.[6] Their weapons were the battle-ax, the spear, and the mace; and, contrary to opinion, a division of the army was equipped as bowmen.

Among the early kings of Sumer in the historic period was Urukagina. He lived about 2900 B. C., reigning only for six years. He was peace-loving, a builder rather than a military commander. He has to his credit the building of temples, the construction of canals, and the codification of the oldest body of legislation which we possess. He executed reforms for the poor and gave liberty to his subjects. He was an enlightened and able monarch, ahead of his age. However, his brief beneficent reign ended tragically. His capital was invaded by Lugalzaggisi, bringing "blood and fire." The homes and temples of Lagash were burned and the people led into captivity. The complaints addressed in verse to the deities of the city are not unlike the laments of the Hebrew psalmists who write in time of misfortune.

In 2750 B. C. the Sumerian cities were invaded by Sargon, a Semitic chieftain, who, encouraged by his success, subdued the neighboring state of Elam, and then led his victorious army northward, conquering the Amorites in Syria and penetrating, so we are informed, the Island of Cyprus. In his old age all his subject territory was in revolt and Sargon personally went into battle to quell the rebellion. Nevertheless, his reign ended disastrously with the empire which he had founded crumbling to pieces. Naram-Sin, his son, regained to some extent the prestige of his father. He is best known for the Stele of Victory, a limestone slab showing the king in the act of leading his soldiers to battle. This notable work of art, a prized possession of the Louvre, is instructive not only as showing the method of warfare the Akkadians followed, but their attainment as artists. Here

---

[6] At Kish have been found toy horses dated during the period 3000 to 2800 B. C., thus indicating that the horse was in use in Mesopotamia six hundred to eight hundred years earlier than was thought.

we find a freedom of execution that their masters the Sumerians never displayed.

During the next period the kings, whether Semite or Sumerian, called themselves rulers of Akkad and Sumer, the two states being federated. However, this did not prevent strife. Had the federation been one in fact as well as in name, their united forces could have more successfully resisted the foreign invasions of Elamites on the east and the Amorites on the north. A breathing spell was permitted when their enemies opposed one another and the clash of arms between Elamite and Amorite permitted the ascendancy of Ur in its third and most brilliant dynasty. The period came to an end in 2282 B. C.[7]

In the next one hundred and fifty years, we have few historical documents to guide us. The southern states were governed by the rulers of Isin and Larsa, who frequently called themselves kings of Akkad and Sumer, but they represented rival and warring dynasties and were unable to stand against the threatening advance of the Amorites in the north or the Elamites who had actually established a state in the midst of their territory. With the end of their rule, Sumerian domination in the Euphratean valley ceased. The Amorites, who now appear on the stage, represent a new Semitic infiltration in the valley, and owe their dominance to the military genius of their leaders.

THE GOLDEN AGE OF HAMMURABI

Hammurabi,[8] sixth in the line of Amorite kings, living about 2125 B. C., made Babylon his capital. Under him a city hitherto unimportant became great. He strongly fortified it, and the wealth gained through trade and his military successes he used for embellishing the city. Of its temples and palaces we know little, for it was destroyed a few centuries later. It was the Babylon of Nebuchadnezzar's day, sixth century B. C., that literature celebrated. Our knowledge of the earlier Babylon can only be derived from what excavations may uncover.

---

[7] H. R. Hall, in *Ancient History of the Near East,* p. 191.
[8] There are alternate spellings of Hammurabi. The author follows Century, Webster, *et al.*

Hammurabi was undoubtedly a military genius and a statesman. His enduring monument is a code of laws inscribed on a black diorite pillar, which once stood in Babylon, but in the twelfth century B. C. was carried away by an Elamitic chieftain and placed in his own city of Susa, where it was discovered by the French. Hammurabi was not, properly speaking, a lawgiver, but he must be credited with collecting a body of legislation long in use, and making it the law of the countries over which he ruled.

"It was no easy task," writes Jastrow, "for even so great a ruler as Hammurabi to hold a vast empire together." During the reign of his son and successor we hear of conflicts with the Cassites, a mountainous people of Indo-European extraction, semibarbarous but capable of assimilating the elements of a higher civilization. By 1760 B. C. the entire country had been conquered by the Cassites but not until there had first been an invasion of the Hittites and many kaleidoscopic changes in the political fortunes of those who sought to govern Mesopotamian territory. These later lords of Babylon did not interfere with the "the sea land" as the Southern Kingdom was called, but nevertheless the Sumerian state existed only in name, its dwindling fortunes giving no promise of a resurrection. The Sumerians maintained themselves politically until 1720 B. C., when the state came to an end with the victory of a Cassite ruler, Ulamburiash.

Gods and Ritual

"The religious life of a people," writes Jastrow, "is always more enduring than their political fortunes." It need not seem strange to us to learn that centuries after the Sumerians ceased to be a nation their priests continued to perpetuate their ancient rites. In the period of Babylonian ascendancy the gods have not changed. Their new names were Semitic equivalents of Sumerian titles.

The bewildering number of deities in the Babylonian pantheon may be accounted for when we remember that the priesthood had catalogued all the deities of the independent city-states of Sumer and Akkad. Such a catalogue would bulk large. Originally the gods were nature deities; that is, they were personifications of the storm, the sun, the moon, and the stars. They were not the inventions of men, so it seemed to them, but discoveries. To name them was to know them and in some sense to gain their favor. There were storm gods like Enlil and Adab; solar deities, Ninib, Shamash and Nergal; the powerful moon god whom the Sumerians called Nannar and the Semites Sin; the seasonal gods, Tammuz and Ishtar; Ea, the ancient god of the sea; Anu of the sky. Religion permeated the whole social and political structure of the state. There was no important function at which the attendance of deity was not desirable. With the ascendancy of Babylon, we find Marduk, an ancient solar deity, accepting a new rôle. He is regarded as the son of Ea usurping his functions. Later he accepts the attributes of all the gods and is well on the way to become supreme. At least so it would appear to a Babylonian but not to a man of Eridu.

The relation of father and son among deities may be explained either as a formula to make place for two important deities like Ea and Marduk; or, as in the case of an aged king, we have the voluntary abdication of an older god to a younger with the consequent transfer of rule.

There were consorts for the gods, but as a rule they were shadowy and vague reflections of their lords. Antum, consort of Anu, is an exception. In Jeremiah's day she was called the queen of heaven and commanded a following on the part of Jewish exiles in Egypt. Ishtar alone among the goddesses stands in her own right. She is a goddess of fertility, of love, and sometimes of war, when, like an Amazon, she leads her people to victory.

For the gods there were temples, highly organized priesthoods, altars innumerable, and sacrificial offerings. The hymns and prayers addressed to deity, and "the penitential psalms," may be regarded as an advance in religious thought, while the magical formulas, and the divination take us back to that early period when men believed that the deity must be coerced. The widespread belief in demonology encouraged the use of magic. Against the "evil eye" and the demons which caused the ills of the body infinite precautions were taken. The medicine man used herbs having an emetic or cathartic quality valuable not because they were good for the patient but bad for the demon.

Religious prostitution was common. Attached to every temple were the women who composed "the god's household." The chief of these was a woman of high caste, often a king's daughter, and acting as high priestess. She was designated as *entu;* then there were women of the second class known as *sal-me*. These did not forfeit the right to marry after their term of service was completed. The third and largest class attached to the temple was known as *zikru* or *kadishtu*. While these were little more than common prostitutes, they had, because of the service rendered the god, a certain social position ordinarily denied women of their class.

Great importance was attached to family relations. Nearly one fourth of Hammurabi's code was legislation bearing upon this. Adultery, at first a venial offense, was later on punishable by death. There was increasing demand that children should perpetuate the family and their paternity be known. A barren woman was held to have forfeited the exclusive rights of wedlock. She might, as in the instance of Sarah, bestow a female slave upon her husband. In such a case the child born would be held as her own.

Inasmuch as the Hammurabi code is a compendium of early laws, it may be regarded as reflecting social conditions in the Sumerian period.

SUPPLEMENTARY READING

J. H. Breasted, *Ancient Times,* Chapter IV, or *Conquest of Civilization,* Chapter IV.

H. R. Hall, *Ancient History of the Near East,* Chapter V.

Morris Jastrow, Jr., *Civilization of Babylonia and Assyria,* Chapters III, IV.

Robert W. Rogers, *History of Babylonia and Assyria,* Vol. I, Chapters XI, XII.

C. L. Woolley, *The Sumerians,* Chapters II, IV.

Cambridge Ancient History, Vol. I, Chapters X, XII.

CHAPTER V

THE STORY OF EXCAVATION AND DECIPHERMENT

It is an astounding fact that the Sumerian civilization continuing for two millenniums, influential to the highest degree, exhibiting a varied culture, artistic, social, and religious, should pass completely from the memory of man.

Pompeii and Herculaneum were buried under the ashes and lava of Vesuvius for seventeen hundred years, but men knew this; the tale of their catastrophe had been written[1] and could at any moment be recalled, but no ancient history, no biblical record has kept alive the memory of the Sumerians. Gibbon wrote of the *Decline and Fall of the Roman Empire,* but no historian so far as we know recorded the vanishing glory of the Sumerian state.

The reason for the oblivion in which Sumerian civilization was buried seems to be the complete absorption of the states of Sumer and Akkad by Babylon. Their literature, their social customs, their laws, as well as their cities and canals, were taken over by the Babylonian state and made their own. Men continued to write in cuneiform character but the language they wrote was Semitic, really neo-Babylonian. Even now some scholars have a preference for the term "early Babylonian" when they refer to the Sumerian civilization though the term is an anachronism and only properly used after 2100 B. C.

The early archaeologists were as oblivious of the fact of a Sumerian civilization as the historians had been. The first excavations were in the north and uncovered Assyrian monuments and the remains of the contemporary or later Babylonian civilization. It was not until the lower Mesopotamian Valley where Sumerian culture once flourished had been excavated, and men had penetrated the lower levels

---

[1] Pliny and Younger (61-113 A. D.).

which mark the earlier period that the ancient states of
Sumer and Akkad were brought to light.

EXCAVATIONS

Excavations began in 1842, when the French government
sent to Mosul the young and able archaeologist and diplomat,
Paul Emil Botta. Trade with Mosul did not warrant con-
sular relations, but the report of travelers and surface findings had intrigued the government. Moreover, the French
had been successful in Egypt and were disposed to heed the
representation of scholars who felt that the era of exploration
in the Tigris-Euphrates valley should give place to excavation. Botta, therefore, went not to explore but to dig.

Mosul was then a thriving Mesopotamian town. It had
given its name to a soft cotton cloth, muslin, which it was
the first to manufacture. Later its importance diminished,
but recently there has been a revival of interest, since it is
near the center of the oil fields of Irak. To the archaeologist
it owes its renown because of its proximity to Nineveh and
other ancient cities. Their sites are marked by heaps or
mounds of dirt and sand, the accumulated debris of centuries.
Cities built of sunbaked bricks are not durable. Earthquakes,
devastating storms, the attack of armies, and the relentless
barrage of time destroy and bury their buildings. When
again men seized the locality as a likely building site, no effort
was made to clear away the rubbish. There was no pains-
taking search in the ashes of the former city for objects of
value, but the ground was leveled off. Such walls as remained intact were employed for foundations, and occasionally the incorporation of the old with the new was
made, if a piece of sculpture or an inscribed stone seized the
fancy of the new builder.

Botta began his labors at Kuyunjik, a small village built
on the mound which he correctly identified as the site of
Nineveh.[2] He worked under great difficulties, due to inex-
perienced native help, the natural hostility of the villagers,

---

[2] He was aided in his indentification by the tradition that the prophet
Jonah was buried near by, his grave marked by the mosque with a
slender minaret.

and the lack of funds. He had insufficient means to buy the site but depended upon the consent of the Turkish government to continue his explorations. It is not surprising that the results were meager and that we find him transferring his work to Khorsabad, a few miles away. Here the village built on the site was removed to another location and the work of excavation proceeded with rapidity. Sargon, an Assyrian king of the eight century, had built here a palace and a fortress. Botta by a lucky chance had lighted upon the exact situation of the royal abode and European eyes could now behold for the first time the glory of Assyrian architecture and decoration. The treasures which the young excavator found he shipped to Paris, where they may be viewed by those who visit the Assyrian antiquities of the Louvre.

Two years before Botta reached Mosul it was visited by an Englishman, Austin Henry Layard, a close student of the Bible, gifted with a poetic imagination and enthusiastic to uncover the cities the ruin of which the prophets of Israel and Judah had predicted. He returned in 1845 with sufficient funds to attempt his work. While he excavated sites of the ancient cities of Calah and Asshur, he was most successful on the site of Nineveh, where Botta had met no success. Here Layard uncovered the palaces of Sennacherib and Ashurbanipal. In the latter he found in two rooms the remains of a royal library. The number of tablets recovered then and in subsequent excavations was thirty thousand. These proved to be most valuable records, rich in myth and legendary lore. However, they were undecipherable at the time and were dispatched to the British Museum, where they were carefully stored away until the key was found which would enable scholars to read them.

Other explorers in the first period of excavation should be named, Rawlinson, Rassam, and Loftus, but the account of their work need not detain us in our hurried summary. It was perhaps fortunate that for several reasons the work of excavation lagged for a time, for it enabled scholars to transfer their interest to the important task of deciphering the records. From the thirteenth century of our era travelers in the East had been fascinated by the inscriptions on the monuments, notably among which were those found in Persepolis. Frequently they were trilingual, that is, written in three languages—ancient Persian, Elamatic, and Assyrian. But this was not at first patent. To Grotefend belongs the credit of distinguishing the Persian from the other two. It was rightly conjectured that the translation of one inscription would furnish the key for unlocking the meaning of the other two. The ancient Persian, an alphabetical writing, was conquered first. Following Grotefend's announcement of his success are the linguistic achievements of other scholars in France and England, and the syllabic writings of Susa and Babylon were deciphered. The year was 1851.

Meanwhile Sir Henry Rawlinson was working independently in the East and securing, apart from the others, the decipherment of the cuneiform. His success was partly due to his twenty-two years residence in Asia, his acquaintance with modern Persia and Oriental modes of thought, but chiefly on account of his remarkable achievement in translating the rock inscriptions at Behistun. Here, on a cliff three hundred feet above the caravan way, which leads from Bagdad to Hamadan, were sculptured figures carved by the artists of Darius's realm and beneath a Persian alphabetical writing. On the left above was an inscription in the language of Elam and below the cuneiform of Babylon. It was obvious that this was the Rosetta stone of Persia, that the three inscriptions were addressed to three races of Darius's kingdom, and that they said the same thing. Rawlinson first tried to read the characters with a spyglass, but failing, he scaled with ladders the face of the cliff and made a squeeze of the writing. Altogether he was twelve years in the work of decipherment (1835–1847).

Cuneiform Writing

"Cuneiform" means "wedge-shaped," and gains the name from the strokes of the pen, which is applied to the tablet of soft clay in such a way as to give a wedge-shaped mark. The Assyrian-Babylonian language is Semitic but its writing is in a character borrowed from the Sumerians. The cuneiform character was at first an ideogram, or picture writing. Examples of such writing have been found and show clearly that in this way the Sumerians began to write. Then the characters were conventionalized and their meaning was extended. Two characters were frequently united; for example, the sign for water united with the eye meant weeping; the ox head with the sign for mountain meant wild ox. In course of time the characters were multiplied and the meanings assigned to them extended until the language became difficult to read and write. Lists of word signs were prepared, and these indicate that those who employed the syllabic character recognized its deficiency. The Persians, as we have seen, adopted the alphabetic character before the days of Darius.

Beginning with 1878 we enter upon a period of systematic excavation in which societies German, English, French, and American take a part, dividing up the territory which they are to survey and work. The first notable work done by Americans was that of the University of Pennsylvania. Their archaeological museum is the accumulated result of years of patient and successful labor.

WORK OF TRANSLATION CONTINUED

When once the key had been found which unlocked the meaning of the cuneiform character, the work of translation was greatly hastened. The two decades following upon 1855 were remarkable in the results achieved. In the year 1872 a curator of the British Museum, George Smith, made a startling announcement before the Biblical Archaeological Society. Rassam had brought to London tablets in which a remarkable parallel to the Flood story of Genesis was recorded. These Smith had translated and read before the society. The effect was electrical. Everyone believed that the account confirmed the Genesis story, and a wave of popular enthusiasm swept over the country. The *Daily Telegraph* sent Smith to Mesopotamia, and he searched even more carefully than Rassam had done the rooms in which the Deluge story had been found. Smith was fortunate in discovering additional fragments which fitted into those previously brought to light. His work admirably supplemented that of Layard and Rassam on the site; for fragments which they had overlooked, but which were necessary for the completion of texts, he recognized as important. Upon his return with this treasure, he threw himself with enthusiasm into the task of preparing a translation for the public. The result was the publication of two books under the titles, *Assyrian Discoveries* and *The Chaldean Genesis*.

It must be kept in view that the seventh-century Ashurbanipal library with its rich legendary lore furnishes copy of the literature which flourished fifteen hundred years earlier, in Hammurabi's time. But back of the Babylonian record is the Sumerian original, and it is not too much to say that we have in the tablets stories which were current in the fourth millennium B. C.

The importance of this epoch of discovery and translation can hardly be exaggerated. In addition to the light which it throws upon late cultures in the Euphratean Valley, it brought to the knowledge of man the story of a forgotten race and shed radiance upon the pages of the Bible.

SUPPLEMENTARY READING

J. H. Breasted, *Ancient Times,* Chapter IV, Sections 13-17. *Conquest of Civilization,* Chapter IV.

Morris Jastrow, Jr., *Civilization of Babylonia and Assyria,* Chapters I, II.

Robert W. Rogers, *History of Babylonia and Assyria,* Vol. I, Chapter V.

CHAPTER VI

SUMERIAN MYTHS AND CULTS

In the preceding chapter attention was called to the rich store of legendary material found in the seventh-century library of Ashurbanipal. These records of myths and legends may be regarded as transcripts from originals in the temple archives of Babylon or Borsippa. But they in turn were derived from Sumerian sources long before the period of the written word, for the origin of the myth lies in the nebulous past.

Primitive man was deeply moved by the manifestations of nature whether violent or periodic—the storm, the midsummer sun blighting vegetation, the change of the seasons, the phases of the moon. In natural phenomena he saw the activity of deities hostile or friendly. To control them to his advantage by recitation or dramatic representation, by the celebration of festivals or magical practices, seemed needful. Inseparably bound up with the myth was the cult which kept it alive, and made it possible for him to live safely. The myth, then, was man's early account of nature. It was born of the effect of natural phenomena upon his consciousness. In time it took on a wider connotation, but at first the nature myth was the only myth he knew.

For the home of the myth, we must look to the fountainhead of civilization and from thence trace the mythology which, despite the change of names and distance traveled, betrays its ancient lineage. The myths and the cults which grew out of them everywhere in the Near East exhibit striking resemblances which hint strongly of borrowing, and give warrant to the thesis of S. H. Hooke and others that early mankind had a pattern myth to which their ritual conformed.[1]

---

[1] Professor Hooke lists as themes of the generally observed New Year festival:
(a) The death and resurrection of the god. (b) The myth of creation. (c) The ritual combat in which the god triumphs over his enemies. (d) The sacred marriage. (e) The triumphal procession in which the king played the part of the god followed by a train of lesser deities.

It will become increasingly clear to the reader as we proceed that the resemblances between religious cults are not fancied but real. The themes frequently and strikingly illustrated in the mythology of the early Babylonians are the creation, the death and revival of vegetation, and the failure of mankind to attain the immortality of the gods.

THE CREATION

The Sumerians had two accounts of the creation. Like the first chapter of Genesis, their early version gives us a vivid picture of a watery expanse; but, unlike the Genesis recital, there is no presupposition of deity already existent (Genesis 1. 1). Rather, out of the deep comes the generation of the ancient gods. These deities, known as Apsu, Mummu, and Tiamath, later on engage in conflict with the gods of a younger generation. Ea slays Apsu and Mummu, while Tiamath, a female monster, is destroyed by Ea's son Marduk. He splits the dragon in twain and out of the halves fashions the sky and the earth. Afterward mankind is created, "that the gods may have temples and sacrifices." These creation tablets, to the discovery of which reference has already been made (Chapter V), record a really magnificent poem in spite of their present mutilated condition. They suggest an order of creation similar to that followed in Genesis, chapter one. The similarity of the Hebrew word *tehom* translated as "the deep" to the Babylonian *Tiamath* has frequently been observed. The Hebrew writer was not unfamiliar with the early Babylonian mythology, while other Old-Testament passages betray a similar acquaintance (Psalms 74. 14; Job 41).

The recension, or perhaps a second independent account of the creation, derived from a Sumerian original, pictures Marduk laying a reed upon the waters and the land appearing like an island rising when the flood recedes. Here undoubtedly we have a race memory of the redemption of the swampland of the Delta. In such a fashion the Sumerians obtained the land upon which they sowed their crops and built their habitations. We can find a parallel in Genesis, chapter two, which gives a second Hebrew account of the creation bearing a faint resemblance to the Babylonian recension.

It has frequently been observed that the Babylonians have preserved no account, if, indeed, they ever possessed it, of the fall of man and his ensuing punishment. However, we find in Sumerian mythology some of the elements of the Hebrew story. Adapa having in anger broken the wings of the south wind which had destroyed his boats is summoned to the court of high heaven to account for his crime. Friendly and powerful deities intercede for him and punishment is remitted. He is offered instead the bread and water of life which would render him immortal. But Ea had warned him:

"When thou comest into the presence of Anu, they will offer thee food of death—do not eat it. They will offer thee water of death—do not drink it."

Ea's prophecy proved incorrect. Adapa had been offered life-giving food and drink, but because of the god's counsel he declined to partake, and thus remained mortal. The same confusion exists here as in the Hebrew tradition (see Genesis 3. 3-4). It is uncertain whether the forbidden food will bring death or life. In paradise, it will be recalled, there was a tree of life, the fruit of which was not forbidden and was destined to make man immortal, but Adam, like Adapa, failed to receive the boon. Professor Sayce, it may be remarked, believes that Adam is the Semitic equivalent of Adapa. When Gilgamesh, the hero of Sumerian legend, returned from a visit to his ancestor Utnapishtim, who had escaped the Deluge, and afterward dwelt eternally by "the confluence of the waters," he brought with him a plant which conferred immortality upon the possessor. But Gilgamesh, while asleep on the bank of a stream, is robbed of his priceless legacy by a serpent. The suggestion here is not of a resemblance to the Hebrew story, but of primitive man's belief that the serpent is immortal, while man is not.

The Babylonians, and presumably the Sumerians before them, felt hopeless concerning future existence. They did not deny the fact of survival but the felicity. They spoke of their dead as dwelling in Aralu, "the land of no-return."

When Ea, a god who always favored mankind, was impor-
tuned by Gilgamesh to bring back his dead friend Engidu, he
acceded to the request and in the interview that follows (compare 1 Samuel 28. 7-19) Gilgamesh is heard saying to his
erstwhile companion, "Tell me, dear friend, tell me the law
of the earth which thou hast experienced, tell me." He
means, of course, the uniform inexorable law of death. To
whom Engidu replies: "I cannot tell thee, my friend. I
cannot tell thee. If I were to tell the law of the earth which
I have experienced, you would sit down and weep the whole
day."

The seasonal gods, Tammuz and Ishtar, and others in their
removal from earth's activities to the lower world, embody the
changes which take place with the dying of vegetation, while
their release is celebrated by the renewal of spring. Here
one does not need to be reminded of the recurrence of a
myth celebrated in many lands. Osiris in Egypt, Tammuz
in Babylonia, Adonis in Syria, and Persephone in Greece are
all seasonal deities, illustrating the "pattern myth" of death
and resurrection.

Ishtar, goddess of fertility, pays a visit to Aralu. It is
pictured as a land of deep darkness, illuminated with no
single ray of light, and from which no traveler returns. Her
entrance is barred, but she threateningly advances, and one
by one the seven gates are opened to her approach to the
inmost palace, where dwells Ereshigal. But at each gate she
is divested of her ornaments and some article of clothing
until utterly naked she stands in the presence of the goddess
of the dead. Here she remains a prisoner while the winter
months pass, and the earth without her beneficent presence
is no longer fertile, nor do the herds yield their increase.
The god Ea in pity for mankind creates a deliverer who goes
to the land of no-return in quest of Ishtar, and secures her
release. Then once more the goddess passes through the
gates receiving at each the garments and ornaments of which
she had been deprived. The release was symbolical of the
renewal of spring and its changes under the beneficent sway
of the fertile goddess.

The mythology of the East was kept not only by oral

tradition and later by literature, but was preserved by ritual and drama, as at a later day the church in a similar way kept alive the memory of the life, death, and resurrection of Jesus. The popularity of the fertility cult was due to its supposed influence upon the growing crops. The traces of this cult in the Old Testament are many, but the subject is somewhat technical and requires a detailed discussion which our space does not permit. It is sufficient to say that beneath and behind the fertility cult is the insistent urge to find an answer to the recurring question, Why does vegetation die and why is it renewed?

RECENT DISCOVERIES IN SUMER

As has been stated, the early epoch of excavation contributed to our knowledge of the mythology of the Babylonians and their predecessors the Sumerians, from whom they borrowed. Recent excavations, on the other hand, are chiefly valuable for their historical contribution enabling us to reconstruct apart from the aid of written records the prehistoric period of the Sumerians. Of outstanding interest are the results achieved by C. L. Woolley, who has uncovered two predynastic cemeteries in Ur.[2] In the royal tombs he found evidence of an early Sumerian art, barbaric in splendor, the nearest approach to which was the First Dynasty art of Egypt. However, the Sumerian workmanship is more advanced and is evidently the culmination of a goldsmith's craft which had acquired its technical perfection only after a long period of preparation.[3]

All told, eighteen hundred fifty graves have been opened in the Ur cemetery. Woolley's exhaustive study of the time sequence is convincing. Apparently, the earliest tombs should be dated c. 3500 B. C.; then follow the graves of the First

[2] The excavations at Ur were under a joint expedition of the British Museum and the University of Pennsylvania.

[3] Among the discoveries were royal headdresses of gold, an electrum spearhead, a golden dagger with a handle of lapis lazuli, a large harp, the sounding board of which terminated in a bull's head, elaborately carved and wrought in gold, rams of gold and lapis represented as erect and caught in a thicket, many toilet articles, and a profusion of gems. The reader is referred to the originals which are deposited in the Sumerian section of the museum of the University of Pennsylvania.

and Second Dynasties and the Sargonoid Period. Sixteen of the number are evidently royal tombs, if we are to judge from the prodigality of the treasures deposited in such tomb chambers as were unmolested. The tombs were plundered in predynastic times and later, only two escaping molestation —Shub-ad's because the roof had fallen in concealing the contents, while the other escaped detection because of its great depth.

The most startling feature revealed by the excavation of the royal tombs is the evidence they furnish of mass burial, the number of human sacrifices found in a single tomb ranging from six to eighty persons. All are in a grave pit, which was approximately thirty feet in depth having a floor area of twenty-eight by forty. Of course the area varied as to its contents. A tomb of brick or stone filled a part or all of the floor space. This was designated for the royal personage and some of his attendants. The remainder of the space was occupied by the court, for apparently we have here a retinue of the king, who have assembled for the last time to do him honor. The inventory of the contents of one tomb listed as P. G. 789 show six of the king's guard, nine court ladies, musicians with their harps, two carts or chariots each drawn by three oxen, the grooms in front and by the chariots the driver, several women attendants, evidently slaves. By each body was a copper cup. Further evidence of the character of the mass burial was the helmets worn by the guards, the musical instruments, the profusion of jewelry, the golden headdress.[4]

Let us picture to ourselves a royal burial in Ur in 3500 B. C. Down a sloping passageway to the tomb chamber is brought the body of a queen. She is not placed in the wooden or wicker coffin, as is sometimes done, but stretched upon a bier, her hands folded across as in sleep. She wears an elaborate headdress of gold, and by her head is a replica. Why? At the foot and head of the bier are crouching attendants. The last service that can be rendered the lovely queen

[4] The necklaces which the Sumerian women wore were of beautifully polished stones, carnelian, agate, and lapis. Their vanity cases held manicure sets, pinchers, and tongs.

is paid. The entrance is sealed by bricking up the passage.
Again figures move down the sloping road until the under-
ground chamber, large as it is, seems filled. The queen's
bodyguard, the chariots, the ladies-in-waiting, the musicians
with lyres and harps, finally attendants and grooms—in short,
all the retinue of the court are here. In the hand of each is
a copper cup filled with hashish or opium taken from a common receptacle. The musicians play, the cups are lifted to
the lips, and death comes swiftly and painlessly to these who,
seated or lying down, compose their features in death. There
is no indication of violence or struggle. Last of all comes an
attendant or two to kill the oxen, then the shaft is filled in,
loose dirt and gravel fall upon the matting of white and
colored drapery, upon the treasures of Sumerian art, upon
the sleeping court. At a certain stage of the filling in, the
ground is trodden with clay and upon the platform rites are
performed, then more dirt until the grave pit is completely
filled.

Of all this there is not a word in the written records. Are
we to surmise that the evidence has been wrongly interpreted?
May it not be argued that the antiquity of the rite and its
eventual disuse before the period of the written word
account for the silence of history? The reason for the dis-
continuance of the custom seems plain enough. The early
Sumerians, like the Egyptians, believed in the survival of the
soul after death, and made provision for it. Moreover, it
must be remembered that the Sumerian king was deified, and
such honors as were performed were appropriate. But the
vision of future life grew less distinct as time went on. The
protest against human sacrifice became stronger and the practice of mass burial was abandoned long before the dawn of
the first dynasty of Ur.[5]

THE DELUGE

Both Sumerians and Hebrews had a written record of the
Flood, as we have already seen. It seems probable that the

[5] For a full discussion see *Ur Excavations, The Royal Cemetery*,
Vol. II, by Sir C. Leonard Woolley, a work to which I am indebted for
the account given.—Joint publication of the University Museum, University of Pennsylvania and the British Museum (1934).

Deluge interrupted but did not altogether dislocate the national life. It certainly did not involve the destruction of the human race, nor even all of the inhabitants of the Delta. Langdon has shown by the excavations at Kish, and Woolley by his diggings at Ur, a flood stratum one and one half feet in depth composed of fine sand, embedded in which were fresh-water shells and rows of small fish. The stratum has been dated with some show of reason c. 3300 B. c.[6] At Kish it extends about twelve miles from the banks of the Euphrates, but covered a much wider area in the Delta, though some of its cities survived. Certainly, it was a catastrophe of such magnitude that it became a landmark in history, and with this we can rest the case.

THE CITY OF UR

As Woolley has shown in his book, *The Sumerians,* Ur enjoyed in historic times two periods of great prosperity, the first and the third dynasties. It numbered at one time a population of half a million. The Euphrates and the canals that connected Ur with the sea gave it great commercial importance. Its hundreds of merchant ships sailed to far distant ports. It had extensive trade relations with the north.

Moreover, it was a very religious city, and those associations kept it alive when its commercial supremacy and political prestige had passed away. Its chief deity was Nannar, the moon god, known by the Semites as *Sin.* That it harbored most of the time a Semitic population coming in from the desert is probable. But the Euphrates changed its course, the canals fell into disuse. Domestic and foreign wars exhausted the resources of the Sumerian city which dwindled in importance and appeared for the last time on the pages of history in the twelfth year of Alexander's reign.

Today it affords a dreary prospect, giving little hint of its former greatness. To be sure, the zikkurat stands forth, a continual reminder and challenge. The sand has been dug away from its foundations revealing a four-squared tower asymetrical with bricks well shaped and laid as if yesterday.

---

[6] Peake and Fleure give a much earlier dating. See *Corridors of Time,* Vol. III, p. 84. Oxford University Press.

To the first platform led a triple staircase. On the level stages once were planted trees to give or suggest the appearance of a wooded slope, for the zikkurat was a sacred mountain surmounted by the shrine of the moon god. The tower rose from a terrace or elevated area adjoining which was the temple of Nannar and the various buildings employed by the large priesthood.

UR, THE EARLY HOME OF ABRAHAM

To the reader of the Old Testament, the chief interest of Ur is its connection with Abraham. While archaeology can throw no light upon the reputed founder of the Hebrew people, it may well be that the family of Abraham lived in the desert vicinity of Ur and that during the reign of the kings of Larsa and Babylon (c. 2050 B. c.) they moved northward, following the course of the Euphrates until it brought them to Harran, a sister city of Ur, likewise dedicated to the worship of Nannar.

SUPPLEMENTARY READING

C. H. Gadd, *History and Monuments of Ur,* Chapter I.
Morris Jastrow, Jr., *Hebrew and Babylonian Traditions,* Chapter I.
Peake and Fleure, *Corridors of Time,* Vol. III, Chapter VI.
C. L. Woolley, *Ur of the Chaldees.*
Illustrated London News, February 8, 1930, Article on "The Deluge," by Stephen Langdon.
Bible, Genesis 1. 1-2. 7, The Creation, two versions. Genesis 2. 8-3. 24, Eden and Fall of Man. Genesis 6-8, The Deluge. For Babylonian account see Jastrow above and Kent's *Heroes and Crises.*

CHAPTER VII

EARLY EGYPTIAN CULTURE

THE men of the Old Stone Age who lived on the south side of the Mediterranean faced different climatic conditions; in fact, they lived in an entirely different physical world than that which mankind inhabiting those same regions today experiences or knows. The prehistoric hunter followed his game through great forests where now there is only sand and rock. Torrential rains occurred frequently in the region of the Sahara, while northeastern Africa and western Asia had long periods of rain corresponding to the glacial epochs in Europe. Under such conditions, the physical contour of the Mediterranean and river basins must have been greatly different from the present, as one may see by consulting the maps which depict the probable land and water surface during the Pleistocene Age.

About the middle of the Old Stone Age, a period of desiccation set in. It forced man from his hunting grounds in the Sahara and north central Africa eastward, until he came to the great basin of the Nile. He was doubtless preceded by the game he hunted, and there found a hunting preserve to his liking. Breasted so argues in *The Dawn of Conscience* (p. 7). But is it not probable that cultures Asiatic in origin first reached north Africa and later penetrated Europe?

It is difficult for a traveler in the Nile Valley today to imagine the region when it was covered with dense forests, the remnants of which one may see in the Fayum district and elsewhere, but such was the country when mankind knew it first.[1] The hunters left their weapons plentifully strewn about, as the

[1] In the neighborhood of Fayum for many miles north and west are the trunks of huge forest trees, some of them seventy feet in length. These are now silicified and indestructible.

It is believed that four periods of abundant rain in north Africa correspond to four glacial epochs in Europe, but Peake and Fleure express a modified opinion. *C. of T.*, Vol. I, pp. 75-76. Oxford Press.

gravel terraces of the Nile reveal.[2] The earliest belong to a period not less than two hundred and fifty thousand years ago. From that time we can follow with considerable certainty the course of Paleolithic man, whose gradual transitions are indicated by the Nile terraces and the weapons he learned to improve. Here was a corridor a thousand miles in length, teeming with animal life, one end in the tropics and the other in the temperate zone of the Mediterranean, timbered with heavy forests and having plenty of arable land. When the process of desiccation began here, as happened eventually, the Nile overflow furnished the fertile soil which men cultivated and the moisture needed for the growing crops. During this and preceding ages the Nile had cut its way through the high plateau to a depth of one hundred and fifty feet, leaving, as all its lateral tributaries did, the gravel terraces to which we have referred. In the end we have the formation of the most important river basin in the ancient world.

TOPOGRAPHY

Egypt today may be described as a vast plain some four hundred thousand square miles in extent, tilted from east to west. On its eastern side it rises abruptly from the Red Sea;[3] on the west it sinks to sea level or below. Bisecting the plain is a great trench from ten to thirty miles across, running north and south and traversed by the river. The trench contains a tract of arable land about ten thousand miles in area.

During the inundation of the Nile, until quite recent times, the arable land was covered by water, which as it receded left a layer of black mud. This greatly enriched the soil of Egypt

---

[2] K. S. Sanford says: "In the terrace gravels of Egypt, we have human implements falling into cultural assemblages each in its own terrace; and, most important of all, the assemblages are of a type and technique similar to those found in like circumstances in Europe." *First Report of the Prehistoric Expedition,* O. I. C. No. 3. University of Chicago Press.

In the final stage of the Capsian industry in north Africa we have the continuance of Upper Paleolithic industries, Aurignacian, Solutrean, and Magdalenian. *C. of T.,* Vol. II, p. 145. Oxford Press.

[3] Some peaks of the eastern range rise to a height of seven thousand feet.

and added to its fertility, justifying Herodotus' statement that Egypt is the gift of the Nile. In fact, there is not an atom of the rich alluvial basin which the Nile in its long course of history has not brought from afar. Today irrigation takes the place of the former inundation of middle and lower Egypt, and by an elaborate system of canals, irrigating ditches, and reservoirs, the water is distributed to the growing crops with a consequent diminution of silt. In the south are basins which receive and hold the overflow, profiting greatly by the sediment deposited while the water is clearing, but this is exceptional. Dr. G. A. Reisner once told the writer that the amount of silt from the Nile overflow in lower Egypt was not more than the thickness of a sheet of paper. Egypt, like all other agricultural states, is dependent upon fertilizing agents. The statement that three or four crops a year may be grown is a gross exaggeration. One crop a year, with the land lying fallow for several months, correctly states the case. Its important crops are sugar cane and cotton, the latter, a long-stemmed variety, is exported in great quantity to the United States, where it is used in the automobile industry.

It will be perceived, since only one fourth of the area of Egypt is arable, that the rest is desert and unproductive. However, the ramparts of sand to the east and west have ever rendered a valuable service to the land in making it immune from attack.

Prehistoric Development

Egyptian history properly begins with the first dynasty, about 3500 B. C., but there must have been a long period of development which we may denominate as predynastic culture.[4] For the Egyptians, prior to the first dynasty, had become agriculturalists, engineers, and artists. They had united their provinces north and south under one government. They had developed commerce both within and without the country. They had mastered the art of writing. They had learned to make their clothing of fine linen, to fashion pot-

---

[4] Peake and Fleure think fourteen hundred and twenty-five years. *C. of T.*, Vol. III, p. 65. Oxford Press.

tery delicate in texture and design. They used copper not only as an ornament, but for utensils and weapons. They had devised a calendar as early as 4241 B. C., and learned to measure time with considerable accuracy.[5] Their year comprised twelve months of thirty days each with an extra five days which they employed as a festival period. For their measurement of the year they observed the time when Sirius appeared on the eastern horizon at the sun's rising, until twelve months later, when it again occupied the same position. Undoubtedly, the greatest predynastic development took place in the five hundred years preceding the first dynastic rule. This Doctor Breasted calls the First Union, during which time the Egyptians had passed definitely from the Neolithic stage to the Age of Metals, and had achieved through a federation of towns a union both in the north and in the south.

The museums render us a great service in following the development of predynastic culture. The Egyptian Museum in Cairo, the British Museum in London, and our own Metropolitan in New York, not to name others, have invaluable collections in which a layman can follow for himself the improvement in craftsmanship of the many objects of utility and of beauty, whether pottery or toilet articles, or beads of semiprecious stones, or the sequence in graves. The latter throw invaluable light upon the earliest civilization, since they contain funerary objects of value and variety. The graves at first were shallow pits, then circular and oblong in form, finally chambers or tombs large enough to contain the body of the deceased and the objects designed for his use and pleasure in the after life. Egypt dealt kindly with its dead, the sands preserving not only the body but the skin, the internal organs and the clothing with which the body was wrapped. Long before mummification was practiced nature had paved the way for the art of preserving the dead perfectly enough for us to detect racial characteristics, even to the pointed beard with the shaven lip.

But earlier even than the predynastic culture just described, we must date the Badarians and a nearly contemporaneous

---

[5] The summer overflow of the Nile demanded a more accurate calendar than a year of lunar months.

people of the Fayum district. The evidence of the Badarian
culture is due to the recent excavations of the Bruntons and
Flinders Petrie at Badari above Assuit. Here lived a people
who at a very early time—Petrie conjectures 13000–10000
B. C., and others guess 5000 B. C.—made the transition to
agricultural life.[6] Their linen clothing indicates that they
sowed flax. Their beads of copper point to trade with Sinai,
where the metal ore was found. Their pottery was of superior color and design, far in advance of that produced in a
much later period. While they display Negroid characteristics, they more nearly resemble ancient peoples of India.

Another people antedating the predynastic period lived in
the Fayum. Apparently, their chief occupations were fishing
and tilling the soil. They produced an excellent quality of
pottery, but since no graves have yet been found, there is a
lack of evidence as to whether or not they were behind the
Badarians in culture. They seem to have no relationship with
the latter. Both cultures must be regarded as isolated links
in a chain which is by no means complete.

The race origin of the Badarians and the people of the
Fayum, together with the dating of the period, when they
flourished, remains a mystery. Petrie, Peake, and Fleure
believe them to be Asiatics, while Childe, Miss Caton Thomp-
son, and the Bruntons think them to be indigenous. All
we can say with certainty is that they were proto-Egyptians
and that they exhibited remarkable artistic traits in a transitional stage which marked the slowly advancing culture of
the Nile Valley.

WHO WERE THE EGYPTIANS?

The discussion brings us to the oft-recurring and perplexing question of the origin of the ancient Egyptian.
There are some who believe that we are to look for his
ancestry mainly in Egypt, others venture the opinion that
he belonged to the Mediterranean race and had close affinity
with Crete, while still others believe that he was Asiatic or

[6] He computes his dating by the rate of deposit of Nile alluvium.
But this must have greatly varied over a long period. Peake and
Fleure estimate the coming of the Badarians to the Nile Valley about
5000 B. C., and think their industry was remotely Solutrean in origin.

more exactly Semitic. Certainly, it is reasonable to suppose that in the predynastic period there were several races in Egypt. The Libyans seem to have entered the country in considerable number. It is more than likely that there was a Semitic infiltration from the East and a Nubian from the South.[7] Of these races there was an amalgamation, or perhaps one proved dominant. This being admitted, it is difficult to arrive at a satisfactory solution of the problem. Meanwhile, as Professor Baikie says, the Egyptian himself is a very solid fact apart from any explanation of his origin; and his culture, however derived, is one of the most wonderful and interesting stories of human development.

EARLY RELIGIOUS IDEAS

Early travelers in the Nile Valley seem impressed not only by the material achievements they report but by their frequent observation that of all peoples the Egyptians are the most religious. It is not hard to see why this conclusion would be reached. The temples, the religious festivals, the reverence paid to many deities, the wall paintings in the tombs all bear witness to the truth of the generalization.

The great natural features with which the Egyptian was confronted profoundly influenced his thought. The dry air and the sand of the desert preserved his dead and instilled in him the belief in immortality. The life-giving Nile and the beneficent sun were his gods. The myth of Osiris, the life, death, burial, and resurrection of the god are derived from the phenomena of the parched fields, the Nile overflow, and the rebirth of nature in the fertility that followed, and ever he was moved by the spectacle of the shining sun. Other elements entered into his religious thought, as we shall see, but these were chief.

RA

The symbols of the Sun-god may be briefly enumerated. The falcon with outstretched wings flying through the heavens seemed to the early Egyptian a fitting representation

---

[7] Peake and Fleure find evidence of six races and regard early predynastic culture as due to foreign influence. *C. of T.*, Vol. III, pp. 79-80.

of the Sun-god Ra; so to other races, for we find the symbol
slightly modified in Assyria, Cappadocia and Persia. The
Hebrew prophet must have had it in mind when he wrote:
"Unto you that fear my name shall the Sun of righteousness
arise with healing in its wings" (Malachi 4. 2), though here
its use is metaphorical. Its wide employment as a travel
emblem has familiarized it to moderns.

A prevailing conception early and late shows the Sun-god
sailing in a bark across the sky. As he descends from the
west, he enters the lower world, sailing its tortuous rivers
in safety and dispelling for the moment the gloom of the
world of the dead. Even the Sun-god is thought to be dead,
but to attain a resurrection with his emergence in the eastern
sky.

The pyramid was not only a royal tomb but an impressive
solar symbol. There was found near the base of a pyramid
erected for Amenemhet III, a beautifully polished capstone
of granite pyramidal in form and apparently designated for
the apex of the monument. On its eastern face was the
symbol of the Sun-god flying across the sky and underneath
a pair of eyes with the words below, "Behold the Beauty of
the Sun." Still lower were two lines which may be freely
rendered:

"The eyes of the King are opened that he may behold
the Lord of the Horizon when he sails across the sky."[8]

The meaning is that when the rays of the morning sun struck
the capstone, the valley yet steeped in mists, the king's eyes
beheld as in life the power and beauty of the Sun-god.

Osiris

Side by side with the worship of Ra was the cult of Osiris,
originally also a nature deity, associated with the fertility
of the fields and the Nile, upon which their fruitfulness
depended. The spectacle of the dying vegetation and its
renewal in the spring after the Nile overflow gave rise to a
myth with which we are already familiar in our study of

[8] James H. Breasted, *The Dawn of Conscience*, p. 57. Charles Scribner's Sons.

the Sumerians. In the myth Osiris is associated with other
deities, who were quite separate originally, but in the development become a part of the Osirian legend. These are
Set, the wicked brother of Osiris; Isis, his sister and faithful
wife; a second sister, Nepthys, inseparable from Isis though
the wife of Set; and Horus, a son of Osiris and Isis. The
myth and the cult by which it was celebrated are reserved for
treatment in a later chapter. It suffices for the present to say
that they concern the death, burial, and resurrection of a
god, whose importance was only second to that of Ra. Osiris
henceforth reigns in the lower world as a god of judgment,
while Horus is god in the realm of the living.

There were many gods in Egypt, temples where they were
enshrined and cults by which they were worshiped. It is to
be observed that the Sun-god and Osiris are before all others,
and with each is bound up the idea of immortality. It is also
to be remembered that Osiris was only associated with the
dead while Ra was god of both the living and the dead.

From the summit of the great pyramid at Gizeh, one sur-
veys the ribbon green valley of the Nile and impinging upon
it the desert, which like a sea stretches before one. On its
tawny surface floats the shadows of clouds, and, like them,
the desert itself seems to have movement sweeping on toward
the Nile; while the cultivated land, the life which we call
Egypt, defies it. Such a contrast of death to life meets us
constantly in Egypt. The pyramid on which we stand and
those close by housed the dead; so did the mastaba, or tombs,
of the nobles which adjoined them, the Valley of the Kings
at Thebes, and a thousand other enduring monuments. But
these tombs cut in the rocks, or built like the earthly homes
of men, are not places of gloom, but are bright with color,
reflecting the occupations, the everyday life, the contentment
and pleasure of men who lived between three and five millenniums ago.

SUPPLEMENTARY READING

James Baikie, *History of Egypt,* Vol. I, Chapter II.
J. H. Breasted, *Ancient Times,* Chapter II, or *Conquest of Civilization,* Chapter II.

H. R. Hall, *Ancient History of the Near East,* "Archaic Egypt."
K. S. Sanford, *Prehistoric Survey Expedition,* O. I. C. No. 3.
Cambridge Ancient History, Vol. I, Chapter VI.
Peake and Fleure, *Corridors of Time,* Vol. III, Chapters II, V.

CHAPTER VIII

THE RELIGION OF EGYPT

In studying the religion of the Egyptians we find a vast amount of material frequently repetitious, often misleading and contradictory in statement. However, we must take the evidence as we find it, remembering that the culture of the ancient Egyptian lasted for thirty-five centuries, that their religion was not static, but, like the great river that flows through the land, ever moving, ever changing its course. Religious ideas at Memphis in the Old Kingdom could hardly be the same as those held in Thebes in the eighteenth dynasty, and equally marked is the change between the Second Empire and the Period of the Ptolemies. However, there are certain governing principles, the keynote of which has been truthfully said to be the desire for life and more life. The Sun-god Ra sinks below the rim of the western sky, traverses the realm of the lower world, conquering darkness and storm, and then emerges triumphantly at the beginning of a new day; while Osiris, a seasonal god, is slain yearly with the inundation of the Nile and the dying vegetation, only to rise triumphantly with the verdant spring. Man himself by magic ceremonies could participate in this life stream which he saw running through the universe, its manifestation in fact.

We shall do well to confine ourselves to a single period and to such contrasts as it presents, reflecting that the limitations imposed by a restricted survey are compensated for by the significance attached to the religious ideas of the men who lived in the eighteenth dynasty (1580–1321 B. C.). At no time did building activity reach such a towering height as in this period. So the temples at Luxor and Karnak bear witness, and comparable to them the Necropolis of Thebes on the western bank of the river.

It is impossible to disassociate the religion of a nation from its political and social life. It is all a part of one

95

complex structure. What the common man believed, what became of him after death was thought to be of no importance. Religion was an affair of the state and not left to the individual to manage for himself. In the eighteenth dynasty we have a synthesis of religious beliefs, a gradual fusion of traditions which in some cases were as awkward to handle as the hyphenated names of deities. In considering the religion of the Egyptians during the First Empire, three questions confront us: What did men believe concerning the gods? How were they served, that is, what rituals were followed? What was the mode of existence in the afterlife?

The Gods

The intelligent Egyptian, it may be presumed, regarded his gods as spiritual beings, existing apart or locally incarnate in some human or nonhuman form. When he conceived of them as spiritual, it was natural for him to visualize them in human form like himself. Men do the same today. When deities drew near to man to become the patron god of the city, he regarded them as incarnate in the cult-image of the temple, or in some plant or animal form. Thus we have Amon present in the cult-image in the shrine of his Theban temple. We have Ptah of Memphis incarnate in the sacred bull. We have the goddess Hathor taking the form of a cow, or a human form, in which she is seen like Aphrodite, the goddess of love or joy, or yet again identified with the sky. It will be at once perceived by the unprejudiced reader that we have here the germ of the doctrine of incarnation which is common to many religions.

It must be conceded that grave dangers are involved in the use of images and graver still in the conception of a divine incarnation in animal forms. We see the deterioration of Apis worship at Memphis under the Persians, who made it the national cult of Egypt. Innumerable instances could be cited showing that the unintelligent or uninformed confused the animal form with deity and worshiped it accordingly.

How, it will be asked, did the belief of gods incarnate in animal forms arise? The roots of such a conception lie in a primitive stage of culture when men were inclined to see supernatural powers in the animal and plant life about them.[1] The Egyptians, as in the case of other races, were unable to escape the totemic stage. Later, they conceived of gods as human but the earlier conception prevailed, and we see two streams of thought running parallel quite separate in idea, but united in symbol.

If the symbolism of Egyptian religion has led to confused thinking, it is due to the fact that we attribute a more extended meaning to symbols than they should convey. When one sees depicted upon the walls of a tomb chamber a human form with the head of an animal it seems to him a caricature of the god so represented. But not to the ancient Egyptian, to whom the representation was like his hieroglyphic writing, merely a designation or a name for a local deity or a god with a particular function. Whatever the origin of such symbolism,[2] to the intelligent Egyptian of the eighteenth dynasty it was a sign and nothing more.

A fatal weakness in Egyptian religion was the multiplicity of its gods. This Ikhnaton, and others like him, saw clearly, but the attempted reforms proved abortive. Egypt was unable to throw off the incubus of a plurality of gods, so divided were its interests, so conservatively religious were its people. Even the state religion established at Thebes supported by the prestige of empire and a powerful priesthood could do little though they had taken a step in the direction of a supreme god.

In the second place, religion in Egypt was handicapped by the animal forms in which the gods were supposed to dwell, for many of them were insignificant, not to say repulsive. On this account there was a growing tendency toward the degradation of man's conception of the divine. Much can be said in favor of the cult of Ra, and of Osiris, and of Ptah, "the master craftsman" of Memphis, but what apology can be offered for the crocodile god of the Fayum, for the cat temple at Bubastis, or for deities like the cobra and the beetle?

---

[1] See Chap. III.
[2] It was probably a compromise between the two conceptions previously mentioned.

MYTH AND CULTS

It is known for a certainty that early mankind had a body of myths, that they performed religious rites, that their gods and their ceremonials were widely disseminated. Moreover, it will be conceded that religion was powerful according to the strength of the state that disseminated it. Since the earliest civilized states were Egypt and Mesopotamia, we may look to them for the origin of the myth and pattern cult which was prevalent in the ancient East.

It may be well at this point to define what we mean by myth and cult. The myth is the history,[3] the original situation; ritual is its enactment in drama or recital. The two are inseparable, for only through ritual was the myth kept alive. Both rose out of necessity. Primitive man faced certain problems, some of them affecting the group, others the individual. To insure the Nile overflow, the bodily vigor of the king who was the embodiment of communal prosperity, to ward off disease, to know the future—all these were pressing problems and called for prescribed actions on the part of the community, whether a benefit was to be sought or some evil was to be warded off.

Thus it came about that in the seat of the earliest civilizations—Egypt and Babylonia—a pattern of actions was evolved. While the pattern was invariably followed in the country of its origin, it was modified when carried abroad. We find, therefore, the elements of adaptation and disintegration present when the myth and its accompanying ritual are diffused. Prof. S. H. Hooke has pointed out as essential elements in the myth and pattern cult:[4] (1) The dramatic representation of the death and resurrection of the god. (2) The recitation or symbolic presentation of the myth of creation. (3) The ritual combat in which the triumph of the god over his enemies was depicted. (4) The sacred marriage. (5) The triumphal procession in which the king played the part of the god, followed by a train of lesser gods or visiting deities. The dramatic representation or recital

---

[3] That is, the account of what was afterward dramatized.
[4] *Myth and Ritual*, Essay 1, p. 8.   Oxford Press.

occurred during the seasonal festivities and was designed not so much to commemorate the past as to affect the present and future by securing in this way the vigor and well-being of the god and the welfare of the growing crops in the coming year.

It must be conceded that while some myths may have been borrowed, many others had an independent origin. They arose out of the consciousness of minds affected by the periodical changes of the seasons, devastating floods, the starry heavens, and other natural manifestations. Such natural phenomena were common to every country. It was otherwise with the cult or ritual by which the myth was dramatically represented. This may have been borrowed, and probably was in many cases. What is more natural than that the Babylonian, observing the Egyptian method of celebrating the death and resurrection of Osiris, should copy details of the ritual. That Professor Hooke is right in assuming a pattern ritual is probable. In fact, not only in ancient times but in the early Christian period there is evidence that the Christians were not unaffected by pagan rituals and celebration of seasonal feasts. As the Church used the Roman basilica for its place of worship, and employed Roman festival days for the celebration of its Christian anniversaries, so it used pagan ritual for representing the death and resurrection of Jesus, which it believed to be historic.

In Egypt and Babylonia the elements of the pattern cult are easily discernible, and to a somewhat less extent in neighboring states. Let us illustrate this by a few examples.

THE DEATH AND RESURRECTION OF THE GOD

The myth of Osiris is well known, but it may prove useful to briefly outline the story as it was told in some parts of Egypt. Osiris had been given by his father the kingship of Memphis. This excited the jealousy of his brother, Set. The latter slew Osiris, placed the body in a chest and set it adrift in the sea. In course of time it was washed ashore on the Syrian coast, where it was found by Isis, the spouse and sister of Osiris. By the aid of Anubis the limbs, which were fallen apart, were joined together and Isis resuscitated the god by blowing upon him with her wings. The dead god thus revived became the god of the lower world in which state he had union with Isis, who bore a son, Horus. When Horus had grown to manhood, he avenged the death of his father in a conflict with Set, who was overcome. Finally, peace was made between the combatants, but Horus was judged to be the victor. Such is the myth. Now for its dramatic representation.

During the month of Choiak, the great spring festival was held in honor of Osiris. On the 24th day of the month the effigy of the dead god, filled with sand and barley, was put in a wooden box and buried. In the development of the rite, we have the resurrection of the god through the raising of a column identified with Osiris. This was on the 30th day. Another rite with the same end in view, but more striking, was the planting of Osiris-beds-of-barley made and watered between the 18th and 25th of the month. The barley was allowed to sprout, thus typifying the resurrection of the deceased individual identified with Osiris.[5] Other ceremonies during the same month included a sham fight or ritual combat, also processions which followed the course of the walls of Memphis. It will be observed that the myth is dramatically presented in the rites which we have just described. Somewhat analogous to this are the Passion plays of the Middle Ages, which celebrated the death and resurrection of Jesus.

THE SACRED MARRIAGE

The elaborate ritual of Amon-Ra at Karnak and Luxor is a striking example of the celebration of the myth of the sacred marriage during the days of the empire. To comprehend the cult of such a god as Amon-Ra, we cannot do better than to imagine ourselves as onlookers in the precincts of the god's temple at Karnak on a festival day. We approach the temple by an avenue flanked with statues, sphinxes with heads of rams. Before us are pylons of the temple,

[5] Cf. *Myth and Ritual,* Essay 2, pp. 19f, 24f. (A. M. Blackman). Oxford Press.

28583

great ramparts defending the sanctuary. Passing between them we find ourselves in a court surrounded by columns culminating in lotus or papyrus plant capitals. The sun is not yet high and the columns cast long shadows across the pavement. Beyond is the hypostyle in deep shadow, for little light comes through the clerestory windows. A little farther and we stand before a chamber after which "the holy of holies" in the Temple of Solomon may have been modeled. Both were windowless, both contained shrines and were accessible only to the officiating priest. The shrine in Karnak may have been of wood or stone, closed by two wooden doors bolted and sealed, or again it might have been a boat-shrine, the cult image within veiled and thus hidden from the presence of all. The boat, while in the temple, rested upon a stone pedestal. When transported, it was borne by priests, who carried it by means of two underslung poles supported on their shoulders. The cult-image was a few feet in height, made of costly wood overlaid heavily with gold and studded with jewels.

In the ritual which followed we see the officiating high priest, frequently the Pharaoh, washing or "purifying" the cult-image, anointing it and placing before it food of which the god was supposed spiritually to partake. The procession forms. The boat-shrine is carried aloft on the shoulders of twelve or fourteen priests down the sphinx-lined avenue to the Nile, where the royal barge is moored. The objective is the Luxor temple, described as the harem, and here the festivity will reach its climax in the marriage rites of the god. The bank of the Nile is crowded with worshipers whose material interest in the proceedings is considerably enhanced by the free distribution of food. As the barge is drawn slowly upstream, the people paralleling its course on the road move on toward Luxor. A good deal of mystery shrouds the ritual in the Luxor temple, but there can be no doubt that the queen was the center. She was the actual high priestess of the god. As Blackman says, the theory was that during the course of one of these festivals the heir to the Egyptian throne was conceived, and was henceforth regarded as of divine descent.

SURVIVAL

To many travelers the chief interest which Egypt affords is the decorated wall surface of the tomb chambers and the corridors leading to them depicting in unfading colors[6] the daily life of the ancient Egyptians. But the paintings were not designed as decoration; they were intended for the dead, who because of certain magic formulas were enabled to enjoy them and actually to be served by the figures in the representations. The magic of the priest was thought to give reality or life to whatever was painted. Doctor Gardiner, commenting upon the tomb of Amenemhet, quotes appropriately the lines of Keats addressed to a Grecian Urn.

> "Fair youth, beneath the trees, thou canst not leave
> Thy song, nor ever can these trees be bare;
> Bold lover, never, never, canst thou kiss,
> Though winning near the goal—yet do not grieve;
> She cannot fade, though thou hast not thy bliss,
> For ever wilt thou love, and she be fair!"

The Egyptians were not alone among ancient peoples in believing in survival after death, but no race has thought so seriously nor made such detailed preparation for the afterlife. Two distinct conceptions can be traced. According to the first, man survived on an earthly plane presumably in his tomb in the carefully mummified body and in the *ka* near by. According to the second view, he survived in a heavenly state with the Sun-god or with Osiris in the Field of Reeds, where he enjoyed a glorified existence similar in pattern to that lived on earth. The abode of the dead was known as "the West," and the dead themselves as "dwellers in the West." The phraseology was derived from the sinking of the sun in the western sky on his way to the realm of the underworld where the dead dwelt.

Ideas changed with the passage of time, they varied with different localities, and it is difficult to present a consistent view where inconsistency prevails. I can hardly do better

---

[6] The painter had only six colors on his palette including black and white. In the earliest time color was applied to the deeply engraved lines as a finishing stage.

than quote Dr. G. A. Reisner, who writes as follows on the meaning to be attached to *ka,* a term evidently descriptive of a mode of existence after death:

"While the Egyptians believe in the afterlife, they were equally certain that it could not be maintained unless materially supported;[7] hence, the funerary objects, the magical formula, and the replica of the deceased in the temple adjoining the tomb. In one part of the tomb was the burial chamber; the other housed the *ka,* a second self, or double. The *ka* was born with the individual and either remained with him as a guardian spirit or lived in the spirit world, it is uncertain which. In either case the deceased joins or lives near his *ka,* the latter to be served and fed by the funerary priest. In early times the *ka* was thought to inhabit a statue of the deceased, which was set in the outer chamber. Then the custom changed and the image was placed behind the wall of the offering chamber, and a hole cut through in order that the *ka* might see the gift bearer" (*Illustrated London News,* February 7, 1931).

A second mode of existence was the *ba,* which carries the meaning of soul. In the release that followed the pangs of death, the *ba* seemed like a bird to fly away. Thus in the tomb representations it is invariably represented as a human-headed bird. It returns frequently to the body, provided the latter has not decayed.[8]

CONCERNING CONDUCT

The fact must not be overlooked that the pious devotion which the Egyptian felt for his honored dead and his certain conviction that he must appear in judgment before Osiris to answer for his sins were important factors in his ethical development. Whether he was in advance of his neighbors of contemporary civilizations it is difficult to say. Doctor

[7] Men continued to live as they did while on earth, provided they were supplied with the necessities of life. At first only the king, the royal family, and the nobles had this honor. Eventually it was extended to all who were not too poor to build tombs or to protect the body from decay.
[8] A vignette in the British Museum shows the soul *ba* visiting the mummy in the tomb.

Breasted seems to think so in his recent book, *The Dawn of Conscience*.[9] During the First Empire we discern traces of a developed conscience in prayers of penitence in which the suppliant says, "Chastise me not according to my many sins;" in admonitions like the following: "Serve thy God and avoid what he abhors," "Pray to him with a longing heart so will he grant thy request."

Of somewhat later date is the text preserved in the British Museum of the tale of The Two Brothers. The chief characters bear the names of divinities, Anubis and Bata, suggesting a mythological origin of the story, but when it gained currency in a popular version, it was told of two brothers, the elder of which, a man of means, shared his home with the younger. Anubis was married. His wife, young and presumably attractive, conceived a strong affection for the younger brother. Bata, however, repulsed her advances, maintaining his integrity and answering her in words like these:

"Lo, thou art with me as a mother, and thy husband is with me like a father, what is, then, this shameful thing that thou hast asked of me? Say it not again, and I will repeat it to no man."

But the woman, incensed by the youth's refusal, gave a perverted version of the affair to her husband. It would have fared ill with Bata had he not been previously warned of his brother's intended vengeance by the cattle whom he had driven and had kindly treated. He fled, and when pursued a stream was caused to appear miraculously, separating the two. From the farther bank Bata told his story. He was believed and Anubis returned to punish by death his erring wife. The legendary and miraculous elements are unimportant. What impresses one is the moral approbation which the tale carries. Mohammed was impressed and wrote it into the Koran. Later it found its way into medieval romance. The story may have been current in the circle of the writers of the book of Genesis, who have preserved among their choice narratives the story of Joseph, whose fortitude was displayed under a similar ordeal.

[9] Chap. VIII, p. 105f.

SUPPLEMENTARY READING

J. H. Breasted, *Development of Religion and Thought in Ancient Egypt,* or *The Dawn of Conscience,* pp. 18-23, and Chapter IX.
Adolf Erman, *Handbook of Egyptian Religion.*
Allan W. Shorter, *Introduction to Egyptian Religion.*
Edmund D. Soper, *The Religions of Mankind,* Chapter III.
Cambridge Ancient History, Vol. I, Chapter IX.
Hastings, *Encyclopedia of Religion and Ethics,* Article on "Egyptian Religion."

CHAPTER IX

THE GREAT PHARAOHS

It does not fall within the scope of the present work to furnish even a brief survey of Egyptian history, the material of which is readily accessible. We may, however, with considerable profit continue to fix our attention upon the most magnificent age in the long history of the Pharaohs, the eighteenth dynasty, ordinarily dated 1580–1321 b. c. It was the period of the First Empire, and important for our purpose because we see Egypt extending its dominion to include Syria and Palestine. Moreover, as we have noted, religious ideas had come to their fruition and the attempt was made to unite and harmonize systems of religious thought hitherto irreconcilable. Finally, it was an era of building temples, the grandeur of which even in their present ruined state impresses the modern world.

Hatshepsut

It is remarkable that among the great Pharaohs of the eighteenth dynasty we should find a woman ruling Egypt. It was contrary to all precedent and could not have happened save for the unusual circumstances that faced Thutmose I as the close of his reign drew near. Aahmose, his queen, had given him no sons but a daughter named Hatshepsut, who was in the direct line of descent and whose mental gifts and aptitude to rule must have been apparent at an early age. However, Thutmose had a son by an inferior wife, a youth physically incapable and without the mental stamina to rule effectively. Moreover, his legitimacy was bound to be called into question.[1] It is probable, as Hatshepsut claimed, that her father promised her the throne, and to make her position more secure married her to her half brother, who later took

---

[1] In Egypt descent was traced through the mother, and this was held so important that the crown prince usually married his sister or half sister, thus strengthening his claim as successor to the throne.

the title of Thutmose II. From the records one judges
Hatshepsut and Thutmose to have been coregents, with the
former as the real ruler. If Hatshepsut hoped for male
issue to support her claim, as she doubtless did, she was disappointed, for the children she bore to Thutmose were
daughters. It was a marriage without happiness, and its
termination by the death of Thutmose must have brought
great satisfaction to his ambitious consort. Now she ruled
alone, supported by a strong faction in the government and
in the priesthood. She knew how to reward those who
served her and, despite the prejudice against a woman ruler,
she managed, with the aid of powerful allies, to hold the
throne.

It has been stated that Thutmose II had no sons by Hatshepsut. He did, however, have male issue by a secondary
wife, Isis. The child, a third Thutmose, was trained for the
priesthood. That the youth felt he had a prior claim over
Hatshepsut was natural, and in his contention he was supported by those of the priests and of the government who
were dissatisfied with the rule of the queen. Hatshepsut,
alive to the disaffection, married her eldest daughter to Thutmose and possibly planned for his accession to the throne
upon her death. At least, she surrendered to the seeming
inevitable.

Through a fortunate exchange between the authorities of
the Metropolitan Museum and the Egyptian government, several remarkable monuments of this queen have been brought
to New York. They are for the most part of red granite,
very beautifully carved. One monument is a figure in marble,
and here Hatshepsut is quite feminine, but in the seated
figures of colossal size which once stood before the portals
of her temple, she is represented as having a beard. This
apparently grotesque manifestation may be regarded with
indifference when one remembers that Egyptian art is not
a portrayal so much as a symbolical rendering of the object
depicted. Hatshepsut was trying to tell her people that
she was really the king; hence the symbol of the beard.
Moreover, the legal fiction of Egyptian courts that their
monarchs must be men was maintained in her case by the

use of masculine appellations and endings. One finds curiously enough such titles as "Her majesty himself" and "His daughter the king of upper and lower Egypt." She appears on the monuments as wearing male attire, which may indicate a fondness of men's dress, for in her nature were strong masculine traits, but it is more likely that she is perpetuating a tradition agreeable to the Egyptian mind. Again, on the walls of her great temple at Del el-Bahri she caused her architect to commemorate her nativity in which she is represented as a male child! Thus, she perpetuated the legend that the Pharaoh of her time was a man.

The biographer of Elizabeth the queen should try his hand at Hatshepsut. He should turn from the sixteenth century A. D. to the sixteenth B. C., from the green fields of England to the golden sands of Egypt. He will find, allowing for time and environment, striking parallels. Few Egyptian rulers have been so interesting.

Did this queen have beauty? She says so on the walls of her great temple, where an inscription runs to this effect: "Her majesty grew; to look upon her was more beautiful than anything; her form was like a god; she did everything like a god; her splendor was like a god; her majesty was a maiden, beautiful, blooming."

She claims to be the daughter of the Sun-god, who in disguise entered her mother's chamber and in the appearance of the queen's husband had all his desire. When afterward he made known his divinity to the king, Thutmose is represented as being overcome by the perfections and bodily graces of the god! How shall we evaluate this legend? The priestly theory was that Amon-Ra was incarnate in the reigning Pharaoh when he visited the queen, and thus the child born of the union was of divine descent. Further, it must be remembered that Egyptian rulers claimed to be the actual sons of the gods, thus deriving their divine right to reign.

The history of the achievements of the queen cannot be fully known. After her death all the bitterness and rancor that Thutmose III felt expressed itself in the petty vengeance of obliterating her name and the record of her achievements wherever found. Fortunately, however, some inscriptions escaped his wrath. There were building achievements and monuments too great, too beautiful for him to dare to destroy, and they stand today testifying to the queen's greatness.

The outstanding monuments are the temple in Del el-Bahri and the obelisk at Karnak. The temple is built against the russet cliffs on the western side of the Nile; the obelisk is on the east side. Concerning the temple Baikie writes of "graceful colonnades of an eighteenth dynasty artist,[2] . . . affording long lines of alternating light and shadow which actually emphasize the height of the giant cliffs behind, . . . while the temple derives fresh loveliness from the majestic setting in which it has been placed." The building was reached by a series of terraces planted with myrrh trees from Punt, myrrh being highly esteemed by the Egyptians, and trees from the fabled home of the gods because of their pleasant associations for the divinity dwelling in the temple. The queen said she had brought them "so that Amon might have a place in which he could walk"—an expression suggestive of the early chapters of Genesis in which it is said, that Jehovah walked in the garden in the cool of the day.

Of her remaining achievements pre-eminence must be given to the splendid obelisk at Karnak brought from the first cataract. Its height is ninety-seven and one half feet; its base seven and three quarter feet in diameter, its weight three hundred and twenty-three tons. The task of carriage and its erection was most difficult. A single slender shaft of granite, which off the perpendicular was likely to break of its own weight—how could it be erected? The problem was solved[3] and it stands today after three thousand four hundred years, an impressive reminder of the greatness of the eighteenth dynasty.

[2] James Baikie, *A History of Egypt,* Vol. II, p. 68. By permission of The Macmillan Company.

[3] The obelisks were brought by barges on the river to their landing place, transported on wooden rollers to their ultimate destination, then hauled to the summit of a high embankment of earth, through which a shaft had been sunk to the proposed base. The shaft was filled with sand which could be removed in baskets through lateral galleries. The obelisk was placed horizontally upon the embankment, its base resting upon the funnel. As the sand was gradually removed the obelisk sunk until finally it rested on its foundation. Cf. *The Problem of the Obelisks,* Robert Engelbach.

Near the base is an inscription which reflects the deep religious feeling of the woman who erected this shaft to the glory of God and not alone to commemorate her name. A translation in language similar to the Psalms reads thus:

"I did it under his command; it was he who led me.
I conceived no works without his doing; it was he who gave me direction.
I slept not because of his temple; I lived not from that which he commanded. . . .
I know that Karnak is God's dwelling upon the earth the august ascent of the Beginning.
The sacred eye of the all-Lord, the place of his heart which wears his beauty and encompasses those who follow him."[4]

Here, surely, the queen is above all pettiness, all earthly vanity, as she seeks after God, who is not far from every one of us by whatever name he may be called.

THUTMOSE III

As was foreseen, the Pharaoh who succeeded Hatshepsut was her son-in-law, who took the title of Thutmose III. For years he had been biding his time, curbing his ambition and nursing his bitterness against a woman who had completely eclipsed his own greatness. He has been described as a man of stocky build, filled with Napoleonic energy. Whether he deserves the title of the Napoleon of Egypt may be seriously questioned, but undoubtedly he was a man of great energy, if we remember that he conducted no less than seventeen campaigns in Syria and Palestine, thus securing for his successors the domination of Egypt in the East, and extended his power southward beyond the Third Cataract. It is essential for us to briefly note the threatening conditions he faced in Syria where Egypt had long maintained a footing.

Eastward and within the great bend of the Euphrates was an Aryan race known as the Mitanni. They entered the country about 2000 B. C., nearly the same time as another invading Aryan people, the Cassites, conquered Babylon. Save for their initial victories neither accomplished much.

---

[4] James Baikie, *A History of Egypt,* Vol. II, p. 88. By permission of The Macmillan Company. Compare Psalm 132. 3ff.

They were, as Baikie states, simply a race of horse-riding Aryan aristocrats who for a time dominated subject races. When Thutmose began his rule, the Mitanni were moving westward to back the Syrians, who were ripe for revolt. The latter were supported also by the king of Kadesh. The Syrian states, impatient of the Egyptian rule, believed that a change of Pharaohs afforded an opportunity to throw off their allegiance and to form an alliance with the backing of the Mitanni.

Apparently Thutmose faced a formidable coalition. In reality the Syrian states had no more coherence than a pack of cards. If Thutmose has seemed to his historians to be a colossus, it must be remembered that he fought against pygmies. As already suggested, he has been called the Napoleon of Egypt, and the comparison is apt in at least one particular—he was a great plunderer. No formidable army faced his troops. In his first campaign the Egyptians do not seem to have lost a man, and the battle of Megiddo could not have been much of a fight. The enemy fled to the protection of the city at the first onslaught, while the Egyptian troops, undisciplined and eager for spoil, seized the goods which the enemy had abandoned in their flight. The carelessness of the Egyptians and their lust for plunder, matched by some Old-Testament stories, led to the escape of the king of Kadesh. While Megiddo was being besieged, a matter of weeks, the Egyptians harvested the grain which had ripened on the plain of Esdraelon, some three hundred thousand bushels according to the Egyptian inventory. Six months from the date of his departure Thutmose with his army laden with spoil returned to Egypt. He gave lavish gifts to the priests of Amon, among them some eighteen hundred slave girls for temple purposes. While he was actuated by a sincere intention, he was making trouble for himself and his successors through the bestowment of gifts in such a lavish manner upon his favorite temple. Next he entered upon an era of building, while his army impatiently waited for the time when they might return to Syria. Thutmose did return the next year. Altogether he visited Syria with an army seventeen times in nineteen years. However, most of his campaigns were in the nature of military parades or plundering expeditions.

In the fifth campaign which was directed against Phoenicia, the Egyptian army was demoralized by the abundance of the wine found in the cellars of those they conquered. When once he got his army sober, Thutmose shipped them home.

An interesting incident occurred in the investment of Joppa by Thutmose's captain, Tahuti. He captured the city by the subterfuge of concealing his soldiers in panniers, and thus his men in the loads which donkeys carried entered the city. A similar ruse was employed by the Turks in taking Edessa, 1038 A. D., and by the Greeks in the capture of Troy. Perhaps the most celebrated account in fiction of such a trick is the version in the Arabian Nights of Ali Baba and the Forty Thieves.

Whatever judgment is passed upon Thutmose's campaigns, he must be credited with the thorough subjugation of Syria, of enriching his country, and of making easy the success of the kings who followed him. For his successors one Syrian campaign was usually sufficient.

Thutmose's character is stained by his treatment of Hatshepsut. After her death he obliterated her name and the name of her favorites from the monuments and the temples she had erected—a wanton and costly destruction, inspired only by spite. The fine obelisk which she had erected in the temple of Karnak he sheathed with limestone, unwittingly preserving it for the benefit of future generations. It may be of interest to note that two obelisks erected in Heliopolis to celebrate his prowess are now in London and New York. The former is called Cleopatra's needle, though Cleopatra had nothing to do with it, and a shaft of granite beautifully inscribed might have a better appellation. It was Thutmose's misfortune first and last to lose his identity in a woman.

AMENHOTEP THE MAGNIFICENT

Amenhotep III was the last of the great emperors, for the tide of empire was on the ebb. Though he campaigned in the south, probably going beyond the last cataract, he felt it unnecessary to wage war in Asia. This is due in part to the

Egyptian policy introduced by Thutmose III of educating
Syrian youth in Egypt and sending them back to become
friendly rulers; due also to the alliance with the Mitanni, and
most of all to the practice of bestowing lavish gifts upon
the rulers of Asiatic states. With one hand he received
tribute and with the other he paid it out. He bought peace
and therefore had it. A pleasure-loving king, indolent too in
the last years of his reign, content to bask in the sunshine of
popular favor, he reigned long and merrily. To do him
justice, we must admit that he promoted commerce and
enterprises of peace, but over against this was the lavish
expenditure of wealth gained by his predecessors. The
Egyptian chroniclers never tire of telling us of his buildings,
his monuments, and his pleasure grounds. A notable commercial enterprise was the trade with Cretans, who sent to
Egypt pottery and damascened bronzes and received in return
the products of the Nile country. The Mycenean artists
were influenced greatly by Egypt and in return must have
contributed much to a country which at that period was
devoted to realism in contrast to an earlier unemotional art.

But there was a cloud upon the horizon. The Mitanni
and the Hittites were engaged in a conflict which involved
Egypt, and Amenhotep found it necessary to send troops to
Syria to meet the Hittite advance. This is the period of
the El Amarna letters which reflect the seriousness of affairs
in Palestine. A letter from the Egyptian governor of Jerusalem complains of the invasion of the Habiru, referring undoubtedly to the entrance of Semitic tribes who are identified
as Hebrews, and whose depredations, so the writer feels,
will lead to serious consequences.

After thirty-six years marked by great material prosperity,
Amenhotep died, leaving his kingdom to a son whose remarkable career we must reserve for a later chapter.

Supplementary Reading

James Baikie, *History of Egypt,* Vol. II, Chapters XXIII,
XXIV.
J. H. Breasted, *Ancient Times,* Chapter III. *Conquest of Civi-
lization,* Chapter III.

S. R. K. Glanville, *The Egyptians,* valuable for depicting social life of ancient Egypt.

W. M. Flinders Petrie, *Social Life in Ancient Egypt.*

Allan W. Shorter, *Everyday Life in Ancient Egypt.*

Arthur Weigall, *History of the Pharaohs,* Vol. II, Chapters VII, VIII.

CHAPTER X

THE REVOLUTIONARY

THE Pharaoh who succeeded Amenhotep III was the fourth of that name to rule, though he is better known in history as Ikhnaton or Akhenaton. He was young when he came to the throne, probably only twenty-four. The year was 1375 B. C. He reigned but sixteen years, and when he died at the age of forty he had only lived through his youthful days. Perhaps much should be forgiven him on the ground of his immaturity.

Two women in the court were of great influence in the life of the young monarch, his mother, Tiy, and his sister and wife, Nefertiti. The last named means "The Beautiful One has come," an appellation which she deservedly carried, as all who have seen the painted limestone bust in the Berlin Museum must own. "Her beauty," writes Baikie, "makes an instant appeal and is characterized by that delicacy touched with a hint of pathos which has always proved most attractive." She was obviously a lady of quality.

It has been said of Ikhnaton that he made religion the center and moving power of his whole life. He was often mistaken in his policy. His methods for the establishment of the religion in which he believed were unwarranted. His neglect of the affairs in the Asiatic portion of the empire was a blunder. But admitting all this he yet remains a challenging personality, and in comparison with the colorless Pharaohs who preceded him he deserves our consideration.

The facts of his life may be briefly summarized. He began his reign in Thebes, where in the temple of Karnak he erected a shrine in praise of Aton, the first step in the formation of a new religion which was to displace the old religion centering in Amon. The latter was originally a nature deity representing the air and wind, which had created life in the midst of chaos. Later as a Theban deity he had adopted the characteristics of a neighboring god Min, and, like him, symbolized the generative powers of nature, becoming a god of marked sexual character. When Thebes became the seat of empire and its priesthood powerful, it was apparent to its religious leaders that the solar doctrine must be associated with the cult of Amon. Thus Amon became Amon-Ra. Doubtless a sun worshiper in Heliopolis would regard the action of Theban priests as a usurpation of powers not Amon's, and their grievance would be increased as they saw the subordinate part that Ra played. All this may help us to perceive how Ikhnaton favoring an exclusive Sun-god would find support for his contention. But the name of the new deity is not Ra but Aton, and the symbol is the sun's disk with rays each terminating in a human hand, a symbol that all could understand.

One could not expect priests and people to surrender cherished beliefs without a struggle. The strongly entrenched priesthood of Amon, which grew rich and powerful through the gifts of Thutmose III and succeeding Pharaohs, stood solidly against the new cult. It speaks something for the force of the king that he dared oppose the priests and eventually to overthrow them. The first step he took was to change his name from Amenhotep, which means "Amon is content," to Ikhnaton, or the spirit of Aton. Next he closed the doors of the temple of Amon. He mutilated statues wherever the name "Amon" appeared. His fanaticism led him to outrageously deface the monuments of his father. His final break with the priesthood was the location of his capital two hundred and fifty miles down the river, where he built a city for the purpose, calling it Akhetaton (Horizon of Aton). It was laid out with a view to the requirements of the new religion and contained no less than three splendid temples for the god. A striking feature of the city was the palaces built in the midst of lovely gardens, while clustering about the garden walls were the cottages of workmen, something like the arrangements we see in the cathedral towns of France and England. Glass manufacture was undertaken, for while the city was chiefly religious and aristocratic, it was also industrial. So far as possible it was designed to be a model community. Art was promoted and was essentially realistic, in contrast to the earlier conventional manner. The limestone bust of the queen, to which I have referred, is an example of the art of the period, refreshingly new and convincing. The houses of the wealthy were spacious and well planned with plenty of living and bedroom accommodations to which lavatories and bathrooms were attached. Baikie calls attention to a feature of the temples which was quite characteristic of Ikhnaton's creed, the open air and sunshine. He writes: "The colonnades where they exist are no longer deep gulfs of darkness but only intervals of shade between courts lit by brilliant sunshine." Here we have light and publicity in place of the darkness and mystery of the old religion.

THE REACTION

But in Egypt there was found no room for Ikhnaton's theology. With the close of his brief life Atonism ended. It had been bound up with the personality of the ruler and met dissolution with him. At the best, we can say of it that it had been a noble experiment, foreshadowing the monotheism of the future. Moreover, Ikhnaton's faith failed in a practical way. Aton was a jealous god brooking no rivals, admitting no compromise; and the last was essential in a country conservatively religious and from time immemorial committed to folk gods, to Ra and Osiris. Atonism found no place for the religion of the common people. It excluded the gods who appeared in moving trees and running water, all household deities, all local divinities. Designed to be universal, it ended as an esoteric cult. "Atonism," said a writer, "began at the top of society and remained there." Most serious of all, so it seemed to his contemporaries, Ikhnaton found no place in his system of religious thought for Osiris and the ideas of the future life associated with the God of Judgment. In Atonism immortality fades into a dream.

It is not easy to estimate the character of Ikhnaton, and widely divergent views are held. In his nature were certain irreconcilable traits. True he was a poet and a dreamer, but he was also an iconoclast, and his religious fanaticism approached madness. His family life was praiseworthy, but what shall we say concerning his disregard of duty to the state?

The excavator who uncovers the capital at El Amarna speaks with unstinted praise concerning its beauty, but Ikhnaton's contemporaries had some justification for believing that the withdrawal from Thebes and the building of a new capital was a selfish, unwarranted piece of folly for which posterity must pay. It is to be noted that El Amarna was a city of pleasure rather than a capital, that Ikhnaton exercised almost no administrative functions, but was solely occupied with religious rites, in the pleasures of his home, in promoting art[1] and in beautifying the city he had built. Meanwhile Egypt lost her Asiatic dependencies, while her domestic affairs pursued a disastrous course, no pilot steering the ship of state.

But if Ikhnaton lamentably failed to establish a universal religion, he has left to posterity the legacy of a sincerely devout nature which found its highest expression in the hymns he addressed to Aton. The reader familiar with the Old-Testament Psalter will at once recognize the parallel between the Egyptian poet and the Hebrew hymn writer. The resemblance of the Aton hymns to the verse of the psalmist, however striking, is probably accidental and not indicative of borrowing on the part of the latter. If Ikhnaton shortly after death passed into oblivion from which he was not rescued until modern times, it is unlikely that his poems would have been known by Hebrew writers of the postexilic

---

[1] The many portrait statues and delineations of Ikhnaton indicate that he was an artistic revolutionary, favoring the exaggeration of physical abnormalities, "the receding forehead, the projection of the head far back suggesting that he was hydrocephalus; his features thin and the jaw long and drooping, his arms slender and his body and legs resembling those of a woman, while the deep sunken eyes smoldered with internal fires above a languid and sensuous smile."—A. W. Shorter, *An Introduction to Egyptian Religion*, p. 94f. By permission of The Macmillan Company.

period. We are indebted to Dr. James H. Breasted for the translation[2] and arrangement of the poems appended.

DAY AND MAN

Bright is the earth when thou risest in the horizon;
When thou shinest as Aton by day
Thou drivest away the darkness.
When thou sendest forth thy rays,
The Two Lands (Egypt) are in daily festivity.
Men waken and stand upon their feet
When thou hast raised them up.
Their limbs bathed, they take their clothing,
Their arms uplifted in adoration to thy dawning.
Then in all the world they do their work.

The sun ariseth, they get them away
And lay them down in their dens.
Man goeth forth unto his work
And to his labor until the evening.

(Psalm 104. 22-23.)

DAY AND THE WATERS

The barques sail upstream and downstream alike.
Every highway is open because thou dawnest.
The fish in the river leap up before thee.
Thy rays are in the midst of the great green sea.

Yonder is the sea, great and wide,
Wherein are things creeping innumerable,
Both small and great beasts.
There go the ships,
There is leviathan, whom thou hast formed to play therein.

(Psalm 104. 25, 26.)

---

[2] From *The Dawn of Consciousness*, pp. 282-284. Reprinted by permission of Charles Scribner's Sons.

UNIVERSAL CREATION

How manifold are thy works!
They are hidden before men,
O sole God, beside whom there
is no other.
Thou didst create the earth
according to thy heart.

O Lord, how manifold are thy
works!
In wisdom hast thou made
them all:
The earth is full of thy riches.
(Psalm 104. 24.)

"While thou wast alone:
Even men, all herds of cattle and the antelopes;
All that are upon the earth,
That go about upon their feet;
They that are on high,
That fly with their wings.
The highland countries, Syria and Kush,
And the land of Egypt;
Thou settest every man into his place,
Thou suppliest their necessities,
Every one has his food,
And his days are reckoned."

Sometime during the eighteenth dynasty or preceding it
certain Hebrew tribes migrated to Egypt. How long they
remained and under what Pharaoh they went out is unknown.
According to the biblical tradition the leader of their Exodus
had been adopted by a king's daughter and brought up in the
palace. In spite of the penetrating fog that envelopes the
history of the Hebrews at this period, making uncertain their
movements, we can envisage the influence of Egyptian myth
and cult upon the religious thought and practices of Israel.
Of this we shall treat later.

SUPPLEMENTARY READING

James Baikie, *History of Egypt*, Vol. II, Chapters XXVIII,
XXIX, XXXII.
J. H. Breasted, *Dawn of Conscience*, Chapters XV, XVI.
Allan W. Shorter, *Introduction to Egyptian Religion*, p. 94ff.
Cambridge Ancient History, Vol. II, Chapter VI.
Encyclopedia—Article on "Ikhnaton" ("Akhenaton").

PART II

THE RISE AND GROWTH OF THE
HEBREW NATION

CHAPTER XI

ISRAEL'S RACIAL HERITAGE

THE student of the early history of Israel is faced with the difficulty of supplying gaps in a narrative which is admittedly disconnected and fragmentary. Doubtless the early narrators had the same trouble, their sources for the Old-Testament material being partial, frequently in duplicate, with differences in detail and requiring careful selection. Their choice was governed not by logical or historical processes but by the desire to preserve didactic values.

The Hebrews had a double ancestry, deriving their early lineage from a nomadic people and their later from an agricultural Canaanitish population among whom they settled after the conquest. Their traditions inform us of a Mesopotamian origin in the family of Terah, of which the most distinguished member was Abraham. As we saw in a former chapter, this family, at first living in Ur, later migrated to Haran on a tributary of the Euphrates. The city, a colony of Ur, had a considerable Semitic population, known more exactly as Aramaeans. From this region Abraham and his immediate family migrated to Canaan, his descendants returning to intermarry with their kinsmen. This identification of the Hebrews of our history with Aramaeans is important and is recognized in the verse, "A wandering Aramaean was my father;" and in the marriages of Isaac to Rebecca and Jacob to Rachel and Leah.[1]

The nomadic strain in the race was always strong and dominant, persisting until a late date. Witness Jeroboam's rallying cry, "To thy tents, O Israel."[2] It is reflected in the stories of the patriarchs, illustrated in the wilderness experiences, and tersely put in the passage quoted from the Deuteronomist.[3] Unless we recognize the influence of a

---

[1] The marriages probably represent tribal migrations and fusions.
[2] 1 Kings 12. 16.
[3] Deuteronomy 26. 5, R. V., m.

desert ancestry and that by instinct and nature the Hebrews were a nomadic people, we shall miss the significance of their early history. Later, when the two strains nomadic and agricultural or urban were fused, Israel entered upon an inheritance, which in spite of the misgivings of the prophets, was richer and more complete than that which the desert could furnish.

The race traditions which we follow concern only a part of the Hebrew people, the Joseph tribes, with possibly other clans associated with them. In a time of drought they enter Egypt and live in an area of the Delta known as Goshen.[4] Ultimately they return to Canaan, not as formerly, restless nomadic clans, but as invaders with augmented forces, a gradual but irresistible force, destined to gather other race elements and out of the fusion to form a great nation.

Israel Leaves Egypt

We may accept as historical the tradition that Hebrews were in Egypt and were detained there for a period in virtual slavery. No nation would keep a record of their bondage to another country unless it were true. It is equally certain that their deliverer was Moses, who after he had effected their escape acted as their leader in the period of wandering that followed. While legends admittedly cling to his memory, we are safe in concluding that he was a man of genius, that he had great organizing ability, that he codified their laws and so impressed his personality upon the race that he has never been forgotten.

As to the duration of their stay and the date of the Exodus, we are left largely to conjecture. The biblical writers do not seem to agree upon the length of the Egyptian period, some making it four hundred and thirty years and others four generations, or, roughly speaking, one hundred and sixty years.

A like uncertainty attends the date of the departure of Israel from Egypt. We apparently find a clue in Exodus 1, verse 11, in which we are told that Hebrew slaves built

---

[4] Genesis 47. 5, 6.

brick cities for Pharaoh, Pythom, and Rameses. One naturally concludes that the reigning Rameses is meant, and the view has been confirmed by Naville's excavations in the Wadi Tumilat, where he has identified the site of Pythom, and established the fact that it was built by Rameses II with Semitic labor. We have a further corroboration in the discovery of a stele in Bethshan, a Palestinian garrison town occupied by Egyptians. On this is listed a city bearing Rameses' name. The evidence seems conclusive and has persuaded many scholars that Rameses II was the Pharaoh of the oppression. He was succeeded c. 1220 B. C. by his son Merneptah, who reigned for ten years. He was an old man at the time of his accession, but a vigorous and able general, as his campaigns against the Libyans and in Palestine proved. He becomes according to this view the Pharaoh of the Exodus, as his father had been the Pharaoh of the oppression.

But unfortunately for those who insist that these are the Pharaohs meant by the biblical writer, we have Petrie's discovery in 1896 in Thebes of a stele with the following inscription:

"Plundered is Canaan, with every evil,
Carried off is Ashkalon,
Seized upon is Gezer,
Yenoam is made a thing not existing,
Israel is desolated, her seed is not;
Palestine has become a defenseless widow for Egypt."

Here in an Egyptian record is the long-sought-for reference to Israel. However, since the tablet was inscribed by Merneptah and indicates that the Hebrews were then in Palestine, it points to an earlier date for the oppression and the Exodus than the time of Rameses II and his son. Additional confirmation is given in the Amarna letters, one of which was written (c. 1402 B. C.) by the governor of Jerusalem imploring the aid of the Egyptian ruler: It reads: "The land of the King, my Lord, is going to ruin . . . all the princes are lost . . . the King has no longer any territory. *The Habiru* have devastated all the King's land." It is reasonable to conclude that by *the Habiru* are meant the Hebrews, but it is not clear that the reference is to Israelitish hosts fighting under Joshua. As Burney suggested, the attackers may have been plundering Semitic bands living on the edge of the desert, who at the time the frightened governor wrote had come in with greatly augmented forces.

Garstang's careful investigation of the site of ancient Jericho should be considered in this connection. He is convinced that the fall of the city occurred in 1407 B. C. and its cause was the invading Israelitish army. If his date is accepted as the beginning of the settlement in Canaan, the Exodus must have occurred prior to 1400 B. C.[5] That, of course, is admissible and will be welcome to those who do not seek exactness in timing events and are undisturbed by the objections raised to an early date. The present writer admits that he has no settled conviction as to the time of the Exodus. To him the citations quoted from the stele of Merneptah at Thebes, the Amarna letters, and the discoveries of Naville at Pythom and Garstang at Jericho, are valuable data not for determining the time a certain event took place but for giving a historical foundation for Semitic movements during a nebulous era.

THE FOUNDER OF THE NATION

Whether or not Moses was of Egyptian descent as some have asserted, he was Egyptian bred. Tradition places him in the household of Pharaoh as an adopted son. He was given the Egyptian name "Mose" (meaning "child"), which was probably prefixed by the name of an Egyptian deity as in the case of Thutmose and Ahmose. We can easily understand why later he would drop the prefix.

In Stephen's address recorded in Acts, seventh chapter, we have in the twenty-second verse the words, "Moses was instructed in all the wisdom of the Egyptians." They embody a familiar tradition which we willingly accept. "Wisdom,"

---

[5] See T. H. Robinson, *History of Israel*, Vol. I, p. 74f. Robinson feels that the Exodus could not have occurred during the period of Egypt's greatest activity (1480-1380 B. C.), and seems inclined, in the light of Garstang's discoveries, to place the date prior to 1480 B. C.

writes Professor Breasted, "meant to the Egyptian social contemplation."

However comprehensive the preparation, it was inadequate for leadership. He needed the discipline of the desert, if he would identify himself fully with the fortunes of his people. The occasion of his flight and his refuge in the wilderness of Sinai is familiar and need not detain us. What is of more importance is the significance of his alliance by occupation and marriage with an important desert tribe. The Kenites, obscurely related to the tribe of Judah, were a nomadic tribe who seemed to have acted as smiths to the scattered peoples of the Sinaitic peninsula. Their deity Yahweh was associated with Sinai or Horeb and was a fire god. There is a division of opinion among scholars as to whether Israel obtained its conception and name of deity from the Kenites. It is interesting to observe that among the writers of the Pentateuch there was likewise a difference, the Yahwist believing that from the very beginning God was known by his name "Yahweh," while the Elohist and the Priestly writer correctly state that God was so known only from the Mosaic period. This seems to be the correct interpretation of Exodus 6. 3. The revelation of the name "Yahweh" in the Burning Bush presupposes on the part of Moses a knowledge which he most naturally would obtain from the Kenites.

Concerning Moses' return to Egypt under a Pharaoh presumably more favorable in his attitude to the Hebrew leader than his predecessor, we have an ample account in Exodus, chapters 5 to 12. We need not linger upon the "miraculous" plagues, disasters which frequently attended the drying up of water in canals and reservoirs when the Nile was low. Their unprecedented severity and their concurrence heighten the dramatic element in the account. The Passover and the passage of the tribes through the Red Sea[6] were race memories indelibly impressed upon the consciousness of Israel.

Of paramount importance during this early period were

---

[6] The passage through the Sea of Reeds (Red Sea) probably occurred in the Delta north of Suez, where the land is only just above sea level and is often covered with water. These "lakes" of shallow depth were crossed through the blowing of a strong wind which left a dry passage. The explanation in Exodus 14. 21 is plausible.

the events which transpired at Sinai, and which we may enumerate as:

a. The adoption of Yahweh as Israel's God.
b. The ratification of the Covenant.
c. The codification of the moral law.

YAHWEH BECOMES THE GOD OF ISRAEL

The meaning of Yahweh is obscure. Doctor Moffatt in his Old-Testament translation renders it "Eternal," but without sufficient support to command general assent. The Hebrews wrote only the consonants leaving the vowels to be supplied. Long ago the pronunciation was lost through their unwillingness to utter the name of Deity, for which they substituted another word, although they continued to write YHWH. This has led to various spellings, all of which is puzzling, no doubt, to the layman. We have in the Authorized Version, Lord, and in the Revised (Amer. tr.), Jehovah. The German spelling is Jahve, and the vocalized form now quite generally employed is Yahweh.

We are on more certain ground when, turning to the biblical account, we seek the characteristics of Israel's God. He was a local deity, a mountain God of Sinai or Horeb, and attributive to him were the earthquake, the storm, the fire. He was also a warrior God. While awe and mystery surround him, he regarded his people with affection and in turn was loved by them. Belief in Yahweh was a formative principle in the development of the nation. Without the religious motive, Moses could have accomplished little.

THE COVENANT RATIFIED

In Exodus 24. 1-8 we have an account of a covenant made between Yahweh and the people Israel. While the passage is somewhat obscure, what took place has been correctly described by Robinson:[7]

"An altar was erected, representing the deity, and over against it stood the people. Victims were slain and their

[7] W. E. O. Oesterley and T. H. Robinson, *History of Israel*, Vol. I, p. 93. Oxford University Press.

blood was drained off into bowls. Part of this blood was then dashed against the altar, and the rest flung over the heads of the people." That is, the life, symbolized by the blood of the victim, was used to cover both parties. Each passing beneath it was identified with the victim and hence with each other. Before the ceremony Yahweh and Israel were separate entities. Now they are one, held together in a vital continuous union.

THE CODIFICATION OF LAWS

The book of Exodus, chapters 20 and 34, contains two decalogues, one moral, the other ritual. It has been frequently claimed that the ritual code is the older, but it presupposes an agricultural stage and feasts, the observance of which would be meaningless to Israel at this time. Obviously, it belongs to the period of the settlement in Canaan. On the other hand, the moral decalogue is timeless. The commands enjoined by the second table, numbered six to ten, were those honored in Egypt and essential to any society, nomadic or civilized. It is difficult to see how Israel could ever have been without those social laws which grow out of the experience of men living a communal life. Concerning the commands written on the first tablet: the *fifth,* which reads, "Honor thy Father and thy Mother," likewise belongs to early nomadic society. The *fourth,* on the observance of the seventh day, in its original form may have survived from the early Mesopotamian contact or it may first have been promulgated at Sinai, like the *first* and *third,* which are peculiar to their relation to Yahweh. The *second* commandment,[8] which forbids the making of graven images, if given at this time, is hard to explain when we remember Aaron fashioning a golden calf or bull, Moses making a brazen serpent as a means of healing the stricken Israelites, Micah's image which was revered by the tribe of Dan, Jeroboam's two calves which were placed at Bethel and Dan as objects of worship, and the veneration on the part of Judah of the brazen serpent until Hezekiah's time. Are we to understand

---

[8] Following the order in the A. V. and R. V. but not the numbering in the Catholic version.

that this commandment was honored in the breach rather
than in its observance? Or was it construed as an injunction
not to make a graven image of Yahweh?

THE WILDERNESS WANDERINGS

We know little of Israel's nomadic life in the wilderness.
To the Hebrew historian of a later date, the delay in entering Canaan seemed regrettable, in fact, downright disobedi-
ence to Yahweh. To us, on the contrary, the delay seems to
have been a precautionary and disciplinary measure. How
long the period lasted is uncertain. Tradition said "forty
years." But forty among the Hebrews had the equivalence
of "many." It was an uncertain numerical quantity. However, the time could not have been less, and to it we must add
the period spent in the trans-Jordanic country before Canaan
was invaded.

For the greater part of the period they were in the oasis
of Kadesh, which furnished them abundant water and pas-
turage. From this as a center they made foraging attacks
upon other desert tribes, and possibly one of the clans entered
Palestine from the south.[9] Questions of the priority of
Moses and the Priestly leadership of Aaron's family were
met, and both Moses and Aaron were vindicated by measures
as dramatic as they were cruel and vindictive.[10] But for the
most part the period was passed over in silence, tradition
having little to recount. At the close a new generation faced
new responsibilities and another leader than Moses took command.

A SUMMARY

Israel's racial heritage on the eve of their entrance into the
promised land comprised the experience and discipline of
nomadic life, institutions which had been born of great
events, laws both written and oral, a deeply seated race consciousness, a belief in Yahweh as present with them and
leading their hosts, and, finally, a literary inheritance.

Too little recognition has been paid to the early stage of

[9] Judges 1. 11-15.
[10] Numbers 16.

Israel's literature, credit being deferred until the writers arrive on the scene. But the folklore of Genesis and other Pentateuchal stories may have reached their perfection, like the parables of Jesus, while in their oral form. Around the campfire in the chill of wintry nights, on the housetop under the light of moon and stars, the families of Israel listened to their bards and story-tellers, who preserved for them and future Israel their literary heritage.

SUPPLEMENTARY READING

John P. Peters, *Religion of the Hebrews,* Chapter IV.
T. H. Robinson, *History of Israel,* Chapters IV, V.
Henry P. Smith, *Religion of Israel,* Chapter III.
Bible, Exodus 1, 4, 12, 19, 20; Numbers 13.

CHAPTER XII

ISRAEL'S CULTURAL HERITAGE

It has been said by a recent writer that Egypt's influence upon Israel was negligible.[1] He was probably thinking of certain periods of history when Israel's resistance to Egyptian influence was especially marked. But taking all factors into consideration, from first to last, Egypt was a dominating influence in Hebrew affairs. For about four hundred years (1600 B. C.–1200 B. C.), Egyptians governed Palestine. Prior to that period, and during part of it, some of the Hebrew tribes lived in Egypt, and must have been to a considerable extent affected by the civilization of that country, unless we are to ignore the environmental factor in molding a race. As their women "borrowed" jewels and raiment from the Egyptians on the eve of their flight, so all along there had been a Hebrew borrowing. The arts and crafts, the customs and manners, the laws and institutions of Egypt had been gradually, perhaps unconsciously assimilated, unless we are to conclude that all Israel had been on the same social level, that all were slaves and incapable of development. The civilization of Egypt was too great, too overpowering, and the Hebrew tribes too assimilative for the latter to escape their environment, although they may have resisted it.

Later on, when Israel entered Canaan, they came in contact with a civilization the ingredients of which were Egyptian and Babylonian. Thutmose III had done his best to "Egyptianize" the country.[2] He had educated the children of Syrian princes in Egypt and later returned them to govern Syrian and Palestinian city-states for him. Egyptian garrisons made the country secure. In some courts the Egyptian language was employed.[3] The gods of Egypt followed

---

[1] T. H. Robinson, *History of Israel*, Vol. I, p. 40f.
[2] Alfred Bertholet, *History of Hebrew Civilization*, p. 81.
[3] *Ibid.*, p. 49.

the army and worship was paid to Osiris, to Ptah, and particularly to Amon. Goods of Egyptian manufacture flooded the country. It is probable that when the Hebrews invaded Palestine the political leadership of Egypt was in jeopardy, but her social prestige still challenged the Babylonian. This culture the Hebrews inherited and assimilated in taking over the country.

From biblical sources we gain some knowledge of the later relationships that existed between the Hebrews and the Egyptians. Solomon married the daughter of a Pharaoh. Jeroboam fled to Egypt and from his exile returned to take command of the Northern Kingdom. In Isaiah's time there was a strong pro-Egyptian party in court. After the destruction of Jerusalem, a remnant of the people went to Egypt in voluntary exile, taking Jeremiah with them. The favorable attitude of the Jews toward the Ptolemies in the Greek period is well known.

It is not a case of occasional contact but of continuous influence political, social, and religious on the part of Egypt. The matter is of more than ordinary interest to us for modern nations have derived the culture of Egypt and Babylonia not directly, but through the impact of those civilizations upon small states in western Asia—Palestine, Phoenicia, Syria, and the islands of Crete and Cyprus.

THE NATURE OF THE INFLUENCE

While the influence, generally speaking, was cultural, more specifically described, it was moral, religious, artistic, and literary. We can only illustrate this in hurried fashion because of the space at our disposal. It is, of course, difficult to say how much Israel received in the first contact with Egypt. Hebrew writers have left little bearing upon this point, and one would presume that a people somewhat isolated[4] and represented as oppressed serfs[5] would receive much less than in subsequent times when they were a dominant race. But even so, I think we may list:

---

[4] Genesis 47. 6.
[5] Exodus 1. 11, 13-14.

a. The environmental influences, unconsciously imbibed and transmitted.

b. The moral and religious preparation of Moses.

c. The impression made by animal cults, namely, bull worship and the veneration of the serpent.

d. Cults and ceremonies.

e. The common law of Egypt under which Hebrew society operated during the sojourn.

f. The value attached to Egyptian arts and crafts. The elucidation of some of these points will be made as we proceed.

BULL AND SERPENT WORSHIP

When Aaron melted the jewels which the Hebrews had taken from the Egyptians and fashioned from them images of calves (bull calves), he cried, "These are your gods which brought you out of Egypt."[6] Here is the reappearance of a familiar Egyptian cult known also in Sumer, Babylonia, Assyria, Canaan, and today in southern India. The bull perhaps better than any other symbol represented the generative power of nature. With the aid of such a god, the worshipers felt that they could obtain the increase of their fields, their herds, their flocks and their own bodies.

In the narrative Moses is represented as being exceedingly angry, and later Aaron and the people are penitent. Nevertheless, bull worship continued in Israel and we find it flourishing in the days of Jeroboam, who made similar images[7] and placed them in the ancient sanctuaries of Bethel and Dan.[8]

An example of serpent worship is found in the story of Numbers 21. 4-9. The wilderness was infested with snakes of a poisonous variety; many of the Israelites had been bitten, and Moses as a cure had made and erected a bronze

---

[6] Exodus 32. 2-4f.

[7] 1 Kings 12. 28, Jeroboam had been influenced by his Egyptian environment.

[8] T. H. Robinson suggests that when this story was related at the Bull sanctuaries in Bethel and Dan, it was said that Moses, not Aaron, had fashioned the images. Neither then nor thereafter was there thought to be any impropriety in worshiping Yahweh under this symbol. *History of Israel,* Vol. I, p. 108. Oxford Press.

serpent, which was designed by sympathetic magic (like cures like) to heal the victims. Serpent worship, as we know, had a tremendous following in Egypt. Writers on modern Egypt speak of the veneration of the snake which still prevails among the peasants. The cult was widely spread. One has only to recall the following of the serpent goddess of Crete, its associations with Aesculapius, and its early appearance in Sumerian mythology[9] and Hebrew folklore.[10]

Its persistent hold upon Israel is suggested by the rally to Adonijah[11] at the Serpent's Stone, and by the preservation of the brazen image which Moses had made and which was still worshiped in Hezekiah's time.[12] The veneration of the serpent was probably due to the popular superstition that it was immortal[13] and therefore a deity.

CULTS AND CEREMONIES

A familiar sight in the wilderness wanderings and in later times was the Ark carried on the shoulders of priests and followed by the procession of the tribes. No religious cult in Israel assumed such importance.[14] The Ark was a chest, and both its name and form would be recognized by Egyptians as borrowed from their temples. As was pointed out in Chapter VIII, the Egyptian shrine was an upright chest or a boat which stood on a stone pedestal in the inmost recess of their place of worship. Poles were slung underneath it and it was supported on the shoulders of priests when occasion called for its removal. The shrine or boat contained the cult image of the god.

The Ark of Israel recalls by its name the boat, by its form the shrine, suggesting that the two conceptions were united. So far as we know, the Ark contained no cult image, although it was revered as the very presence of deity,

---

[9] See Chap. VI.
[10] Genesis 3. 1f. See also G. A. F. Knight, *Nile and Jordan*, p. 306f.
[11] 1 Kings 1. 9 where "stone of Zoheleth" should be rendered "Serpent's stone." Evidently, an altar on which sacrifice was offered to a serpent deity stood here.
[12] 2 Kings 18. 4.
[13] See Chap. VI.
[14] 1 Samuel 4. 5, 21; 2 Samuel 6. 12f.; Psalm 24.

and addressed as such. When the Ark moved into battle the priests chanted:

"Arise, O Lord, and let thy enemies be scattered,
And let them that hate thee flee before thee."

The corresponding chant upon the Ark's return ran:

"Return, O Lord, to the myriads
Of the families of Israel."[15]

The cult of the Ark marked a new departure in Israel's religious practice. So far as we know, there was no suggestion of its presence in the early nomadic stage. On the contrary, the deities were local and associated with sacred places.[16] In Egypt where the religious procession was featured, the gods were transported usually by means of Nile barges. Under what more fitting and familiar symbolism could Yahweh be conceived than the Ark, by which he became one with his people, traveling like them from Sinai to his ultimate home in Canaan?

The tent in which the Ark was housed[17] was at first simply furnished, each article having a special significance. Before it there was a court where matters of judicial inquiry were handled and decisions made by those who acted for Yahweh. This gave the sanctuary its ordinary name, The Tent of Meeting.

THE TEMPLE

In connection with the Ark, we may appropriately mention the Temple which was designed as its repository and not as a royal chapel nor as a place of public worship. It was built for Solomon by Phoenician workmen, but the design was Egyptian. There was the same ground floor plan. In place of the twin obelisks, standing before Egyptian and Phoenician temples, were two bronze pillars. The lighted seven-branched candlestick reminds us of the lights that burned before Egyp-

[15] Numbers 10. 35, 36.
[16] Chap. II.
[17] The elaborate account of the Ark described by the Priestly writer in Exodus 36 should not be taken as descriptive of the original form.

tian deities, while the innermost chamber, "the holy of holies," containing the Ark, had, as we have seen, its Egyptian counterpart. It is a matter of little consequence whether the Temple pattern was the tent in the wilderness or a Phoenician adaptation; in either case, we reach an Egyptian origin.

THE RITE OF CIRCUMCISION

Opinion has been divided as to the practice of circumcision among the Egyptians, but the weight of authority now leans strongly toward Professor Elliot Smith's view that all adult Egyptians from predynastic times were circumcised.[18] Such is the evidence derived from prehistoric cemeteries and tomb reliefs. The Priestly writer traces the rite among the Hebrews back to Abraham,[19] but it is evident from other sources that it was not practiced during the period when Israel was in Egypt.[20] Certainly the most plausible interpretation of Joshua, fifth chapter, verse 9, would indicate that the Egyptians had reproached the Israelites because they were uncircumcised. This is in harmony with the interpretation of Exodus 4. 23f. As obscure as the passage is, it apparently means that Moses was uncircumcised until he received the rite vicariously through Zipporah's action.[21] However that may be, the Hebrews were all circumcised before they were permitted to partake of the Passover feast (Exodus 12. 48). Again, a second time, as we are reminded by the Priestly author of Joshua 5. 2-9, the nation was circumcised at Gilgal, the rite having lapsed during the wilderness period.

However, we are not justified in concluding that the rite had an Egyptian origin, although some writers claim this.[22] All Semitic tribes seem to have practiced circumcision upon their males when they had attained the age of puberty, a rite preparatory to marriage or tribal membership or both. Therefore Egyptians and Hebrews were following a pattern-cult, varying in mode and significance and so ancient that its origin is obscured.

---

[18] *Ancient Egyptians,* p. 62f.
[19] Genesis 17. 10.
[20] Joshua 5. 2-9.
[21] A case of transference by magic.
[22] J. H. Breasted, *Dawn of Conscience,* p. 353.

The Cult of the Dead

In the closing chapter of Genesis (verses 2, 3, 26), we have an account of the death and embalming of Jacob and Joseph, and we are told that the "embalming" was after the Egyptian manner, that is, it was mummification. Whether this careful disposal of the dead was prevalent in Canaan in Israelitish times is undetermined. Certainly, the presence in graves of many funerary objects including food is significant of the belief in survival after death. The tombs of Phoenician kings in Byblos on the Syrian coast north of Beirut reveal Egyptian workmanship and funerary objects similar to those found in Egypt. There is also evidence that like ceremonials for the dead were followed.

It is difficult[23] to define the attitude of the early Hebrew on the subject of life after death. Some passages in the Psalter are expressive of hope,[24] others of despair.[25] Perhaps the Hebrew alternated between the Babylonian, to whom the place of the dead was the Land-of-no-Return, an existence void of feeling; and the Egyptian, with his confident view that all would be well for him in the future. It is to be remembered in this connection that Yahweh was the God of the living and that there was no Osiris in their future.

Diffusion of Egyptian Culture in Canaan

It is not likely that the Hebrews in Canaan ignored the craftsmanship of the Egyptians. Having no predilection for creating art for themselves, they were not unappreciative of what others produced, as the excavations everywhere in Palestine reveal. The expedition of Harvard University in Samaria found ivory plaques used as incrustations on the furniture of the palace.[26] They were engraved with figures of Egyptian deities, among them the goddess Maat, who personified righteousness. The museums at Megiddo[27] and

[23] See Alfred Bertholet, *History of Hebrew Civilization,* p. 77.
[24] Psalm 139. 8.
[25] Cf. Isaiah 38. 18.
[26] J. H. Breasted, *The Dawn of Conscience,* p. 360. Chas. Scribner's Sons.
[27] Compare Alfred Bertholet, *History of Hebrew Civilization,* p. 87. Geo. G. Harrap & Co., London.

other excavated cities display objects of exquisite workmanship by Egyptian craftsmen. These belong to both Canaanite
and Israelitish periods. The inventory that Isaiah furnishes
of a woman of fashion doubtless included toilet articles of
Egyptian manufacture.

Trade relations, as we have remarked, were continuous
between Egypt and Palestine, the Hebrews usually acting as
middlemen. The extensive stables at Megiddo were used by
Solomon for the trading of horses bought from Egyptians
and sold to Hittites.

The diffusion of Egyptian literature is probable during a
literary age like the ninth century and later. Breasted com-
pares its spread with that of the classics among the Western
European races in the Renaissance.[28] This, as far as the
Hebrews may be concerned, is probably an overstatement,
although the story of The Two Brothers,[29] to which reference has already been made, is an example of tales widely
current. The proverbs of Amenemope, an Egyptian moralist of the tenth century, were sufficiently well known for the
writer of Proverbs 22. 17 to 24. 22 to take them over in part
under the caption "The Words of the Wise."

It is not so evident that the prophets of Israel and Judah
were inspired by Egyptian social reformers, as Doctor
Breasted believes.[30] Possibly Psalm 104 shows Egyptian
influence as the parallels exhibited in chapter 10 indicate.

In Bethshan stood two Egyptian temples built during the
Egyptian occupation of the stronghold. One was a temple of
Mikal, the other presumably belonged to his consort. Later,
when the post was abandoned and the Hebrews occupied the
site, they took over the temples and without architectural
changes employed them for their worship. It was somewhat
anticipatory of the Christian movement after Constantine
when Roman and Greek temples were converted into Christian edifices, and Roman feasts became the festivals of those
who followed Christ. In fact, the early Israelitish period in
Canaan may be described as a borrowing of an earlier cul-

[28] *The Dawn of Conscience,* p. 383. Scribners.
[29] See Chap. VIII.
[30] *The Dawn of Conscience,* p. 364.

ture religious, artistic, literary for which they were no less indebted than they were for the harvests of the fields which they had not sown and the wine of the vineyards which they had not planted.

SUPPLEMENTARY READING

Alfred Bertholet, *History of Hebrew Civilization,* p. 78ff.
J. H. Breasted, *Dawn of Conscience,* Chapter XVII.
John Garstang, *Joshua and Judges,* pp. 105-115.
A. T. Olmstead, *History of Palestine and Syria,* Chapter X.
Bible, Exodus 32; Numbers 21. 4f.; Exodus 37. 1f.; Numbers 7. 89; 9. 15-23; 1 Samuel 4. 5f.

CHAPTER XIII

THE LAND OF PROMISE[1]

PALESTINE'S limited area offers no indication of its importance. On a chart of the ancient world, it appears as the state of Vermont on a map of the United States. In fact, its area is about the same as the little New England commonwealth. While its northern boundary line has varied with the fortunes of war, and the southern is quite obliterated by the sand, it is fair to say that the distance north to south is one hundred and fifty miles and the mean average width is seventy. On the west lies the Mediterranean, on the east the desert. As it happens, both are protective barriers. Only a people of the desert can come in from the east. On the west, while Phoenicia boasts a few good harbors, from the Carmel promontory south we have an almost unbroken shore line with no welcoming bays for the mariner, but instead dangerous reefs where the sea breaks.

Crossing the country from west to east one is amazed at the diversity he encounters in the natural features of the country, the soil and its products, the climate and the people. First comes the Maritime plain or the coast land. It has always been fertile enough to support populous cities, and one need not be greatly surprised at the growth of modern towns like Tel Aviv. The products of the land are in the main grains and citrus fruits.

Lying between the Maritime plain and the Central mountain range are the hills known as the Shepelah. While some valleys are fertile and some hillsides are cultivated for the vine and the olive, most of the hill country is used only for

[1] Palestine has been likened to a bridge across which armies, caravans of trade, and the emissaries of kings have passed from one great nation to another. But it has also been an object of desire, a land of promise. So to the early Semite, a desert dweller, who longed to possess its green pastures for his flocks, to the children of Israel emerging from the desert of their wanderings, the Crusaders, the pilgrims of the present day who seek out its sacred shrines, the Zionist, who passionately longs to possess the land of his fathers.

grazing purposes. Its great need is moisture, which it might have if a way could be found for conserving the winter rains. The territory has never figured prominently in the history of Israel. One remembers it as the boyhood home of Samson and the scene of some of his exploits, and later as debatable ground between the Philistine and the Israelite.

To feel the contrast between the fertility of the plain by the sea and the central rocky tableland, the motor road between Jaffa and Jerusalem should be followed and thence to the Jordan. Beyond Jerusalem the deep rifts and broken ranges offer a desolate, almost terrifying aspect. But even so, in the spring months there is enough outcropping herbage for a few herds and flocks of sheep and goats.

The most unusual feature of the topography of Palestine is the deep trench known as the Jordan Valley and its terminal, the Dead Sea basin. The river finds its rise in the Lebanon range, flows through the Sea of Mermon, and by a series of waterfalls and cascades finds its way to the Sea of Galilee, six hundred and eighty feet below sea level. The stream continues to descend toward the south following a winding course and traversing, as the crow flies, three times the distance to its objective the Dead Sea, one thousand two hundred and ninety feet below the Mediterranean.

The Dead Sea is alive with interest. No part of Palestine so quickens the pulse as the descent from the Judean range to this sunken depression in the earth's crust—a valley and a lake two thousand six hundred feet below the level of the sea, if we measure from the lake's lowest depth. While the surrounding shores are desolate, the far-away views are superb. In size and appearance it resembles Lake Geneva. No outlet carries away the vast volume that its tributaries pour in—six and a half million tons daily.[2] But nature cares for this through the sun's hot rays. The excessive rate of evaporation leaves the water, impregnated with salts, about five times the density of sea water. There are no fish in the sea; no birds fly on its shores or across its expanse. A bathing pavilion on the north beach attracts a colorful throng,

---

[2] Karl Baedeker's *Palestine and Syria* (1912), p. 132.

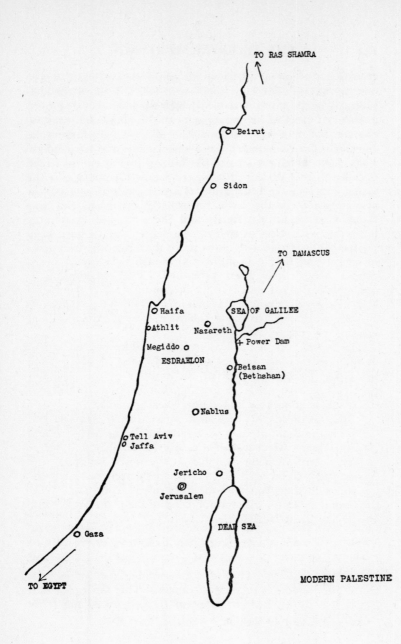

TO RAS SHAMRA

Beirut

Sidon

TO DAMASCUS

SEA OF GALILEE

Haifa

Athlit

Nazareth

Power Dam

Megiddo

ESDRAELON

Beisan
(Bethshan)

Nablus

Tell Aviv
Jaffa

Jericho

Jerusalem

DEAD SEA

Gaza

TO EGYPT

MODERN PALESTINE

who find the unique pleasure of swimming in water where one cannot sink but only bobs about like a cork on the surface. A small gasoline launch which accommodates perhaps a score of persons is anchored near the shore and may be chartered for a trip around the lake—an unforgettable journey. On the southern and eastern shore are crystalline formations which are shaped like human forms, one of which is called "Lot's Wife." Elsewhere, below the surface of the water, one sees the foundation of a town indicating the slow rise of water in the basin. Formerly the Dead Sea was thought to be utterly sterile and the surrounding country unproductive. Not so today. Its saline waters have been pumped into evaporating pans more than five hundred acres in extent and thus a bromine and potash industry of incalculable wealth has been promoted. The evaporation is accomplished most successfully in summer when the torrid heat of the valley reaches its maximum, but living conditions for the workmen are made tolerable through the excellent housing recently constructed.

The fourth zone is the Eastern tableland known as Bashan in the north, Gilead farther south and called Moab opposite the lower Jordan.[3] Much of the country in the past and present has been used for grazing, but its soil especially in the north is admirably suited for wheat growing.

In the northern part of Palestine separating Samaria and Galilee is the Plain of Esdraelon, known also as Megiddo and Armageddon. Its characteristics are its fertility and accessibility. Any invading army from the north following the Syrian coast could leave it at Acre and march the intervening miles to the plain without physical interposition. This has been done times without number and the plain has become one of the great battlefields of history.

CLIMATE, SOIL AND PRODUCTS

The topography, soil, and climate of a country are anticipatory of its history. They are determining factors in promoting or hindering race development. This George Adam Smith has shown in his *Historical Geography of the Holy*

[3] The names used are biblical.

Land, and Rudolph von Ihering when he wrote, "that geography is latent history."

Palestine, unlike Egypt and Babylonia, had considerable rainfall, doubtless more in ancient times than today. There is good reason to believe that the Hebrews entered the country during a pluvial period. There are, roughly speaking, two seasons in Palestine, a wet and a dry, but the beneficial rains occur in the fall and spring and are known in the Bible as "the former and the latter rains."[4]

To desert tribes entering the Fertile Crescent at almost any point, the land must have appeared as a veritable Eden, compared with the arid regions whence they came. However, physical conditions varied greatly especially in Palestine. The country east of Galilee (Bashan), the Plain of Esdraelon, the fruit-bearing hills of Ephraim (Samaria), the Valley of the Jordan, and the Maritime plain were all arable, but the Central mountain-range country, the Shepelah, and the desert south of Judea were in the main grazing lands. Wheat and barley were the agricultural staples; the olive was widely cultivated, figs, grapes, and in later times citrus fruits.

Formerly there was a great deal of game. The word "lion" occurs one hundred and thirty times in the Old Testament and frequent mention is made of other beasts of prey—the leopard, the bear, the wolf. Of the smaller game there were wild fowl and foxes—"the little foxes that spoil the vines."

The climate presented marked contrasts: the proverbial cold of winter on the Judean range and the torrid heat of the Jordan Valley; chilly nights following hot days; the dreaded Sirocco and the welcome northwest and westerly winds. Twice in the Old Testament we read of a lion wandering from the Jordan thickets back into the hills, where it was caught in the snow. It was a land in every way suited to breed men of virility, not excepting the debilitating climate of the Jordan Valley.[5]

[4] The heavy rains of midwinter are often destructive, washing away the soil of the terraces, spreading ruin and desolation.
[5] Jericho is today a prosperous town, the center of a fruit industry which has reached great proportions.

The Roads

The thoroughfares of Palestine were an important feature in its development. They were arteries through which flowed the lifeblood of the nation. The ordinary channel of trade between Egypt and Babylonia led through Palestine or Syria. If one followed the all-land route from the Delta of the Nile, he either crossed the Sinaitic peninsula, thence northward keeping on the east side of the Jordan, and from Damascus by Palmyra proceeding to the Valley of the Euphrates. It was a caravan route direct but dangerous, and probably used more today than in ancient times. The other better and more frequently traveled route hugged the sea, leading through Philistia and Sharon to Carmel, where it divided, one branch going north to Syrian cities, while the diverging route led through the Megiddo pass to the plain and thence to Galilee, Damascus, and the East. Roads of secondary importance connected the main highways, giving one the impression of a network of highways, roads, and paths designed to promote the commercial importance of a people who were fast becoming the middlemen of the ancient world.

Armies, of course, followed the main roads. Between 1479 B. C., when Egyptian troops under Thutmose III negotiated the Megiddo pass, and 1918 A. D., when General Allenby's cavalry rode over the same rough road, innumerable military expeditions have passed through this gateway to Armageddon either meeting their foe here or passing on, not without taking their toll of grain and wine as they proceeded. One does not forget other travelers, men of a different sort, bent neither on trade nor war, but carrying a precious merchandise, some priceless roll of writing. These too followed the highways promoting the kinship of races.

The People of the Land

Concerning its earliest inhabitants, we have had in recent years surprising evidence. The remains of Paleolithic man have been found in the neighborhood of Galilee, and on the western slopes of Carmel near the Crusaders' city of Athlit.[6]

---

[6] Neanderthal man. See Chap. I for his period and industry.

Neolithic man has been prolific in scattering the evidence of his trail. One thinks of Macalister's discoveries in Gezer, of findings at Megiddo in the cave dwellings which honeycomb the mound, and especially the megalithic monuments east of the Jordan. So stupendous were some of their achievements that we need not wonder at the awe with which they were invested by early biblical writers. "There were giants in the earth in those days."[7] While archaeology has given slender evidence of the presence in Palestine of men of great stature at any time, we can understand the primitive judgment that only a great race could produce the prehistoric causeway of Megiddo or the megalithic monuments in trans-Jordania. But of Neolithic man and his predecessors we have no immediate concern. So far as we can tell now, he is linked in no way with the later races of Palestine.

Early in the third millennium before Christ we have the first of three invasions of Semites. The newcomers were called Amorites. Already they had made their presence felt in Babylonia, where they had furnished a line of kings. They were men of medium height, regular features, warlike, bearing a close resemblance to the Arab of the present day. They were succeeded by the Canaanites, when, we do not know. Bertholet[8] guesses that the latter entered the country about 1500 B. C. and drove their predecessors into the hills. This is in harmony with biblical evidence which represents the Amorites as occupying the hill country, while the Canaanites were in the plains. Professor Robinson offers a modified view. In his opinion, Canaanite means a trader, and he especially designates the Phoenician.[9] The third invasion was the Aramaean. From this stock came the Hebrew. The Aramaeans are first met on the upper Euphrates and its tributaries,[10] but because of the pressure of northern races upon the Hittites and these in turn pressing upon the Aramaeans, we have the consequent invasion of Palestine.

It must be recognized that only tentative views concerning

---

[7] Genesis 6. 4.
[8] *History of Hebrew Civilization*, p. 46. Geo. G. Harrap & Co., London.
[9] *History of Israel*, Vol. I, p. 36. Oxford Press.
[10] See Chap. XI.

early tribal movements are possible, and their periods conjectural. That there should be wide difference of opinion
among scholars is not surprising. This much is ,certain, that
the invading peoples were Semitic, that they had similar customs and spoke the same language with dialectic differences.
Moreover, they inhabited the land long enough to leave their
name. Palestine has been called in turn the land of Amurru,
the land of Canaan and Philistia. The last appellation seems
undeserved.

The Philistines were a non-Semitic race. They were late
comers and occupied only a limited area, the lower part of
the Maritime plain. There is some obscurity about their
origin. Apparently, they were Aegeans living in Crete prior
to the Dorian invasion. Driven from their country, they
moved southward by an overland route and by boat.[11]
Eventually attacking Egypt, they were repulsed by the army
of Rameses III. On their retreat they reached the Maritime
coastal plain and settled there, forming a confederacy of five
cities. There is no reason for regarding them as barbaric or
uncouth. On the contrary, they belonged to a cultivated race
and brought with them their arts, although it is possible to
credit them with too much. That they should have entered
Palestine about the beginning of the Iron Age is probably
fortuitous. Certainly, it does not furnish us sufficient basis
for believing that they introduced iron in the country.

THE HITTITES

Until we know more about the Hittites, we shall be unable
to decide if they were a dominating influence in the population of Palestine. Their Syrian center was Kadesh on the
Orontes, and they do not seem to have gone farther south
than the Dog River. If they penetrated Palestine in large
numbers, it seems strange that so artistic a people should not
have left more evidence of their culture than they did. We
can explain objects of Hittite workmanship found in Palestinian excavations as importations, while the scattered references to them in the Old Testament may refer to a few

[11] Peake and Fleure, *Corridors of Time*, Vol. VIII, Chap. V. Oxford
University Press.

colonists who had become landowners, to slave girls, and to military adventurers.

Does the anthropological feature, the broad, fleshy or hooked nose common to Anatolian monuments and characteristic of Jewish physiognomy, offer sufficient evidence upon which to build a theory of race kinship? The suggestion is tempting but intermarriage between the Hittites and Semitic peoples, if it ever took place, must have occurred long before the settlement of Hebrews in Canaan. The broad, fleshy nose is a racial characteristic of several Semitic peoples.

RACE CLASSIFICATION

It has been found convenient to classify mankind by races distinguished by physical characteristics, language, etc. But it must be owned that the problem of race is extremely difficult. Language is an insufficient basis for classification, for a conquering people may adopt the tongue of the race conquered, or a change may take place in the structure of the language over a period of a few hundred years; Latin becomes Italian, Anglo-Saxon the English of Shakespeare's day. We are on safer ground when we argue from physical character, for people frequently resemble one another in those characters which likewise distinguish them from other groups. But the racial characteristic may be derived from only one parent and thus transmitted.

There is no pure race. Into the composition of the larger groups of mankind enter many elements, namely, intermarriage, the absorption of one people by an alien conquering race, and frequently small outlying groups are drawn into the orbit of a larger more progressive people, taking their name. Nor would it be desirable to preserve the purity of a race. Whenever there is a group intrusion with other *mores,* a new religion, or different social conceptions, the group receiving such is benefited. A pure race would be stagnant. Their only hope of progress is the infiltration of ideas and customs from extraneous sources.

GOVERNING RACES

As has already been stated, the Egyptians governed Palestine for four hundred years, half of which time covered the Israelitish occupancy.[12] The excavations bear increasing witness to the important part that Egypt played politically and culturally. But the dominating external influence was Babylonian. It was their culture chiefly that the Canaanites absorbed and the Hebrews inherited. This was natural, for trade relations between the two countries were continuous and there were affinities in customs, manners, and speech. Most important of all, their religious cults followed the same general pattern.

SUPPLEMENTARY READING

Alfred Bertholet, *History of Hebrew Civilization*, Chapter I.
John Garstang, *Joshua and Judges*, pp. 67-103.
A. T. Olmstead, *History of Palestine and Syria*, Chapter I.
John P. Peters, *Religion of the Hebrews*, Chapter V.
T. H. Robinson, *History of Israel*, Vol. I, Chapter II.
George Adam Smith, *Historical Geography of the Holy Land*, Chapter I.
Illustrated London News, May 12, 1934, p. 720.

---

[12] Chap. XII.

CHAPTER XIV

THE CULTURE AND CULTS OF CANAAN

The people who formed the basis of the population of the land in pre-Israelite times and who gave their name to the country were Canaanites. As has been stated, they were a second wave of Semitic migration who came into Palestine and Syria about the middle of the second millennium B. C. There was no clear demarcation line between the two cultures Amorite and Canaanite[1] save that the Amorite was older. Like the Hebrews, with whom they were affiliated by race, the Canaanites had a nomadic origin, but had passed long since from the pastoral to the agricultural stage. Culturally they thrived but seem on the whole to have been less virile than their predecessors. However, they endured as a race until about 1000 B. C., when they were engulfed by the rising tide of Hebrew civilization. The sources of our knowledge of the period are derived from biblical writers and the discoveries which have attended the excavation of Palestinian cities, more exactly, the Canaanitish levels.

The Old-Testament writer, as one might expect, was in revolt against the religious practices of Canaan, and the more so because he saw the undoubted influence they exerted upon the impressionable Israelites. It is significant that the most explicit condemnation is from the book of Deuteronomy (c. 650 B. C.), indicating that the customs had prevailed for a long period. It may be taken as axiomatic that what the prophets prohibited was practiced by the Canaanites and their docile pupils, and from their alleged vices we may gain some descriptive information of the cults.

The culture of the Canaanites prior to and following the Hebrew invasion is evidenced by recent discoveries, which, added to the early findings, have given us a rich store of

---

[1] The terms "Amorite" and "Canaanite" seem to be used interchangeably in the Old Testament, although J. shows a preference for "Canaanite" and E. for "Amorite." Robinson believes the designation to be literary; Stace, geographical; and Bertholet, racial.

material. Archaeology has given the name Late Bronze Age
to the period roughly corresponding to the Canaanite occupancy. Weapons of bronze, funerary and domestic utensils,
temple and palace decorative pieces in brass and bronze have
been found in abundance; more rarely gold and silver. A
hint of what cities like Jericho once contained is found in
Joshua 6. 24; 7. 21. What Megiddo possessed we know
from Thutmose III, who left an inventory of the articles he
carried away, namely, two gold-mounted chariots, bronze
shirts of mail, silver-mounted tent poles, swords, drinking
bowls, figures in ivory, ebony, and wood, "vessels of bronze
and much clothing."

Iron was more rarely found. Who first introduced its
use in Canaan we do not know. Perhaps the Philistines, but
more likely the Hittites, who had plenty of iron ore in the
north and knew how to reduce and work it. This may have
a bearing upon the date of the Hebrew invasion which seems
to have occurred in the Late Bronze Age.

It will be perceived from the foregoing remarks that our
knowledge of the Canaanite civilization is derived directly
from the Canaanites themselves—from what they have left
us in tombs, temples, palaces, and their dwelling places; while
our knowledge of their cultic practices is derived from what
the Hebrews of a later period have said against them.

There is, however, a noteworthy exception, a Phoenician[2]
poem of eight hundred lines discovered in the spring of 1929
by the French expedition working at Ras Shamra on the
northern Syrian coast. In the poem are embodied two
ancient myths. The first records a conflict between El, an
old god who dwells by the seashore and whose consort is
Elat, known also as the Ashera of the sea, and a younger
god, Baal. Against him El sends the *aquqim,* divine beings
having the horns of bulls and faces like Baal. The issue is
not clear but apparently Baal is slain.

In the second myth the antagonists are Aleion, son of Baal,
who personifies the sky, winds, and rain, and Mot, god of
the earth and its products. Aleion is slain by Mot and

[2] The Phoenicians are regarded by the writer as a division of the
Canaanitish people.

goes to the underworld, where he is held a prisoner. Meanwhile the clouds and rain are withheld and the earth becomes a desert. Anath, the sister of Aleion, seeks him, demanding of Mot the knowledge of his whereabouts. Mot pretended innocence and tried to persuade Anath to search in the underworld for pitchers of the water of life, which poured out upon the desert would convert it into fertile fields. In the end Mot is brought to justice. He is condemned by a tribunal of the gods and handed over to Anath for punishment. She slew him with her sickle, cast him into the fire, ground him between the millstones and finally scattered his remains over the fields.[3] Aleion delivered from the lower world is exalted and hailed as king and judge. He is honored by El and Ashera, and a temple is built for him of the cedars of Lebanon.

Evidently, we have here myths in a transitional stage. They are Babylonian or Egyptian in origin and on their way to becoming Greek. Aleion recalls Osiris, the two kings having several features in common. Anath's quest for her brother in the lower world brings to mind Gilgamesh seeking among the dead for his lost friend Engidu, or Ishtar searching for her lover Tammuz, Astarte's grief for Adonis, and Demeter's search for Persephone. Deities with different names but unchanged characteristics appear. The poem is a stage in the westward march of a goddess. She who was Ishtar among the Babylonians is now Astarte, cr Ashera. Later she will be known as the Cyprian Aphrodite, and after that the Roman goddess of love. Likewise, Tammuz becomes Adonis, for whom, as for the lost Babylonian god, women lament.[4]

---

[3] Professor Hooke observes that the figures of speech are drawn from agricultural operations. *Myth and Ritual,* Essay IV, p. 81. Oxford Press.

[4] There survived from the later rites of the Phoenicians an interesting and picturesque ceremony known as the Gardens of Adonis. As described by Professor Hooke, the rite was performed in the summer when women lamented the death of Tammuz-Adonis. In baskets or jars of earth they sowed barley, wheat, lettuce, anemones, and various flowers. These were watered, diligently cultivated, and sprang up quickly. Quite as rapidly they withered away, and after eight days they were carried out with the image of the dead Adonis and flung into the sea or river. The resurrection of the god was implied in the act. *Myth and Ritual,* p. 83. Oxford Press.

Canaanite Festivals

As has been stated, the myths of early peoples, the Egyptians, Babylonians, and Canaanites, were celebrated in the annual festivals, where by drama or recitation they were presented. Invariably other ritual observances were added, and it is not difficult to see how the cultural enrichment and religious instruction of the worshipers might have been advanced. Unfortunately, the religious and ethical values were too often lost in the not infrequent sensuality that marred the occasions.

When the Hebrews invaded Canaan, they saw in the agricultural feasts of their neighbors a national expression of the joy which men find in the harvest period. That they participated in the festivals is not surprising, nor is it strange that they should adopt for their own use the Canaanite ritual, and worship the gods whose blessing attended the harvest.

While the agricultural festivals in Canaan followed in general their Babylonian prototype, there was undoubtedly such adaptation and change as would suit their environment. The seasons were certainly not the same as in Babylonia, but, on the other hand, there was the fixed idea that the vernal and autumnal equinox and the summer solstice were divine changes and should be observed by religious feasts.[5] The festivals were therefore solar in origin and continued to be the feasts of sun worshipers, although in time added significance was given to their celebration. That the Hebrews were oblivious of sun-ritual may be greatly doubted from what we know of a later period in which traces of it still lingered. See 2 Kings 21. 3; 23. 5, 11; and Ezekiel 8. 16.

Canaanitish Deities

As one would expect, a country which harbored many nationalities would have many gods. We find in the period before and following the Hebrew occupation Egyptian temples and deities, Hittite and Babylonian gods, and the shrines or high places where the baals of Canaan dwelt. As

---

[5] See W. O. E. Oesterley, *Myth and Ritual*, Essay VI, p. 111f. Oxford Press.

Bertholet said, "Baal was not one god. He was many. In his essential nature, he was, speaking generally, everywhere the same, but in reality he was divided into a multiplicity of locally differentiated figures."[6] "Baal" is a common noun unless localized, in which case the designation becomes a name hyphenated with the name of the place. Thus we find localities called Baal-Hermon, Baal-Peor, Baal-Judah, Baal-Gad. In Phoenicia the designation "Melkart" was ordinarily given and his consort was Astarte, she who was called in Canaan Baala or Ashera.[7] The tendency in Canaan was toward the unification of local baals in one supreme Baal, a process that had been anticipated by the Phoenicians. It was to check this movement that all the energies of Elijah were directed (ninth century B. C.).

Baalism was a fertility cult. Its shrines harbored prostitutes who were dedicated to the service of Ashera. While the festivals were designed to commemorate the change of seasons, or celebrate the ancient myths, inseparable from their performance was much that was shameful.

THE CANAANITES ADOPT THE ALPHABET

Among the sites recently excavated in Palestine is Kiriath-Sepher, which means "the book town." As the name indicates, it was a center of scribal activity. The great mass of the Canaanites could neither read nor write, hence the need of a professional group who could perform the service. Until the discoveries at Ras Shamra it was believed that the scribes contented themselves with merely transcribing letters, business documents, and court annals. This appears to have been the case in Canaan proper. At least there is no evidence to the contrary.

What gives significance to the writing movement is the fact that the Canaanites were beginning to use an alphabet and employed new writing materials, namely, papyrus, ink, and brushes.

---

[6] See *History of Hebrew Civilization,* p. 106f. Geo. G. Harrap & Co., London.
[7] Frequently called Ashtoreth. Her prototype was the Babylonian Ishtar.

ORIGIN OF THE ALPHABET

The credit for inventing the alphabet apparently belongs to a Semitic people occupying the country in the neighborhood of Sinai. Professor Sprengling calls them the Seirites, identifying them with Mount Seir. Perhaps he is correct. At any rate, they were employed by the Egyptians to work the mines in the southern part of the Sinaitic peninsula. Inasmuch as they spoke only their own tongue, it was necessary for interpreters to be employed, and to explain in a small measure the meaning of the hieroglyphic writing carved on the face of the rocks at the mine entrances. To these syllabic signs of the Egyptians, the Seirites gave their own values simplifying the sounds to the initial letter. This should not have been difficult, for the Egyptian language in the process of time had come to have many simple consonantal signs. Just as we contract "I have" to I've and "you are" to you're, so their syllables were worn away to single consonants.

The initial letter was treated by the Seirites not as a sign but was pictured. For example, their word "ox" pronounced, as nearly as we can show it in English, *alph* was indicated by its initial letter pictured as an ox head. A house called *bet* was represented by drawing a simple floor plan, and giving it the *b* sound. To this very day, the two sounds are recalled by our word alphabet. Altogether the Seirites devised twenty-one alphabetic signs. Unfortunately, they were all consonants. The deficiency of vowels in the Egyptian language was characteristic here also.[8]

THE SPREAD OF THE ALPHABET

The newly devised manner of writing found its way into Arabia, not without modification, for the signs were increased to twenty-eight letters. About the same time it moved northward into Palestine, where it was used by Canaanites, Phoenicians, Aramaeans, and eventually by the Hebrews. It is probable that Sprengling is correct in dating the origin

[8] For full discussion, see Martin Sprengling's *The Alphabet, Rise and Development,* O. I. C. No. 12. University of Chicago Press.

THE SCRIBE

about 1650 B. C., but its use was retarded in the north by the
employment of cuneiform. The chief agents in transmitting
it were the Phoenicians, who carried it to the Greeks, who
in turn passed it on to the Romans. Meanwhile Aramaean
traders were spreading its use in the east, and eventually
it reached India. Its early use was restricted to commercial
purposes, to inscriptions on monuments, and to royal decrees.
The Hebrews seem to be the first to employ it in the creation
of a literature, although an apparent exception to this are
the Ras Shamra writings.

THE RAS SHAMRA TABLETS

The fascination felt for the newly discovered tablets at
Ras Shamra (1929) is partly owing to the fact that while
the language is Phoenician the writing is in the cuneiform
character with syllabic signs replaced by an alphabet of
twenty-eight letters. The question at once arose whether we
have here a transitional stage in the evolution of a Phoenician alphabet, simultaneous to the movement in the South,
or do we have an adaptation or imitation of the Sinaitic
alphabet? The general opinion favors the latter view. It
is not difficult to see that the letters in the Ras Shamra tablets
were made in imitation of the earlier alphabet, the wedge-
shaped markings of the stylus replacing those made by the
graving tool, or the brush employed in the South.[9]

SUPPLEMENTARY READING

S. H. Hooke, *Myth and Ritual,* Essay 4.
A. T. Olmstead, *History of Palestine and Syria,* pp. 90-93.
Martin Sprengling, *The Alphabet, Rise and Development,* O. I. C.
No. 12.
Illustrated London News, November 29, 1930. Article by Pro-
fessor F. A. Schaeffer.

---

[9] See A. T. Olmstead, *History of Syria and Palestine,* p. 235f. Charles
Scribner's Sons.

CHAPTER XV

CULTURAL AND RELIGIOUS ADVANCE IN A TRANSITIONAL AGE

WE may accept as historical the traditional entrance of the Israelites into Canaan. That the initial stage was attended by conflict is more than likely. Probably Garstang and others are right in their surmise that the calcined walls of Jericho are due to the destruction and burning of a hostile invading force. Dates, of course, are conjectural, and we may regard as imaginary the detail that embroiders the biblical legends of the period, but that does not invalidate the fact of an invasion, nor preclude the possibility that it was Israelite.

Our biblical sources for the early settlement of Hebrews in Canaan are the books of Joshua and Judges. Both are descriptive of the period and in their early chapters roughly contemporaneous. Joshua is a relatively late writing among Old-Testament books. According to its viewpoint, the invasion was a conquest compressed within a generation. The author is in doubt as to the completeness of the conquest, for he informs us that Joshua, when he was very old, said to the assembled tribes or their representatives, "There remaineth very much land to be possessed"[1]—a surprising admission when we recall that the conquest had been represented as complete rather than partial, and that successful campaigns had been waged on both sides of the river, in southern, central, and northern Palestine. The Priestly writer may be regarded as compressing into a single generation the results attained by three hundred years of more or less desultory conflict.

The book of Judges in its final form was also late—a recension of the Deuteronomists, but it rests upon written documents of considerable historic value. Like the book of Joshua, it begins with initial conquests, but the leader is not

[1] Joshua 13. 1.

Joshua nor are the twelve tribes engaged, but only Judah and Simeon, who make a sally from the trans-Jordanic country into southern Palestine.[2] Other invasions follow,[3] minor conflicts take place. Gradually the restless tribal movements cease and the Hebrews come down from their occupancy of the hills into the plains from which at first they could not dislodge the Canaanite.[4] Presumably by trade, intermarriage, and in other ways they effected a peaceable settlement. No great battles are staged for us until the settlement is regarded as complete, and then the Hebrews are attacked rather than an attacking force.[5]

The counterpart of the early Hebrew settlement in Canaan is now before our eyes as we watch the colonizing movement of the Zionists in present-day Palestine. There is the inevitable conflict with the Arab who outnumbers him seven to one, but the outcome—a Jewish state—seems certain.

THE SURPRISING CONTENT OF JUDGES

The novelty of the book of Judges lies not in the viewpoint that the Hebrew occupation was a settlement rather than a conquest but in the nature of its contents. It reflects with surprising candor the barbarism and the vices of a people who were making the great transition from the desert to urban and agricultural life. With blunt directness the author particularizes the moral failures during this unsettled and troubled age. Rape, sodomy, image worship, senseless and destructive civic feuds, the capture of brides by stratagem are enumerated.[6] If the author does not always condemn the crimes he assigns to Israel, he takes grim satisfaction in showing that the punishment meted out to them was a fit consequence of their folly. With monotonous regularity he states that "in those days there was no king in Israel, but every man did that which was right in his own eyes."[7]

The tales of Samson are, in the first instance, folklore with a slender ethical content. In their final form it is made clear

---

[2] Judges 1. 1-10.
[3] Judges 1. 22f.
[4] Judges 1. 34.
[5] Judges 4. 1f.; 6. 1f.
[6] Judges, chap. 17ff.
[7] Judges 17. 6; 18. 1; 19. 1; 21. 25.

to the reader that Samson had failed in his life purpose, that he had worked singly when he should have led others, that he had been tripped up by his own unchecked sensuality. But even so, Samson is an attractive personality, an adventurer whose counterpart we may find in any age of license. His boisterousness, his love of practical jokes, his adventures in sex, his quick anger, his heroism, his incredible feats of physical strength, his reverence for the gift within him, and his tragic end are depicted in unfading colors and with characterizations unforgettable.[8] He has been remembered while far better men are forgotten.

By this time the reader, recalling the title of the chapter, will inquire how we can regard the period as an advance. Any transition from a nomadic stage to agriculture and communal urban life should be considered an advance if it gives promise of betterment. The so-called "dark ages" of Israel, like the medieval period in European history, was the seedtime for a future flourishing era. The writers who insist that this was an age of decadence are not disposed to judge it leniently, forgetting that it was a time when society was in the making. Strictly speaking there was no decadence, only the rankness that comes with growth, the barbarism that was redeemed by virility. All that the Hebrews did in three hundred years, we do in a single day, if the morning paper which we peruse can be relied upon for the accuracy of its reports. Too often the period is judged adversely by those who have an exaggerated sense of society in the Mosaic Age. Are we to regard the Israelites in the wilderness as living under the law? Were they more moral than their descendants? Were they an exception to other desert tribes? Such is not the view of those who are positive that they see in the period of the Judges a change for the better whether material or moral.

The gravest criticism of life under the Judges is the lack of cohesion among the tribes. This was felt as much then as now. Deborah voiced it in a stinging rebuke. It was the basis of judgment against Jabesh-Gilead. It was the

---

[8] Judges, Chaps. 13-16.

recognition of this weakness which led directly to the mon-archical movement.[9]

The close of the period of early settlement found Israel in possession of considerable territory. At the time they were not so much race conscious as they were aware of tribal relationship. One wonders what had become of Levi, Simeon, Reuben, once powerful tribes, but now obliterated save for a Priestly order that derived its descent from the first. Either they had been assimilated by the more impor-tant clans or had been engulfed by the Canaanite civilization. On the other hand, tribes like Ephraim had become power-ful through the acquisition of territory. Tribal boundaries, generally speaking, were well defined. The distinction be-tween North and South which seems to have risen at first, because the Plain of Esdraelon long held by the Canaanites interposed a barrier not easily crossed, still prevailed, though the physical cause had been overcome. There was also the consciousness of race, a latent nationalism. They were keenly alive to the importance of traditions. Moses' great contribu-tion had been to give them an awareness of Yahweh and their relation to him. Their deliverance from Egypt had been kept alive by the Passover feast. Whatever it meant to their remote ancestors,[10] to them it was significant of the birth of a nation.

They possessed no epic poems recounting their early struggles, but some verse had survived in oral form, for example, the Song of Vengeance attributed to Lamech, a ballad of deliverance known as Miriam's Song, and the Song of the Well. The scribes had mastered the Sinaitic alphabet, but while there was writing the possibility of creating a literature had not yet dawned upon their minds.

Their language, Hebrew, was really a Canaanitish tongue called by an Old-Testament writer, "The lip of Canaan." It was one language in the family called Semitic. More par-ticularly, we speak of it as Western Semitic to distinguish it from the Eastern or Babylonian branch, but, unlike the latter, it was written not with syllabic or word signs but with

---

[9] Judges 21. 25.
[10] It was probably a moon festival at first.

an alphabet of twenty-two letters. These were formed like
the Phoenician signs and are readily traced through the
Phoenician to the Greek and Latin alphabets. Unfortunately,
the vowels were sounded, not written, and we shall never
know how some Hebrew words were pronounced. The language is called triconsonantal, because commonly three
consonants make up the stem of the word. There were only
dialectic differences between the languages of Palestinian
races. The Moabite Stone of the ninth century is written
in a language not essentially different from Hebrew, and
there is every indication that the spoken tongues and afterward the written language of Canaanitish peoples were the
same.[11]

It was only to be expected that the Hebrews, learning
agriculture from the Canaanites, should adopt as their own
the agricultural festivals. The land which they cultivated
belonged to Baal. He was the god of the land, the Canaanites
explained, the landlord, the possessor, and without his blessing the crops would be a failure. This implied a change of
gods—an unwelcome transition for the Hebrews; so by a
process which we call syncretism, they kept the name "Yahweh" but gave him the characteristics of Baal. Just as Israel
changed from a nomadic to an agricultural people, so Yahweh
left off being the God of Sinai to become an agricultural
divinity.

"Religion," writes Bertholet, "clings to the soil of the country."[12] Whoever conquers a new country must adopt its gods
and pay homage to them. Otherwise disaster will be the
lot of the offender. This is illustrated by a remarkable passage in 2 Kings 17. 25, where we are informed that the
Assyrian colonists, who had been placed in Samaria to till
the land for the king of Assyria, had neglected to worship
the god of the territory and that the offended deity sent lions
into their midst. Whatever construction we place upon this,
the fact remains that men feel that they owe the god of the
country something. While they have conquered the people

[11] Cf. *Cambridge Ancient History*, Vol. III, p. 432. Cambridge University Press.
[12] *History of Hebrew Civilization*, p. 146f. Geo. G. Harrap & Co.,
London.

of the land, they have not subjugated the gods, nor would this be desirable. They court the favor of the deities upon whose blessing the prosperity of the country depends.

We perceive this in reference to the shrines. Where men have always worshiped they must continue to pray. "Sanctity clings to the spot," says the modern. "God is there," said the ancient. Saint Paul's in London was built on the site of the Roman Temple of Diana. It is doubtful if a single shrine of Israel, Bethel, Shiloh, Gibeah, or Dan, had not first been a Canaanitish place of worship.

Equally important was the need of following the ancient ritual in its general features. In time there were modifications but the persistence of the cult pattern is remarkable. When the Hebrews adopted the agricultural festivals, it is doubtful if they made any immediate changes, although there were features of Canaanitish ritual which outraged the religious sentiments of the prophets. How often we read that the "high places," that is, the shrines, were allowed to remain. The work of reformation stopped short of their abolition. Popular feeling would not have permitted their destruction. So the prophets contented themselves with the adaptation of the Canaanitish cult to their own use. They obliterated in the ritual all traces of myth. There was to be one supreme deity and to him was ascribed the creation; he was the owner of the land, the husband of the soil, and upon his favor rested their material prosperity. But the agricultural festivals of Canaan, and elsewhere, were fertility cults. Just here the prophets met their greatest opposition and had their most disheartening results. The persistence of the fertility cult which involved licentious rites even in the sanctuary[13] and "sacred" prostitution in the temple precincts[14] is an admitted feature of the Hebrew cult until the time of the exile.[15]

The essential modification of the agricultural feasts included both a change in terminology and ritual. Yahweh took the place of Baal. Myths which embodied plural gods and rituals which involved license were obliterated. The

[13] 1 Samuel 2. 22.
[14] 2 Kings 23. 4-10.
[15] Jeremiah 2. 20.

ceremonial observances celebrated the creation, the deliverance from Egypt, thanksgiving for the harvest, prayers for continued favor. Dancing was also a feature. The festival at the beginning of the barley harvest was merged, as we have said, with the Passover, the evidence of their early separate origin being lost. The ritual consisted of offerings of the flocks or herds, the sacrificial meal, and the sprinkling of blood over the doorway of the tent or home of the worshipers. The feast was celebrated at the time of the full moon nearest the vernal equinox. It was, therefore, a spring festival.[16] Seven weeks later occurred the Feast of Weeks, a midsummer festival terminating the barley harvest. An important feature of the ritual was the offering of two loaves of leavened bread. "This was analogous," writes Oesterley, "to the waving of the sheaf in the Feast of Massoth."[17]

The most important festival of the year occurred in the fall after the harvest had been gathered in, and just before the fall rains, which were so essential to the fructification of the soil and its preparation for the plowman. It fell near the autumnal equinox and in time was identical with the Babylonian New-Year festival. That it was recognized as such is suggested by the descriptive phrase "at the turning of the year." It was called by the Hebrews "the feast of tents" or "the feast of ingathering." The former appellation rose from the custom of the people who erected as dwellings either tents or booths made of leafy boughs. In these they lived for the duration of the festival. No feast was celebrated with so much joy, none had greater significance. The rites of a later day included the pouring out as a libation water drawn from the Pool of Siloam and the lighting of a great candelabra in the court of the Temple. The sacred processions, which were a prominent feature of the festival, are frequently referred to in the Psalms,[18] but for detailed and interesting description we must turn to late Jewish writings, namely, Mishnah, Sukkah 4. 9, 10, and the Talmud, Rosh Hashana 16a.

[16] Exodus 23. 15, 16; 34. 18; Leviticus 23. 10; Deuteronomy 16. 1f.
[17] *Myth and Ritual*, p. 121ff. The Clarendon Press, Oxford.
[18] Psalms 68. 1-4, 25; 24. 7-10.

While the festivals under Canaanitish influence not infrequently led to license and continued to do so until the fertility cult, which had been an early important feature, was
obliterated, on the other hand they were productive of good.
They were the natural expression of the joy of the people in
their harvest. They were observed at important centers and
therefore were a unifying factor in the growth of the
nation.

Supplementary Reading

H. T. Fowler, *Origin and Growth of Hebrew Religion,* Chapter
III.
J. Garstang, *Joshua and Judges,* pp. 51-54; 119-148.
John P. Peters, *Religion of the Hebrews,* Chapter VI.
T. H. Robinson, *History of Israel,* Vol. I, Chapter VIII.
Henry P. Smith, *Religion of Israel,* Chapter IV.
Bible, Judges 1-2, 5, 13-16, 21.

CHAPTER XVI

EARLY KINGS OF ISRAEL

THERE is no indication in the book of Judges of Egyptian government in Palestine, although we know for a certainty that such existed. Likewise the books of Samuel make no direct statement of the Philistine lordship over Israel, which succeeded that of Egypt. There are, however, hints in the text of the subordinate relation of Israel to the maritime people, for we read of Philistine garrisons,[1] of a Philistine law which implied that Israel was barred from using iron weapons,[2] and of Bethshan, a former Egyptian fortress, now in the hands of Philistines.

The situation apparently was this: Philistia aspired to take Egypt's place as a foreign power governing the country. The latter had withdrawn her troops because of domestic troubles;[3] Babylonia was in no position to interfere,[4] and the Philistines pressing their advantage had pushed the Israelites back into the hills. The inevitable conflicts which followed were in the nature of guerrilla warfare rather than open campaigning. The Israelites were at a disadvantage in their equipment; their leaders were ineffectual and their troops badly organized. From the Philistine point of view, Israel was a subject people rebelling against authority, while the Israelites on their part would have none of the Philistines, regarding them as outsiders, barbaric, uncouth. Their attitude was summed up in the derisive epithet "uncircumcised."

SAUL

All this has an important bearing upon the institution of a monarchical Hebrew state. The Hebrews waited with an intense expectancy for a deliverer, who like the heroes of old,

---

[1] 1 Samuel 14. 1f.
[2] 1 Samuel 13. 19-21.
[3] Trouble with Lybians and Ethiopians during the 21st dynasty.
[4] Now subject to Assyria.

Barak, Gideon, Jephthah, would free them from oppression. Gradually the idea took shape of a national deliverer who should be their king. In Saul they believed they had found such. He had delivered Jabesh-Gilead, a trans-Jordanic town, he had fought the Amalekites successfully, and now promised to throw off the Philistine yoke. He had the title rather than the prerogatives of kingship. His headquarters were in his home town, Gibeah. He had no palace, no court, and no standing army, if we except the king's guard, a selected group of warriors who followed him always.

His battles for the most part were skirmishes; they could hardly be more than that under the conditions that prevailed. On at least two occasions these took the form of battles[5] and his followers were augmented to a large force.

He was distinguished for his courage,[6] his irrepressible fury[7] under provocation, his impatience at deferred action.[8] He inspired devotion in others who saw in him a man "head and shoulders above his fellows." In short, he had those qualities of character which at that time were most esteemed in leadership.

Posterity has done Saul scant justice. He suffered by comparison with David. "Saul," sang the women of Israel, "hath slain his thousands, but David his tens of thousands." While David has been praised overmuch, Saul has been underestimated. In his contest with David he is made to appear on the wrong side, as futilely, madly, waging war against God's anointed. But we should like to hear Saul's side of the story. It is not difficult to guess what he would have said about this young man who owed his rise in the army to him, who sat at the king's table, married the king's daughter, and seduced, so it seemed to Saul, the king's son, while all the time he was a secret aspirant to the throne.[9] Saul undoubtedly meant to follow the example of other nations, to make the title of king hereditary, and to found a dynasty, Jonathan being his successor. To him David's

---

[5] 1 Samuel 17 and 31.
[6] 1 Samuel 11. 5f.
[7] 1 Samuel 11. 6, 7.
[8] 1 Samuel 13. 8-12.
[9] T. H. Robinson, *History of Israel*, Vol. I, p. 188. Oxford Press.

conduct seemed little less than treason.   One may reasonably reply to this that David did little more than allow the winds of circumstance to blow his sails.

The change in Samuel's attitude toward Saul, finally culminating in an open break, had a dire effect upon the king. The seer's pronouncement of doom, his unrelenting attitude after death,[10] affected sadly a mind not too stable at any time. Saul must have felt himself accursed, like some medieval monarch, whose sentence of excommunication has deprived him of spiritual ministrations in this life and salvation in the next.

There was much that was lovable in Saul.   His ecstatic moments were the measure of his depression.   He readily forgave, was generous to a fault, and had he been surrounded by wise counselors, the issue of his reign would have been far different.   There are two accounts of his death: one that after being wounded on the field of battle he committed suicide;[11] the other that he was killed by a member of a tribe which had reason to hate him, an Amalekite.[12]   The latter is most probably the true version.

He was honored in death, even by the Philistines, who, having hung his headless body on the walls of the Bethshan fortress, sent his head to each of the five cities of the confederacy, and by so doing boasted that they achieved the death of one whom long they had feared.   A far different motive actuated the men of Jabesh-Gilead, who crossed the Jordan, penetrated the lines of the enemy, and carried away from Bethshan the bodies of Saul and his sons for interment.

To the modern much that was inexplicable to the contemporaries of Saul is plain—his melancholy which was induced by the fear he felt of Samuel's displeasure and which later by the growing popularity of David led to momentary madness, and his superstition which caused him to seek from a clairvoyant an interview with the dead Samuel, only to receive like Richard[13] the ominous message, "Tomorrow thou

---

[10] 1 Samuel 28. 15f.
[11] 1 Samuel 31. 4.
[12] 2 Samuel 1. 10.
[13] A striking parallel to the séance of 1 Samuel 28. 19 is found in Shakespeare's *Richard III*, Act V, Sc. 3.

shalt die." Whatever David felt concerning the justice of his own cause, it did not prevent him from recognizing the greatness of Saul in one of the most touching eulogies found in the Old Testament, 2 Samuel 1. 19-27.

Generally speaking, Saul's work was constructive. He had achieved in part the consolidation of the kingdom. He had never adopted kingly ways; his tastes had been simple, as befitted one who was first and last a soldier. In so doing he had endeared himself to a democratic people.

DAVID

Few characters in history have suffered more from adulation than David. It obscured his real greatness, which lay in the accomplishment of having united and consolidated the tribes of Israel, while it invested him with a fictitious grandeur as misleading as it was undeserved. It is remarkable that we should have missed the real David, since the source material for his life is so abundant—the second half of the First Book of Samuel, all of the Second Book, and the opening chapters of First Kings, more in content than the life of our Lord, as given by any one of the evangelists. With this material supplied from almost contemporaneous sources, it ought to be possible to make a just appraisal of the achievements and character of the David of history.

The David of tradition is quite a different person. The exaggerated estimate placed upon his virtues and achievements is due in part to the Chronicler to whom David was an ideal, "a man after God's own heart," in part to late Jewish thought which regarded the Messiah as a second David, and chiefly because of his reputation for writing more than half of the Psalter, the devotional quality of which is manifest. If David was the author of the psalms attributed to him, this factor must be taken into account in our estimate of him. But critical opinion[14] assigns only three or four psalms to him, and these may have been composed rather than written, just as the troubadors of France and bards of Ireland composed and sung but did not themselves write their

[14] Ewald.

songs. In David's age writing was an accomplishment of
scribes, and while no one has the right to deny him the
ability, it would be natural to conclude that in his active warring life he found no time to perfect himself in an art
which was yet in its infancy among the Hebrews.

Legend has been busy with details concerning his early
life. The express statement of 2 Samuel 21. 19 that Elhanan
killed Goliath[15] is said of David in 1 Samuel 17, and the
story is given with elaborate detail. If we accept the tale as
true, we are confronted with two versions of David's introduction to Saul: the first, that his reputation as a musician
brought him to play before the king;[16] and, the second, that
his extraordinary feat in the vale of Elah brought him to the
attention of Saul.[17]

The biblical material in the books of Samuel readily lends
itself to the analysis of David's life. A chronological
sequence is followed in which we discern four stages in his
career: (a) his early life in Bethlehem and later in the army
of Saul; (b) his experiences as an outlaw, when he fled to
the wilderness of Judea and to the Philistine territory; (c)
his reign of seven years in Hebron over the Southern tribes;
(d) his reign over united Israel with Jerusalem for his
capital.

DAVID'S MILITARY SUCCESS

Our records imply that Saul, hoping for David's death,
sent him against the Philistines. But it is reasonable to
suppose that Saul employed him, certainly in the first instance
to carry out his own set purpose of ridding the land of
Philistine dominion. To this task, then, David, like Saul,
was dedicated and while interruptions occurred, and fortune
was frequently adverse, eventually the Philistines were forced
to retire to their cities on the Maritime plain.

The conquest of Jerusalem, still a Canaanite stronghold,
was not less difficult. Because of its situation, it could defy
attack, and it was not until David was king in Hebron and

---

[15] The Chronicler notes the discrepancy and corrects it to read "the
brother of Goliath" (1 Chronicles 20. 5).
[16] 1 Samuel 16. 17ff.
[17] 1 Samuel 17. 55f.

needed it as a capital that he risked defeat in seeking its capture. In the end it was taken by a clever strategy engineered
by Joab, who entered it by one of the water conduits.[18]

In his subjugation of surrounding peoples David proved
himself a strategist and an able general, but merciless in
his treatment of his foes. One can understand his desire to
protect the eastern border, and to exact tribute from those
he conquered, but his treatment of Moab[19] and Ammon[20] was
unjustifiable, and placed him on the level of contemporary
oriental kings. In contrast one notes his more favorable
treatment of the Aramaeans (Syrians), whose center was in
Damascus. Here he seemed content with taking the spoils of
war and the collection of tribute which he effected by garrisons placed in the capital.[21]

He had no war with Phoenicia, but concluded a treaty
which was apparently of mutual satisfaction. In return for
protecting trade routes which the Phoenicians followed he
received valuable concessions of timber.[22] The Phoenicians
had no desire for territorial aggrandizement. Theirs was a
nation of traders, turning covetous eyes westward for commerce and colonies. They desired, however, protection along
the eastern trade route to the Euphratean Valley, and this
was indirectly afforded by the Syrian check.[23] The Amalekites, a wandering warlike Sinaitic tribe, David all but ex-
terminated, thus removing an ancient and continuous menace
along the southern border.

This, in brief, sums up his military successes by which he
enlarged the Palestinian state, freed it from all foreign
dominion, and added to the wealth of the nation. At no time
before or after was the Hebrew state so politically great,
prosperous, and unified as under the rule of David. This
was the outstanding achievement which must be placed to
his credit. It was not his fault that the state did not endure.

---

[18] I Chronicles 11. 6.
[19] 2 Samuel 8. 2.
[20] 2 Samuel 12. 31.
[21] 2 Samuel 8. 3, 5. A like policy was followed in the case of Edom.
[22] So conjectured.
[23] The Aramaeans were the chief traders between the Mediterranean
and the Euphrates.

David Chooses a Capital

Jerusalem because of its impregnable position was admirably suited for a capital. It was capable of sustaining a long siege, and only on three occasions in ancient times did it surrender—to David, to Nebuchadnezzar, and to Titus. Moreover, it lay between the South which David had been governing and the disaffected Northern states which he hoped to win over. He fortified the city, enlarged its walls, and ultimately designated a contiguous area for the Temple site. While the building of the Temple was left to his successor, Solomon, the idea of a central sanctuary was David's.

Among the factors that helped to consolidate the tribes into a national government was the deposition of the Ark in a sanctuary in Jerusalem. This had a most important bearing upon unification, for the Ark was the palladium of their ancient freedom; it held in custody precious relics and above it, "in a cloud," was thought to be the very presence of the God of Israel.

The Character of David

Regrettable as was David's conduct in his adulterous relation with Bathsheba and the death of Uriah, the incident in the end was not without some redeeming features. What other king of his time would have hesitated to take the wife of one of his subjects if he so desired, or having done so would have felt concerned for her husband or public opinion? But David in his repentance expresses a feeling of moral responsibility. He stands rebuked before the prophet, his own conscience, and God. Such an attitude on the part of a man in any age merits our respect.

There were lovable traits in David, as we see in his ability to inspire the devotion of others. The love of Jonathan[24] for David is classic. Michal, the king's daughter, loved and married him.[25] Saul himself at times bore a strong affection for one who was to him as a son.[26] The women of Israel

---

[24] I Samuel 18. 1.
[25] I Samuel 18. 20.
[26] I Samuel 16. 21f.

followed his triumphal return from a sally against the Philistines and celebrated his praise in song.[27] Men followed him to the wilderness when all he could offer them was hunger, thirst, weariness, suffering, and perhaps death. What was superstition in Saul was religion in David. His reverence for tradition, his dependence upon the guidance of God through Abiathar, the priest, his religious ecstasy all speak of one who, in spite of glaring faults, was sincerely and deeply religious.

SOLOMON

The third of the kings of the United Monarchy lived in reflected glory. Save for his building achievements in Jerusalem and border towns there is little to be said of Solomon's reign. His reputation for wisdom rested upon his fondness for the proverb[28] and judicial decision, in which the victim is made to condemn himself.[29] Shrewdness he undoubtedly displayed, nor was he always honorable in so doing, as we see in his gift of the Galilean towns to Hiram as payment for material and labor for the Temple.[30] But wisdom in ruling or in discerning true from false values he did not have. Only a late age confusing glamour for greatness could be mistaken in a king whose reign began with intrigue, was baptized by blood, marked by ruinous extravagance and senseless folly, and ended in an eclipse of apostasy.

It remained for Rehoboam to complete the ruin of that which Solomon had begun to destroy. While there was dissatisfaction, murmurs of revolt, as long as Solomon lived somehow things held together, due no doubt to the faith of a people who felt that the foundations laid by Saul, completed by David, would have built upon them an enduring structure. With Rehoboam's accession complaints are voiced, and when unheeded, bring on a revolution. The Northern tribes are split away from the Southern and henceforth we have two kingdoms.

[27] I Samuel 18. 6, 7.
[28] I Kings 4. 32.
[29] I Kings 3. 16f.
[30] I Kings 9. 10-14.

SUPPLEMENTARY READING

T. H. Robinson, *History of Israel,* Vol. I, p. 141f.; Chapters IX-
XI.
Bible, Saul, 1 Samuel 8-10, 11, 14-15, 28, 31; 2 Samuel 1. David,
1 Samuel 16, 18, 22, 25, 27, 30; 2 Samuel 3, 5, 6, 11, 12, 15,
18, 24. Solomon, 1 Kings 1-5, 9-10, 11.

CHAPTER XVII

SOLOMON'S ACHIEVEMENTS IN
ANCIENT MEGIDDO

Solomon's building achievements were many and varied. These reflect whatever glory we may ascribe to this overrated king. In addition to the Temple, he built in Jerusalem his own palace, a building for his chief queen, and an armory. He erected also at strategic sites store-cities, one of which was Megiddo. It is only of the latter that we have clear knowledge. The Temple area would undoubtedly yield results if archaeologists were given a free hand, but it must be remembered that the ground is now occupied by the Mosque of Omar and other Moslem shrines. It is hardly to be expected that Mohammedans who regard Jerusalem as only second in importance to Mecca would permit the profanation of sacred sites. It is otherwise with Megiddo, and it may not be amiss at this point to review the labors of those who have uncovered a lost city or, more accurately, the Solomonic level of this northern outpost.

Megiddo is conveniently reached by motor car from Haifa. While the road is not surfaced save for part of the distance, it presents no real obstacle. Moreover, it traverses a country fraught with interest. First, one has the prospect of the coast that lies between Haifa and Acre across the bay—a stretch of blue sea breaking in white foam upon the sand. As the road turns toward the south, the town of Haifa melts away; the terraced gardens and vineyards of Mount Carmel give place to rougher slopes. Close by is the cement plant recently erected at a cost of two million dollars. Its output is enormous and the company has no difficulty in filling the orders for silicate bricks which Tell-Aviv and other modern towns demand. By this time we are fairly in the plain, known variously as Esdraelon, Megiddo or Armageddon. Its western boundary is the Carmel range which we have been skirting; on the east is the rounded summit of Mount Tabor and farther south Mount Gilboa, separated from the former by the Valley of Jezreel, through which one passes to the Jordan. The northern boundary of the plain terminates in Galilean hills, where nestle Nazareth, Cana, and other towns associated with the gospel story. To the south is Jenin, much improved over the town I visited in prewar days and far more attractive. The road through Jenin goes to Jerusalem; that which passes through the Valley of Jezreel proceeds to Damascus.

The Plain of Esdraelon is of strategic importance. The Canaanites held it separating the northern tribes of Israel from their powerful neighbors in the south. Thutmose III thought it necessary to gain control of the plain not only for rationing his army but as a gateway to all Palestine. General Allenby found its capture necessary in 1918. When the Seer of Patmos visualized the battlefield where the nations were to wage their last conflict, he named it Armageddon.

We may inquire at this point how ancient cities long buried in the sand are brought to light. Can their location be traced through local traditions or through history, or must the discovery be left to chance? In answering let it be confessed that the excavator frequently is led astray and finds that he has uncovered a place of no importance. One cannot depend upon the Arab equivalent of the name, for ancient cities lost their names which in turn were adopted by other towns. On the other hand, important strategic sites like Beisan tend to be perpetuated. The Egyptian account of a victory at Megiddo was sufficiently detailed to make the identification fairly certain.

The site in the first instance was chosen because easily defended, and on account of the proximity of springs, which would furnish an adequate water supply. Usually it was an elevation. At Megiddo only the upper half represents the accumulated debris of the successive cities which were here

built. The lower part is a natural formation honeycombed
by caves.

Such an elevation partly artificial is known as a mound, or
Tell, the Arabic for hill. It is distinguished by its rectilinear
profile, and in the case of Megiddo by a steplike formation
where the city wall followed the contour of the hill. During the winter and spring months it is unusually verdant as
compared with the rather colorless limestone range in the
vicinity. With this much evidence Schumacher, the German
archaeologist who visited the place first in 1903, must have
been confident that his quest for a buried city would be
rewarded.

As we approach Megiddo, we note that the mound rises
from an elevation somewhat higher than the plain. The
extensive and pretentious buildings of the Chicago Expedition are in the foreground. A group of women are washing clothes, scrubbing them over stones which appear on
inspection to have been the surfaces of ancient altars.
Through the holes where dripped the blood of sacrificial victims the soapy water trickles, but the end in view, the removal of defilement, is the same. As we pass the women
flash us a glance. Their eyes are lovely but their faces dis-
figured by tattooing marks.

The pass of Megiddo is discernible. It is a rough trail over
the range from the arterial highway that once followed the
sea from Egypt to Syria. It was followed by Thutmose III
in the spring of 1479 B. C., who made a surprise attack on
the rebellious Syrian states and their allied forces. It could
not have been much of a battle, although the victory is ex-
ploited in the Egyptian records. So eager was the invading
army to plunder that they fell upon the spoil of the camps,
permitting their enemies to reach safety within the high
ramparts of Megiddo, while the king of Kadesh escaped in
his chariot. As an example of the repetition of history, one
may recall that thirty-four centuries later, to be exact, September 19, 1918, General Allenby made a night attack over
this same road, falling upon the Turkish forces camped on
the plain. Their German general, Von Sanders, narrowly

escaped capture, riding away in his pajamas in a motor car!
The next day Beisan,[1] the eastern gateway to the plain, fell.
The troops holding the city made slight resistance. Allenby
continued to follow the fleeing Turks northward to Damascus
and still farther north to Aleppo. At this point they surrendered and the war ended as far as Turkey was concerned.
Once more Megiddo was the scene of a decisive victory in
world conflicts.

But enough of history. We are at our destination, where
we are cordially greeted by the director and his associates
of the Chicago Expedition. The buildings, which include a
museum, working quarters, and pleasant living rooms, are
approached by a garden where flowers are blooming in profusion. Without delay we ascend the mound to the fourth
stratum, now cleared and revealing a Hebrew city, once so
carefully laid out that it contained not one crooked
street!

Schumacher had been content with cutting a trench twenty
meters wide and about twelve meters deep, uncovering on
the lower level a series of well-built stone buildings. He had
found accidentally, or by sinking a shaft, bedrock at seventeen meters. Above this he computed that seven or eight
cities had been built. How long mankind has occupied
Megiddo it is difficult to say, but Schumacher and the later
excavators have found abundant evidence pertaining to the
Neolithic or Late Stone Age. The first homes were caves in
the honeycombed slopes of the mound. To the present-day
investigator it seems remarkable that the German should have
accomplished so much by the simple expedient of running a
trench through the mound. Vertical digging, it must be
remembered, is only a test, to be abandoned as soon as the
excavator has demonstrated the value of his discovery. Undoubtedly, Schumacher felt this and resigned himself to the
idea of being merely a pioneer. For twenty years the work
halted and then in 1925 Mr. John Rockefeller, Jr.'s interest
was enlisted and he furnished the necessary funds for a

[1] Called Bethshan in biblical times.

thorough and scientific investigation at Megiddo. His generosity enabled the University of Chicago to send out an expedition, to house them permanently, to well equip their staff, to install modern machinery, and, what was most important, to buy the land. The Expedition was fortunate in its field directors, first, Mr. C. S. Fisher, 1925-27, whose experience in Egypt and elsewhere in Palestine made him a valuable acquisition to the staff. He was followed in the summer of 1927 by the present director, Mr. P. L. O. Guy.

The mound may be regarded as a huge layer cake, its levels where objects of value are found are the icing. To the archaeologist the latter was the most important part of the cake. Now Schumacher had cut out a slice, counted the layers, and revealed enough to show future excavators what to expect.

It is clear that in any work of excavation, the surface soil on the summit must be removed so that the level of the last city to occupy the site may be reached. Objects are left *in situ* until photographed and cataloged. Cameras on extended tripods or attached to balloons are employed since aerial photography is indispensable. When the preliminary work has been completed, objects are removed by the expert assistance of Egyptian foremen and carried to the local museum for study, or in the case of pottery for cleaning and repair. It will readily be perceived that the work of excavation proceeds in direct ratio to the ability of the recorders to keep abreast with the discoveries. Eventually a lower level or stratum will be uncovered but the work proceeds slowly, and when I asked the field director how long the work of excavation at Megiddo would continue, he was nonplused. The Expedition reached stratum IV in 1929, but now, five years later, they are still cataloging objects of interest which belong to this period.

Mr. Guy believes that stratum IV reveals the foundations and walls of a city laid out under Solomon's direction, and built by skilled Phoenician workmen. One is reminded of

Pompeii, the streets are laid out with such care. Considerable space was given to the stabling of Solomon's horses, three hundred of which could easily have been accommodated. Attempts at the reconstruction on a small scale of these stables have been successful and one gains the idea that Solomon felt that the breeding and trading of horses was most important. He was probably interested because the horse was a novelty in Palestine among the Hebrews, although a thousand years earlier the Hyksos in Gaza had them in plenty. The Old Testament refers eleven times to Megiddo, indicating its importance and in one instance, 1 Kings 9. 15, 19, stating that Solomon built it as a store-city for his horsemen and his chariots. He imported the last from Egypt and probably his horses also. The reference to Megiddo as "the city of horses and chariots" ties in with the large number of chariot wheels which have been found in the excavations.

A well-constructed tunnel leads to a spring outside the walls, which was thus made accessible in time of siege. The expression "the waters of Megiddo" owes its rise to the abundance of the water supply, for there are five springs in the vicinity of the town.

At one time the wall rose much higher than the city. As was said, it followed the contour of the hill and must have given the early beholder a sense of the impregnability of the stronghold. Certainly, one gains that feeling today as he looks upon the plain below. On the south side it is thirty meters from the plain to the base of the wall—quite a scramble for the foe, and not up yet!

Some of the other features of the fourth stratum city are the Governor's House, from the flat roof of which one could look over the ramparts and down upon the distant plain, and the Astarte temple which seems to have been built by Solomon. The latter contained an altar adorned by sphinxlike figures which may be identical to the cherubim of the Temple of Jerusalem. The incense altar found in the same building recalls the six-horn altar described in Exodus, chapter 30. As a door jamb to the temple were shafts of stone sur-

mounted by Proto Ionic capitals.   The shafts were square
and bore no resemblance to the lovely Ionic columns which
the Greeks evolved, but the capital with its lily pattern
exhibits a transition to the later more developed Ionic form.
I say transition, for a member of the Megiddo staff has
found clear evidence of Proto Ionic capitals earlier than
Megiddo, and, of course, several centuries before their employment in Greek sculpture.   One confesses to some degree
of amazement when he considers the Hebrew king building
the Astarte temple and worshiping therein the goddess of
love.   But there is excellent authority confirming this.   The
passage 1 Kings 11. 1-5 concludes, "For Solomon went after
Astarte,[2] the goddess of the Sidonians."

The walls of the temple contained stones carefully cut and
laid diagonally, while in the case of the governor's palace
rubble was used in the foundation and dressed stone above.
The evidence of skilled workmanship in building is abundant,
but it must be remembered that the town contained for the
most part buildings so frail that not a vestige of them
remains.

How, one may ask, are cities destroyed and then rebuilt
on the same site?   An invading army looting, destroying,
burning leaves nothing of value.   Even the inhabitants are
carried away captive.   Or a sweeping, devastating pestilence
carries off the inhabitants, while the few who are left for-
sake the city.   Again, a city may be voluntarily abandoned
for a more strategic location, or for a more favorable trading center.   In the case of Megiddo, abandoned in the middle
of the fourth century B. C., it was malarial fever most
probably.   Even today it devastates the countryside and the
Expedition has given much effort to checking it.

After a lapse of time the site again is visited.   Men level
off the debris, all usable material is retained, and on the
broad platform thus gained and furnished, the new city
rises.   If a new fashion in building has come in, if men
use iron instead of bronze, it will be indicated.

---

[2] Called Ashtoreth in the Old Testament.

While occasionally an inscription is found, like the Shishak Stele at Megiddo, which gives a dating, one usually has to follow the broad guiding lines laid down by pottery sequence or by the stone, bronze, and iron ages, the limitations of which are pretty well known. Shishak, who is called in the Old Testament Sheshonk, a ruler of Egypt during the days of Rehoboam, having been affronted by something Israel had done, came to Palestine and invaded Jerusalem with an army. Rehoboam offered no resistance but quite calmly submitted to the indignities which the Hebrews suffered at the hands of the Egyptians. Shishak carried away in addition to the other plunder three hundred golden shields which formerly hung in the armory in the Temple precincts. Rehoboam replaced these, we are told, by shields of brass. Shishak proceeded then to Megiddo, which he destroyed, although he thoughtfully left a calling card in the shape of an elaborately carved stele. The Expedition recently unearthed a fragment showing quite clearly the royal cartouches which identify the Pharaoh in question.

The building which houses the Expedition has ample facilities to care for the material comfort of its personnel. At the time of my visit the staff numbered ten or twelve who were in active service as surveyors, draftsmen, photographers, and recorders. The Museum contains many objects of interest. Some have been recently found and their ultimate destination will be the Oriental Museum of Chicago University, provided the government grants permission to the Expedition to move them. The drafting rooms are extensive, for great stress is placed on epigraphic work, that is, the recording of inscriptions. Photography and reconstruction are both important. One room of considerable size is used for shipping; another for the repair and reconstruction of pottery, which is invariably found in fragmentary condition. The cataloging is extensive and not only contains a record of whatever has been found but the exact zone in which it was discovered. Pieces that do not fit into the picture puzzle are carefully filed away for future reference.

SUPPLEMENTARY READING

Alfred Bertholet, *History of Hebrew Civilization*, Chapter III.
Clarence S. Fisher, *The Excavation of Armageddon*, O. I. C. No. 4.
P. L. O. Guy, *New Light From Armageddon*, O. I. C. No. 9.

CHAPTER XVIII

INDUSTRY AND VOCATIONS

THE transition of the Hebrews from a nomadic to an agricultural and urban life is now virtually complete, and at this point we may appropriately consider the nature of their occupations. There were, of course, herdsmen on the trans-Jordanic tableland and on the mountain ranges of Judea, where the soil was only suitable for grazing. These represent the connecting link with the past, but most of the population were on farms or in towns engaged in industrial pursuits. They were probably the counterpart of the population crowding into Palestine today, eager, industrious and assimilative. They were only one among the many races in Palestine but they were dominant. Under David they had become a political entity.

AGRICULTURE

An ancient seed catalogue of Palestine, had such existed, would have listed among common cereals, barley, wheat, and flax. The fruit-bearing trees were the olive, the fig, and the sycamore. The latter produced a fruit known as the mulberry fig, the harsh juice of which was extracted by pinching while it still clung to the tree. Amos described himself not only as a shepherd but as a pincher of mulberry figs. The vintage wines were most commonly made from the red grape, if we attach value to the expression "the blood of the grape," so frequently employed in the Old Testament. Among vegetables we have melons, the pumpkin called a gourd, and the cucumber or gherkin. These were produced early in the season before the ground cracked under the scorching summer heat.

Agriculture required not only the work of men's hands but the blessing of God. The god of the Canaanites was Baal, the owner of the land, and when Israel learned agri-

184

culture, they implored the aid of Baal in seed-sowing and returned thanks to him in the harvest. It was long before Yahweh, who had been the God of Sinai and of battles, was recognized as the God of the land. Meantime Israel seems to have confused the two deities and to have given the name and attributes of the Canaanitish Baal to Yahweh.[1] But when the God of Israel became the sole possessor of the land, that is, when Israel was everywhere dominant, there was prophetic insistence that the name Baal should no longer be employed.[2]

BUILDING

A people accustomed from early days to tents, or caves, or mud dwellings erected against the face of a rock will not suddenly make a transition to a building era. We are informed by the biblical records that those who taught Israel the art of building pretentiously and well were the Phoenicians. This is stated directly and is also implied. Ahab was said to have an ivory palace, which was perhaps due to the inspiration of his Phoenician queen, who also furnished the workmen. At any rate, we know that Solomon's Temple was built by Hiram and that his fleet was Phoenician also, termed "ships of Tarshish," not on account of his trading relations with a port in Spain but because of its builders. Only the groundfloor plans of the Temple have been described and efforts to reconstruct a model have been as futile as they have been various. In the seventeenth century A. D., we have a reconstruction in Renaissance architecture, while in the following century we have one in Rococo![3]

ENGINEERING

A good deal of ridicule has been wasted upon a tunnel designed to carry the water of Gihon, now called the Virgin's Well, to a place available to the inhabitants of Jerusalem. It was five hundred and ninety-four yards in length and extremely crooked, since in a direct line the tunnel would have

---

[1] See Chap. XIV.
[2] Hosea 2. 16, 17.
[3] Alfred Bertholet, *History of Hebrew Civilization*, p. 204. Geo. G. Harrap & Co., London.

been only three hundred and seventy-two yards, but the zigzag course was due to the desire of the builders to avoid the obstacle of almost impenetrable rock. The chisel marks on the walls and the accompanying inscription indicate that the work was commenced simultaneously at both ends. After following such a course as we have described, that the workmen should meet with an error of only a foot or two seems almost miraculous.

FINE ARTS

In the field of plastic art or culture the prohibition in the Decalogue[4] which forbade the making of images was held as a bar to progress in this direction. But there were many infractions of the rule and some without protest. Even in the Holy Place, the innermost shrine of Solomon's Temple, were two cherubs carved from olive wood. One suspects that the command belongs to a late period, when image worship had become a distracting feature in the Hebrew cult, or else it was a command more honored in the breach than in the observance.

In painting the Hebrews were deficient. The word meaning "to paint," "to smear," "to anoint" is the same; one word designates red and brown; one, yellow and green. Ezekiel speaks of figures in vermilion painted on the Temple walls designed to advance idolatrous practices.[5]

Among allied industries may be noted pottery, dyeing, spinning and weaving, cutting precious stones.

In music we should expect the Hebrews to make great progress. Unfortunately, their musical terminology is confusing, and we are at a loss to find a satisfying glossary of terms sufficiently descriptive to inform us as to what the instruments really were. We gather from the Psalter that their string instruments were the harp and the lyre. Frequent mention is made of the flute and pipe which pertain to their pastoral life. The bugle and the ram's horn could hardly be termed musical, since each sounded only a single

---

[4] Exodus 20. 4.
[5] Cf. Alfred Bertholet, *History of Hebrew Civilization*, p. 306f.   Geo. G. Harrap & Co., London.

note, which must have fallen unpleasantly upon the ear. The percussion instruments in common use were the cymbal and the tambourine. In the Hellenistic period we become familiar with new instruments.[6]

SCRIBAL ACTIVITY

When Israel invaded Palestine, they confronted a people whose speech, the Canaanitish, was similar to their own.[7] That the Canaanites had at a previous time borrowed the Accadian written language we know from the Amarna letters. But recent discoveries indicate that they also employed alphabetic signs which they probably obtained from the Seirites.[8] It is a fair inference that by the beginning of the fifteenth century B. C. the new alphabetic language was making progress though hindered on account of the reluctance of the scribes to abandon the cuneiform syllabary.

We must avoid the fallacy of regarding the invaders as able to read and write. It was centuries before this achievement obtained. One does not learn to read without the stimulus of books to peruse, and the paucity of reading material is evident from the excavations. We find pottery sherds with characters indicating that a receipt was given, proclamations which people could be made to understand though they could not decipher them, but nothing comparable to the writings of a much earlier date (3000 B. C.) found in Egypt and Mesopotamia. Should we expect more from a people who had served a long apprenticeship in the wilderness, struggled to gain a foothold in Canaan, and had only recently achieved political stability? Fowler is probably right in assigning 1040 B. C. as the earliest date for any Hebrew writing of importance. We have no copies of their first "books." We would not know that they existed, if they were not referred to in the biblical writings. Two are mentioned, the Book of Jasher (Jasher probably meaning "Israel") and the Book of the Wars of Yahweh. Undoubtedly, their contents belong to a much earlier period,

---

[6] *Ibid.*, p. 307f.
[7] "The lip of Canaan."
[8] A. T. Olmstead, *Palestine and Syria*, pp. 93, 235. Charles Scribner's Sons.

and were transmitted orally, as were several isolated poems. Whatever writing existed among the Hebrews was due to the activity of the scribes, who were alone in mastering the art of writing. It is interesting to note in this connection that their office is mentioned for the first time during the reign of David.[9]

Traders and the Working Class

That the Hebrews were chiefly interested in trade is not surprising, since the propensity was an inheritance from their Aramaean ancestry. As the Phoenicians were the merchants of the sea, the Aramaeans were land carriers, middlemen for the Babylonians and Assyrians, whose goods they forwarded to western nations receiving in exchange goods and money. Considering this fact, it seems remarkable that the trading class had little voice in the government. The case in Europe during the Middle Ages was analogous until the time of the French Revolution, when we see emerging as a political power the Third Estate. But in Israel in spite of its democracy or because of it neither the merchant class nor the proletariat had a class consciousness, but continued to exist "within the shelter of the ancient clanship."[10] That the proletariat or laboring class was submerged was due to the preponderance of slaves in industry. Hired labor when such existed could command only a pittance. As a result Israel did not advance economically but continued to be a primitive state socially speaking. On the other hand, democracy was furthered by the ideal of the brotherhood of all Israel.

Supplementary Reading

Alfred Bertholet, *History of Hebrew Civilization.* Book II, Chapter II.
John P. Peters, *Religion of the Hebrews,* Chapter I.
Henry P. Smith, *Religion of Israel,* Chapter V.
Louis Wallis, *Sociological Study of the Bible,* Chapter VII.

---

[9] 2 Samuel 8. 17; 20. 25.
[10] Louis Wallis, *Sociological Study of the Bible,* pp. 60, 61. University of Chicago Press.

CHAPTER XIX

HEBREW FAMILY LIFE

It is significant that the Septuagint, the Vulgate, and the English versions place the charming idyl of Ruth immediately after the book of Judges, as if to tell us that even in that dark age a light was shining.[1] The light was the family, fraternal affection, and love between the sexes. No estimate of the religious and moral life of a people of any age would be complete if it omitted the consideration of the family and its value to society.

The Hebrews from early times had high regard for family life. Their domestic customs are reflected in the stories of the patriarchs. The laws of the Deuteronomic and other codes protected the home. Their census was based not on the numbering of individuals but of families. The prejudice against David's census lay in the fact that it departed from the previous custom of counting by families or houses. The family was the unit of the social structure, the foundation stone of the Hebrew commonwealth.

The Hebrew household was often large, comprising the family proper, frequently kinsmen, domestic servants, and slaves. This was particularly true in patriarchal times. Abraham's household included, we are told, three hundred and eighteen persons, some of whom are named—Eliezer, a steward; Lot, a kinsman; Hagar, a female slave.

Before taking up the constituent members of the family, it may be well to inquire concerning the housing of so great a number.

DESERT DWELLINGS

On the desert, shelter was provided by tents, usually made of goat skins and invariably dark in appearance. In the

---

[1] This does not preclude the view that the book of Ruth in its final form was a late writing and had a polemic purpose. It was perhaps an old story rewritten in postexilic times.

Song of Songs we find the simile, "As black as the tents of
Kedar." Tents were placed close together for protection
and for the convenience of the occupants, who thought that
the near proximity of their neighbors was no hardship. We
gather from the book of Numbers that kinsmen were often
grouped together. Such a unit would be a clan, the larger
groups a tribe. Where several generations live together they
are known as a sept, or household.[2]

In the genesis of communal life in Canaan it was natural
for the Hebrews, where they were free to do so, to arrange
their town dwellings compactly, as they had their tents on the
desert. It was amazing how they packed themselves in. The
larger dwelling houses were built around courts but the
rooms which opened off from them were small. The towns
and cities were usually walled. The Canaanites had seen
to that, and their successors repaired or rebuilt them when
damaged or destroyed. But the villages, or hamlets as we
would call them, were as unprotected as camps in the desert.
Nevertheless, they afforded some security, and one could see
issuing from them in the morning people going to their work
in the fields and vineyards and at night returning to them.
Isolated farmhouses so common among us would have been
regarded by the Hebrews as unsafe. Communal life to them
was a necessity like the caravan in the desert. Another type
of dwelling was open to them. Many hills in Palestine are
honeycombed with caves, having connecting passages. These
had been the dwellings of Neolithic man, and we may suppose that his Semitic successors used them likewise.

The town dwellers, who possessed sufficient wealth, often
built pretentious houses. Amos complains of the extravagance of Samaria in this respect.[3] We are told that Ahab
had an "ivory house," by which was probably meant a lavish
display of ivory in the trim and in the decoration of furniture. Solomon's palace for his favorite wife was cedar from
Lebanon. Wood was scarce in Palestine during the Hebrew

---

[2] The word "family" is sometimes used where we would employ the
word "clan" (Joshua 7. 14). In this chapter we are using it in its
restricted sense. Compare Alfred Bertholet, *History of Hebrew Civilization*, p. 148f. Geo. G. Harrap & Co., London.
[3] Amos 3. 15.

occupancy. Stone was sparingly used, but when employed, as at Megiddo, the courses were laid in a decorative pattern. The ordinary building material was unbaked clay and rubble. To support such frail structures wooden beams were employed. Brick was used extensively, invariably stamped with a factory mark. But, speaking generally, even the best towns were composed of buildings which were too frail to be permanent.

The book of Deuteronomy makes provision in the case of flat-roofed dwellings for a parapet in order that those who sought the roof for the coolness of summer nights might be protected, particularly the young.[4]

The Members of the Family

The head of the house is the father, the patriarch, or chief. His word is law. He provides for the marriages of his sons and daughters, distributes his inheritance, and is so completely the representative of the family that with his fall or punishment all are involved.[5] He may have one wife or several. Plural marriages appear to be the exception; more often he had two wives. His wives, of course, were property. In the case of kings, marriage alliances were usually political. We know the names of seven of David's wives, and of Solomon it was said that he had seven hundred in addition to three hundred slave girls. The numbers are suspiciously large and should perhaps read "seventy" and "thirty." Many men were monogamous by nature, content with the love of one woman. If Abraham, Jacob, Elkanah, and others had two wives; Isaac, Joseph, and multitudes of others had only one.

A bigamous relationship was not necessarily a concession to sensuality. The law made provision for such unions, it is true, but its intent seems to be the continuance through children of the home. Procreation was the fundamental reason of the marriage relationship, and if children were not born, the husband had the right of divorce or to take as a second wife a female slave. A wife could easily be divorced

---

[4] Deuteronomy 22. 8.
[5] Joshua 7. 24, 25.

on the husband's part. He had only to say, "She is not my wife, and I am not her husband." This constituted a bill of divorcement. But obstacles[6] were placed in the way of an easy performance of the act.

Bigamous or plural marriages are not to be defended. Their drawback, aside from moral considerations, was just as apparent in early times as today. A second wife was called a *sara,* meaning "the enemy," and was regarded as such by the first wife. If she bore children, while the other had not, or if she were a sister, the case was aggravated. It is probable that the legislation against marrying a *deceased* wife's sister grew out of the reform which forbade a man to take two wives if they were of the same family.[7]

Considerable latitude was given in the matter of concubinage, the slave girl being usually the spoil of war.[8] But such unions gave rights to the slave, and her children were regarded as legitimate. In fact, illegitimacy was unknown in Israel. If a son could trace his paternal descent, he had a share in the patrimony. Jephthah is a case in point where the real cause of his expulsion from the family was that he might not share in the inheritance.[9]

One might outside of marital relations take a woman and not be guilty of adultery according to Bertholet. He quotes Stade as saying, "A man cannot sin against his own marriage but only against the marriage of another."[10] This assumption rested upon the idea that the wife was a man's property. But this construction is contrary to the Christian view and did not meet the approval of the prophets, who draw no such distinctions. No doubt then as now society extended a leniency to man which it denied woman. A woman's infidelity was punishable by death, nor could she obtain divorce save with the greatest difficulty.

We are not to conclude that a wife was held in low

[6] Deuteronomy 22. 13-19, 29. See Alfred Bertholet, *History of Hebrew Civilization,* p. 154f. Geo. G. Harrap & Co., London.
[7] Leviticus 18. 18.
[8] Deuteronomy 21. 10f.
[9] Judges 11. 2.
[10] Alfred Bertholet, *History of Hebrew Civilization,* p. 154. Geo. G. Harrap & Co., London.

esteem. Not infrequently she won a place of influence through her personality, her cleverness, and her capacity to give as well as to receive. Such a woman is described by Lemuel in Proverbs 31. 10ff.

There were many love marriages among the Hebrews. We need only cite as instances: Jacob serving seven years without pay for Rachel;[11] Boaz's thoughtful regard for Ruth;[12] Elkanah comforting his despairing childless wife with the words, "Am I not more to thee than ten sons?"[13] Hosea's pitying love for Gomer;[14] and the immortal lyrics of the Song of Songs which celebrate wedded love.[15]

When a son was about to marry, the negotiations were effected by his father, who interviewed the parents of the girl. Her father was about to lose a valued member of his household, a person of sufficient maturity and strength to be an asset. Accordingly, a purchase price known as the *mohar* must be paid. The price depended upon several factors, but on the average it amounted to about fifty silver shekels ($30). While this was the father's money and he could do with it as he pleased, he was thought to act ungenerously if he did not share it with his daughter. The bride on her part brought a dowry. In the case of the wealthy, it amounted to a good deal. We read of Solomon receiving Gezer,[16] a border city, from the King of Egypt as a dowry brought by the princess. Another bride brings a "well," a precious possession to desert tribes;[17] Sarah, a female slave;[18] and Rachel, a nurse.[19]

The bride was brought to the son's home and became a part of his family. In nomadic times she occupied the first night her mother-in-law's tent, but later had a tent of her own.[20]

Children while young were assigned some duty in the house or in the fields. There were no schools, and what they learned was received in the women's quarters.

---

[11] Genesis 29. 18-20.
[12] Ruth 2. 8; 3. 9f.; 4. 5.
[13] Such the meaning of 1 Samuel 1. 8.
[14] Hosea 1. 3ff.; 3. 1-3.
[15] Song of Songs 8. 6-7.
[16] 1 Kings 9. 16.
[17] Judges 1. 15.
[18] Genesis 16. 1f.
[19] Genesis 35. 8; Compare 24. 59.
[20] Genesis 24. 67.

SERVANTS IN THE HOUSEHOLD

For the most part the servants in the household were slaves. The wage-receiving servant was rare. An exception might be the steward,[21] who was either a freedman or free born, whose capacity to rule had entitled him to a place of responsibility and honor.

Slavery was a recognized institution among the Hebrews, as among all ancient peoples. It was regarded as a great improvement upon the barbarous custom of slaying captives in war. In fact, many of the slaves were more kindly treated and had more advantages than the wage-earning class. Provision was made in the Levitical law for the freeing of slaves every sabbatical year.[22] Whether this was carried out in practice in the majority of cases we have no way of knowing. Like some of our laws, it may have been neglected. Frequently the slave satisfied with his condition had no wish to become free but preferred to live with his master on somewhat different terms for the remainder of his natural life (Exodus 21. 2-6). But the law did not apply to foreigners who had been taken captive, but only to the Hebrew born. Most Hebrew slaves were such because of debt. A man unable to meet an obligation would give his son or a daughter into virtual slavery for the payment of the debt. Doubtless in many cases he intended to redeem his pledge after a time, but was unable to do so.

The household consisted not only of the persons mentioned, who were an integral part of it, but of kinsmen. There are allusions in the Old Testament to brothers of the householder living with him.[23] Other kinsmen too are noted, Lot with Abraham, Jacob with Leban, Ruth with

[21] Genesis 24. 2f.; 39. 4f.

[22] Analogous to the sabbatical year for the freedom of slaves was the Deuteronomic law for the release of obligations and debts of any kind. According to this law there was to be a clean slate every seven years. It was especially stipulated that men should not hesitate to loan money in the sixth year knowing that a few months later the debt would be discharged without any payment on the part of the debtor. The provision seems to anticipate the impracticable features of a law, which probably was never put into execution.

[23] 1 Samuel 10. 14. Saul is met by his uncle when he returns to his home.

Naomi. In addition there were "the poor relations" who
depended upon the bounty of the well to do.

Supplementary Reading

W. F. Bade, *Old Testament in the Light of Today,* Chapter II.
Alfred Bertholet, *History of Hebrew Civilization,* Book II, Chap-
ter I.
T. G. Soares, *Social Institutions,* Chapters III, IX, X.
Louis Wallis, *Sociological Study of the Bible,* Chapter VI.
Bible, Genesis 24, Wooing of Rebecca. Book of Ruth. Proverbs
6. 20f., Instruction to sons. Proverbs 31, Ideal wife and
mother.

CHAPTER XX

SOURCES OF HEBREW LITERATURE

THE Hebrews by the middle of the eleventh century had become proficient in writing, in which accomplishment they were undoubtedly aided by the use of the alphabet. It may be noted in this connection that they were the earliest people to employ letter signs in extended narrative writing.

It is a mere commonplace to say that there must be a period of achievement and development before a nation can excel in writing. A literary renaissance does not follow immediately the dark ages of ignorance and superstition. Between such periods lie preparatory stages. In a preceding chapter[1] attention was drawn to the "lost" books of Israel concerning which no knowledge would have been had, were it not for allusions, or quotations from them, in the historical books of the Old Testament. It is tempting to think that there were other similar books known and used by biblical writers, although no reference is made to such sources.

THE FIRST NARRATIVE WRITING

The earliest narrative writing preserved in the Bible is the greater part of Second Samuel and the opening chapters of First Kings.[2] The author lived when the events happened and has given us the record of one who was not infrequently an eye-witness. The vividness of his recital,[3] the absence of "tendency,"[4] the fullness of detail, and the selection of characteristic incident are quite journalistic. The subject of the narrative is David, his family, his friendships, his battles, the frailty of his old age, and finally his death, but not until an intrigue of Bathsheba supported by the prophet Nathan had put Solomon on the throne.

---

[1] Chap. XVIII.
[2] 2 Samuel 1-6 and 9-20; 1 Kings 1, 2.
[3] Especially 1 Kings 1, 2.
[4] Or purpose.

Encouraged by the reception of the first attempt, the author pushed back his narrative—the only direction it could take —to the early life of David, to Saul and to Samuel.[5]   Then followed the stories of heroes—the original draft of the book of Judges.[6]   Such writing is not properly termed history, but is biographic or, as Bertholet felicitously calls it, "incipient history."   It was invaluable material for later writers who in their recensions usually treated it with reverence.   When there were two versions of the same battle,[7] or two accounts of Saul's election to kingship, both were spared.[8]

THE EARLY NARRATIVES[9]

The time[10] was ripe for undertaking an ambitious project. There was an urgent demand for a narrative that would go back to the beginning of human life, that would relate the stories of the founders of the race to the nation which was formed in the Mosaic period.   In a word, the writer was to put into permanent form the sagas of the race.   Whoever should attempt the task would find at his disposal a vast amount of material, some of it written, most of it oral tradition.[11]   This must be assembled, sifted, and so much of it saved as would illustrate the ways of God with man.   That the historian was discovered, that he had collaborators, that the work was well done, does not need to be retold.   The writing contained elements valuable to a high degree.   The author set out to write a history of the world and to show its religious intent; he ended having created literature.

THE CONTENT EXAMINED

It is to be remembered that the knowledge possessed by the Hebrews was practical rather than theoretical.   They were without scientific information however richly endowed in other respects.   What they had to tell men about the crea-

---

[5] The material of First Samuel.
[6] In its later form a work of the Deuteronomists.
[7] Judges 4 and 5.
[8] I Samuel, Chaps. 8 and 9-10.
[9] Not "first" to be written, but so designated because they cover the early periods.
[10] About 850 B. C.
[11] See *supra*.

tion of the world, the beginning of life on the planet, the stars, the origin and growth of nations may be described as "guesses at truth," but this does not detract from the value of their work, nor are they to be regarded as more limited in their outlook than other ancient peoples. That Hebrew writers were not historians in the modern sense of the word, nor scientists, nor distinguished for erudition is a small matter. That they were endowed with literary genius, that they had a high sense of moral values, that for the most part they were deeply religious men is highly important. There was time enough in the long course of human events for the introduction and impartation of scientific knowledge. To know how to live, to obtain social justice was more essential than the knowledge of the origin of life, and to this task the writers successfully applied their talents.

THE JAHVIST

A Judean writer was the first to essay the task of writing a world "history." That he remains anonymous does not greatly matter. He is known to posterity as the Jahvist because of his preference for the divine name "Jahve."[12] He began with the creation of man[13] and continued the history of his descendants through the Hexateuch.[14] He is recognized by his power as a storyteller, his style, his diction, his use of Jahve, and the immaturity of his theology. The incidents chiefly characteristic of his writing show him to be reflective. He mused much on the presence of evil in a world which began as a paradise. Man he felt was "prone to do evil as the sparks fly upward." The consequences of wrongdoing follow in his train. The blood of an injured man cries from the ground where he was slain.[15] He has a sense of the dramatic; his recitals are vivid; he has the power of awakening conscience, and he still speaks through his writing to disquieted men. He was not averse to using fragments

[12] The German spelling for Yahweh which will be followed in this chapter to avoid confusion.
[13] Genesis 2. 4f.
[14] Designation for the first six books of the Bible.
[15] Genesis 4. 10.

of myths[16] or falling back upon parable,[17] if by so doing he could explain the origin of human traits, or the rise of institutions. He endeavors to satisfy the curiosity of his readers by explaining why men have to work so hard for the bare necessities of life,[18] why they wear clothing,[19] why they marry,[20] why the rainbow follows the storm.[21] He is not a misogynist, nor does his outlook upon life seem unduly pessimistic, although he undoubtedly reflects the period in which he writes. He impresses one as writing objectively, but not dispassionately.

THE ELOHIST

In the Northern Kingdom at a somewhat later date, a writer stimulated by the success of the Judean narrative attempts a similar work. He has other sources at his command, has advanced religious ideas, and shows a marked preference for the use of "Elohim" as a divine name, believing rightly that Jahve was not employed until the covenant of the Mosaic period brought Israel into a definite relationship with a tribal deity.[22] To the Elohist God is a spiritual Being and does not assume a human form as the Jahvist had thought.[23] When he converses with men, he sends an angel[24] or communicates by dreams.[25] He rejects the cult of human sacrifice, and one of the most pathetic and powerfully told incidents of Genesis is the story of Abraham's test, his offer to sacrifice Isaac, and the substitute victim by which the lad was spared.[26] Like the Jahvist, he continues his narrative through the book of Joshua.

After the fall of Samaria,[27] the narrative of the northern writer found its way to Judea. The circumstances were not dissimilar to those attending the exodus from Constantinople in 1453. After the fall of the city, scholars fled with their precious manuscripts to Italy and thus opened a new field of culture. The presence in Judea of two narratives

---

[16] Genesis 6. 4.
[17] Genesis 3. 1f.
[18] Genesis 3. 17, 18.
[19] Genesis 3. 7, 21.
[20] Genesis 2. 23, 24.
[21] Genesis 9. 12-16.

[22] See Exodus 6. 3.
[23] Genesis 2. 18-22; 3. 8.
[24] Genesis 21. 17.
[25] Genesis 20. 3.
[26] Genesis 22. 1f.
[27] 722 B. C.

similar and yet divergent tempted the scribes to make a recension. Before the two writings were combined forming a document known to scholars as JE, it was necessary to delete, to dovetail, to interpolate, but in several instances the reverence of the scribes for ancient writings led to the inclusion of parallel accounts of the same incident notwithstanding divergencies in names and other details.[28] We do not recognize the hand of the Elohist in the composite document until Genesis 17. Inasmuch as he must have given an account of the earlier period, we are forced to the opinion that his work was greatly abridged. How much both writers lost by the compilation we shall never know. Similar recensions are common in Arabian literature and were frequently made in the Middle Ages.

THE DEUTERONOMISTS

The book of Deuteronomy, which purports to be a series of addresses given by Moses on the eve of Israel's invasion of Palestine, is, in fact, a late writing. The addresses are prophetic in tone and embody legislation designed to correct the abuses of Manasseh's evil reign. The reflective reader may conclude upon comparing a section of Deuteronomy forbidding certain cults[29] with a passage in Second Kings, in which these "strange" rites were said to flourish, that Moses had he returned to earth in Manasseh's day, far from regarding Deuteronomy as "a pious fraud" would consider it the revival of his own spirit. Deuteronomy is a great book, easy to read, its legislation humane and in advance of the enactments found elsewhere in the Pentateuch. While the Deuteronomists engaged in other literary labors, the Pentateuchal writing was their *magnus opus*.

THE PRIESTLY WRITER

In the exilic period a writer, heartened by the glowing pictures which Ezekiel painted of a restored Jerusalem, a rebuilt Temple, and a purified priesthood, wrote an ecclesiastical history which, like the early narratives, started at the

---

[28] Genesis 12. 11-20; Chap. 20; 26. 1-11.
[29] Deuteronomy 18. 9-12 with 2 Kings 21. 3-9.

beginning of created life. He was, no doubt, actuated by the desire to pave a way for the return to sacrificial cults, and to justify the institution of the priesthood. He incorporated "the law of holiness," a code prepared by one of Ezekiel's immediate followers. He was indefatigable in his quest for genealogical tables. To him we owe the chronological sequence, and much of the numbering in the Hexateuch. To regard him as often mistaken in his calculations is not to forfeit our respect for his diligence. Even as late as the seventeenth century we have Archbishop Usher declaring that the creation of the world took place in 4004 B. C. The Priestly writer's crowning achievement is the first chapter of Genesis in which he rises, in spite of his tendency to be repetitious, to sublime heights. He conceives of God as spiritual, transcendant, benign, and the Creator of all life.

EARLY TRADITIONS, POEMS, LAWS, CUSTOMS
PRIOR TO 1040 B. C.

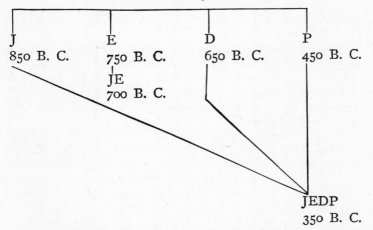

J 850 B. C.

E 750 B. C.

D 650 B. C.

P 450 B. C.

JE 700 B. C.

JEDP 350 B. C.

J stands for the Yahwist (German spelling Jahvist), or the Judean narrative; E for the Elohist, or the Ephraimitish narrative; D for the Deuteronomists; and P for the Priestly writer. The diagram indicates the relation of each to the preceding, the editorial symbols and the approximate dating.

The Completion of the Task

During the fourth century in the days of Ezra the scribe,[30] we have a compilation of narrative and laws, essentially the material found in the Hexateuch as we now have it. Because legislation occupied a preponderate place in the six books, they are collectively known as "The Law," and were esteemed as the most important division in the Old-Testament canon. The preceding diagram may aid the reader in summarizing what has been written concerning the composite nature of the Hexateuch.

The Prophets and Other Writings

While the six books were gradually taking form under the supervision of writers in Judea, Israel, and Babylon, other important additions were made to Hebrew literature. Prophetic discourses or sermons were put into writing either by the prophets themselves or their followers.[31] Although the prophets were not immediately influential, and their moral reforms proved abortive, their written words remained to challenge posterity, and to constitute a most important part of the Old Testament.

Poets contributed songs which in time were compiled in the Psalter, the hymn book of the Jewish Church. Sages collected proverbs, aphorisms, shrewd and witty sayings, and these when brought together became one of the books of Wisdom,[32] to which we must add Ecclesiastes, Job, Ecclesiasticus and Wisdom of Solomon.[33]

To the historians' credit must be placed a work known in the Hebrew Bible as "The Book of Kings." Originally the designation covered the four books familiar to readers of the English versions as First and Second Samuel, First and Second Kings. Reference has already been made to the books of Samuel as the earliest narrative writing.[34] To this important source material later historians added the annals of

---

[30] Scholars quite generally agree on a late date for Ezra rather than the traditional fifth-century period.
[31] Jeremiah 36. 4.
[32] Proverbs.
[33] The last named are Apocryphal.
[34] See page 196.

Judah's kings, the chronicles kept in the court of the Northern Kingdom, and the collection known as the Elijah-Elisha stories.[35] A late ecclesiastical history known as First and Second Chronicles by the author of Nehemiah and Ezra complete the historical portions of the Canon.

If such a survey seems to do violence to the inspiration of the writings, the reader is reminded that inspiration ("a breathing into") is said of men. They and not their writings are the subject of the divine afflatus.[36] When the word is transferred to their productions, it is to be used in a general sense and should not convey the idea of a mechanically inspired book, as the Koran or the Book of Mormon is said to be.

A PARALLEL

The growth of Old-Testament literature is comparable to the course taken by New-Testament books. Here, as in the older canon, we distinguish stages in the development of a single book or a group. Take, for example, the four Gospels. There was first the stage when the events occurred and the words of Jesus were spoken; a second stage of oral tradition which continued for some fifteen years until a compilation of the sayings of Jesus[37] was put in written form with a bit of narrative added. In a fourth stage we have the Gospels of Mark, Matthew, Luke, and John, written at different centers and circulated in adjacent regions. Eventually the Gospels were collected together, and by the close of the second century they were included with the writings of Saint Paul and others in the canon of the New Testament.

What would have happened if the separate writings of the evangelists had been combined? Exactly what occurred in the case of the Hexateuch. In fact, Tatian nearly accomplished this in the second century, when he published the "Diatessaron," a compilation of the four Gospels. The work

---

[35] The authors ordinarily refer to their sources.

[36] Hebrews, Chap. I. I.

[37] Hypothetical; however, the view is sustained by evidence, which stops just short of complete verification.

was received with such acclaim that the bishops of the early church suppressed it.[38]   Had the Pentateuchal writers been thus restrained, would we have profited by having separate rather than compiled writings?[39]

THE IMPORTANCE OF THE DOCUMENTARY SOURCES

Undoubtedly, the recognition of the documentary sources of the Hexateuch is important, without which we cannot make a true valuation of the contents.   However, the question of origins is a technical problem and need not long detain the lay reader, whose chief concern is with the Old Testament as literature, or a book of devotion, or a manual of conduct.

At what stage can we assign the literary quality which distinguishes such a writing as the book of Genesis, which has unsurpassed value as a series of related short stories each perfect in itself?   Certainly, prior to the editorial recensions.   It is difficult to see how the document known as J could have been improved by being incorporated with other writings.   Its literary quality lies in its content and is inseparable from it.   In fact, the charm of the stories which constitute Genesis may go back to the period of oral tradition, that is, to the storyteller's art.   One might deduce as a parallel the parables of Jesus which owe their perfection to him and not to those who transmitted them.   This is also true of the document known as E.

SUPPLEMENTARY READING

E. C. Baldwin, *Types of Literature in the Old Testament,* Chapters I, II.
J. A. Bewer, *Literature of the Bible,* Chapters I, II, IV-VI.
S. R. Driver, *Introduction to the Literature of the Old Testament,* Preface.
I. A. Matthews, *Old Testament Life and Literature,* Chapter III.

[38] At least discouraged its use.
[39] Attempts to print a Bible in which the original documents are indicated by italics, parenthesis marks, etc., or by colored inks are not wholly successful.   In Kent's *Shorter Bible,* we have an edition of the text of J which stands by itself and is worth repeated perusal.

John P. Peters, *The Religion of the Hebrews,* Chapter I.
D. C. Simpson, *Pentateuchal Criticism,* Chapters I, III, IV, V.
J. Patterson Smyth, *The Bible in the Making* (entire).
Wood and Grant, *The Bible as Literature,* Intro., Chapters XVI-
    XVIII.

PART III

RELIGIOUS AND MORAL VALUES IN HEBREW PROPHECY

CHAPTER XXI

THE ORACLES OF ISRAEL

IN an earlier chapter mention was made of shrines which marked the places where God had once spoken to men. It may have been under a "whispering oak,"[1] or on a rocky hilltop,[2] or by a fountain in the desert.[3] That Israel regarded such places as sacred and persistently visited them until a late period we may believe. Where God had once spoken, he might again appear.[4] But the shrines adopted by Israel were celebrated as altars of sacrifice, or were centers for religious festivals, or became in time temple sites. They were not places of oracular response such as the Greeks knew. The oracles of Israel were the sayings of the prophets, vital and binding because they were the words of living men. But this is to anticipate. Long before the prophetic period there was a preparatory stage in which we have mere intimations of prophecy, when the means at man's disposal for learning the will of God do not seem to differ essentially from those of contemporary nations. Abraham, who inquires concerning the future when he enters a strange country,[5] does not differ from any earnest seeker whether in Canaan, or Babylonia, or Greece. Each is conscious that whatever befalls him depends upon a higher Power, nor dare he enter upon any important undertaking without an intimation of the outcome.

THE MEANS EMPLOYED

The measures men employed for a knowledge of futurity were by no means on the same spiritual level. The inspection of an animal's entrails, the inquiry at the Delphian oracle

---

[1] Genesis 12. 6 to be translated "whispering oak."
[2] Genesis 28. 11, 18, 19.
[3] Genesis 16. 7, 14.
[4] See Chap. II.
[5] Genesis 15. 1-5.

and the consultation with the prophet differ as credulity from
reason and magic from religion. Where there was a developing religious sense, as in the case of Israel, we may look
for stages in man's advancement. The Hebrews progress
from what we may term the intimations of prophecy to the
true prophetic word. The advance when it once started was
phenomenally rapid, as we shall see. But at first there was
groping, a twilight stage, when the Israelite differed in no
degree from his neighbor. He employed magic, undoubtedly
believing that thus he could influence the future. The impli-
cation in magical rites is either that men are without God or
that they can influence Deity to do their will. It will be at
once perceived that Israel's religious leaders sternly opposed
practices of this nature. Deuteronomy, the eighteenth chapter, gives us a list of the proscribed cults, divination, sorcery,
necromancy, astrology, and augury—rites familiar to
Canaanites but forbidden Israel. But what the Deuteronomists forbade we may be certain was customary, even as late
as Manasseh's reign.[6]

Divination was apparently harmless, since it consisted in
the study of the entrails of animals, particularly the liver,
or in the use of the divining cup. A reference to the latter
may be found in Genesis in the silver cup discovered in
Benjamin's sack and restored to the rightful owner, Joseph,
who is made to say, "Did you not know that a man like me
would use divination?"[7] The method most likely employed
was to fill the cup to the brim and to pour on its surface a
few drops of oil, the movement of which was watched and
interpreted by the diviner.

Sorcery implied recourse to evil spirits through whose
powers desired ends would be gained. This, it will be perceived, was a species of devil worship, and anything but ethical in its nature and results.

Necromancy was consultation with the dead, the spirits of
whom still lived, were localized and accessible to men through
mediums. A classic instance of the rite was Saul's interview
with Samuel, whose return from the place of the dead was

effected by the Witch of Endor.[8] We may regard necromancy as a rite of ancestor worship and forbidden on that
account to Israel.[9]

Astrology taught that the stars were deities and presided
over the affairs of mankind. Probably no ancient superstition has continued so long or been so influential among enlightened peoples. To this day the planets and constellations
bear the names given them by star worshipers thousands of
years ago. While astronomy has replaced astrology and
science outdistanced superstition, the latter still prevails
among large sections of people. That the Hebrews did not
escape star worship we know from the passage cited in
Second Kings and elsewhere.[10] What the prophetic viewpoint was may be learned from a postexilic writer who
regarded the stars as points of light, placed in the heavens
by their Creator, and moving there to mark the course of the
seasons and to distinguish day and night.[11]

It is difficult to see why augury should have been forbidden,
unless there were objectionable features in the rite. Ordinarily it refers to some practice[12] designed to obtain knowledge of coming events.

The practices described lingered long in Israel. We find
the prophet Isaiah[13] scornfully enumerating the diviner, the
charmer, the enchanter as holding honorable places in Jerusalem, who will be missed by their followers, when the city
is besieged and its great ones are taken away![14]

The common and legitimate sources to which Israel turned
for ascertaining the knowledge of the divine purpose, especially of futurity, were dreams, the sacred lot, and the word
of the prophet.

DREAMS

The patriarchs we are told received divine communications
through dreams. The well-known vision of Jacob at Bethel

[8] 1 Samuel 28. 8f.
[9] 1 Samuel 28. 3.
[10] Judges 5. 20.
[11] Genesis 1. 14-18.
[12] Perhaps a sacred lot; compare Ezekiel 21. 21.
[13] Isaiah 3. 2, 3.
[14] The ironical strain in the passage should be observed.

occurred while he was sleeping. Solomon shortly after his coronation goes to Gibeon, a shrine or high place of considerable importance. Here he offered sacrifice and slept in the sanctuary, hoping thus to induce a dream of significance.[15] Nevertheless, dreams are not on a level with the prophetic saying, and the time came when Jeremiah declared:[16] "The prophet that has a dream let him tell his dream, but he that has my word let him speak my word faithfully. What is the straw to the wheat?"

THE SACRED LOT

One form of the sacred lot was the *Urim* and *Thummim*. The words are not translated because it is not quite clear what they signify. Probably, as suggested by H. P. Smith, they were two disks, white on one side and black on the other. When the white fell uppermost the answer was affirmative; when black, negative; and when both white and black appeared, the answer was withheld. These sacred emblems were in the hands of the priest and kept in the ephod of the high priest. David had the lot to guide him after Abiathar, the priest, escaped the massacre at Nob and joined him.[17]

Ezekiel relates the form which the sacred lot took in Babylonia.[18] He says that the king was undecided whether to wage war against Rabbah-Ammon or Jerusalem, and so shook from his quiver one among several marked arrows. The lot indicated Jerusalem as his destination.

PROPHETS AND PROPHESYING

Long before the eighth century there were certain prophetic movements in Israel which indicate to us the spiritual lineage of the writing prophets. We can distinguish, on the one hand, the sons of the prophets, who seem to be best described as guilds of ecstatics, into the maelstrom of

[15] I Kings 3. 4f.
[16] Jeremiah 23. 25, 28.
[17] I Samuel 22, 23f. The sacred lot was employed in the New-Testament times, and the first chapter of Acts records the use to which it was put by the apostolic band. What form the lot took we are not told.
[18] Ezekiel 21. 21f.

whose emotions was drawn the first king of Israel; on the other, solitary figures, whose insistence upon democracy and ethics makes them the true forerunners of Amos and his contemporaries. It is necessary for us to consider this double ancestry of the prophets.

Near the close of the period of the Judges we first note the appearance of bands of religious enthusiasts whose frenzied rites drew to them the attention, if not the sympathy, of Israel. Their affinities were with the sect known as the Rechabites, and, like them, they protested against Canaanitish civilization. They would banish agriculture and city occupations, returning to the nomadic way of life. Their sacred dance was accompanied by music—the lyre, fife and drum—and by such means they induced an ecstatic state, during which they tore off their clothing and finally fell to the ground insensible.[19]

In a later period there seems to have been some modification in their practices, or something added. We gain the impression that the bands over which Elisha presided were industrious[20] and relatively sober. Certainly, some of their number had not disdained marriage.[21] While Elisha identifies himself with the movement and is at times subject to an induced ecstasy,[22] Elijah apparently keeps aloof.[23]

In the eighth century the reputation of the ecstatics suffered considerably, probably because they were commercialized[24] and not on account of a change in their methods and ideals. We hear Amos indignantly deny that he was one of their number.[25] But certain values had been conserved and their influence continued to affect in a marked degree the prophet of the eighth and seventh centuries.

Prophecy throughout its history was characterized by displays of emotion. We find that the Temple police were ordered to arrest Jeremiah as one "who was mad and played the prophet."[26] Ezekiel we know was subject to hypnotic trances,[27] and of more than one prophet the companions of

---

[19] I Samuel 10. 5, 6, 9-12; 19. 23, 24; 2 Samuel 6. 14, 16, 20.
[20] 2 Kings 6. 1f.
[21] 2 Kings 4. 1.
[22] 2 Kings 3. 15.
[23] 2 Kings 2. 3, 16.
[24] 2 Kings 5. 20f.
[25] Amos 7. 14.
[26] Jeremiah 29. 26.
[27] Ezekiel 1. 1; 2. 1; 3. 12, 14.

Jehu might have asked as they did of Elisha's emissary,
"Who was that mad fellow?"[28]

THE FIRST PROPHETS

The isolated prophets from Samuel to Amos differ from
those who follow them in one respect only. Their messages
were not written either by themselves or by their disciples.
Only two had biographers, if such an appellation is appropriate to those who wrote the stories of Elijah and Elisha.
At least their writing can be called "incipient biography."[29]
These tales are valuable chiefly for the light shed upon the
relation of the prophet to the common people.[30]   True, in
the background are kings and courts, but little value is
attached to such. The prophets rise from the common people and invariably represent their interests when they come
in conflict with the assumed prerogatives of the sovereign.
Thus we have Nathan reproving David in the matter of
Uriah on the ground that the latter has been robbed of his
one valuable possession.[31]   Elijah confronts Ahab for the
crime of taking as his own the vineyard which belonged to
one of his subjects.[32]   "The prophets"—to quote Robinson
—"were in a very real sense the inheritors and guardians of
the democratic principle which Israel had preserved from
nomad days."[33]

The political interference of the prophets is indicated by
many examples illustrative of the influence they exerted in
affairs of state. It has been said of Samuel that he made
and unmade kings. Nathan placed Solomon on the throne,
although Adonijah had a strong following and a prior claim
to kingship.[34]   Ahijah of Shiloh backed the revolution under
Jeroboam, foretelling his success, and may justly have been
regarded as a social agitator.[35]   Elisha did not hesitate to

---

[28] 2 Kings 9. 11.
[29] See Robinson, *History of Israel,* Vol. I, p. 449.   Oxford Press.
[30] 2 Kings 4. 1ff.
[31] 2 Samuel 12. 1ff.
[32] The act was Jezebel's, not .Ahab's.   The latter knows nothing of
the plot until it is accomplished.   1 Kings 21. 4-7, 8-10, 14-16.
[33] *History of Israel,* Vol. I, p. 325.   Oxford Press.
[34] 1 Kings 1. 5, 6, 11f.
[35] 1 Kings 11. 29f.

foment a conspiracy which led to dynastic change and cost the lives of many persons.[36]   Elijah on more than one occasion addressed Ahab in stern, unrelenting terms, predicting the disaster which would overtake his house.[37]   Not always does the prophet seem to be politically constructive, unless we view as salutary words which first burned but afterward proved as healing as the balm of Gilead.

The sanctity attached to the person of the prophet explains his escape from imprisonment and death, either of which would have overtaken him in courts other than those of Judah and Israel, where kings dared not violate a personage esteemed by men and approved of God.   To have slain a prophet would be an act of apostasy and be held as the repudiation of Yahweh himself.[38]   Only thus can the expulsion of Amos from Bethel and the imprisonment of Jeremiah be explained, when circumstances would indicate the death of either.   Against Jehoiakim, alone among the kings of Israel and Judah, is the specific charge laid that he slew a prophet of God.[39]

The prophet in early days was attested by miracles, according to the common view.   This may account for the miraculous element which looms so large in the stories of Elijah and Elisha.[40]   But later with only occasional exception[41] the prophet depends for his recognition upon the nature of his message, to the popular esteem in which he is held, and his own integrity.   No miracles are related, none are required for attestation.

THE TWO STREAMS MEET

It must always be borne in mind that there were two Israels, that the real line of division was not political but social and religious.   Opposing those who had assimilated the civilization of Canaan was the nomad element who eschewed it.   From the latter came the early ecstatics and

[36] 2 Kings 9. 1-3, 6-8, 14-37; 10. 1f.
[37] 1 Kings 21. 17f.
[38] Robinson, *History of Israel,* Vol. I, p. 404.   Oxford Press.
[39] Jeremiah 26. 21-23.
[40] 1 Kings 17. 6, 8-16; 18. 30-46.   2 Kings 2, 3, 4, 5, 6, 7.
[41] 2 Kings 20. 8f.

prophets like Elijah, but mediating the difference between the nomad and those who represented urban and agricultural interests were the later prophets. Not even the shepherd Amos champions the nomadic ideal, but, like all the eighth- and seventh-century prophets, he regards Israel and Judah as religiously and socially one.

The prophet was essentially a messenger. The Greek and English equivalent of the Hebrew *nabi,* meaning "one who speaks for another," is accurate. The history of the word[42] and the prophet's consciousness that he was a mouthpiece of Yahweh are sufficiently clear. But it is an error to suppose that the predictive element was unimportant or even subordinate.

> "Surely the Lord God will do nothing
> Except he reveal his secret
> To his servants the prophets."[43]

SUPPLEMENTARY READING

E. C. Baldwin, *The Prophets,* Chapter II.
John P. Peters, *The Religion of the Hebrews,* Chapter X.
T. H. Robinson, *History of Israel,* Vol. I, pp. 447f., 404, 325.
Henry P. Smith, *Religion of Israel,* Chapter VI.
J. M. P. Smith, *The Prophets and Their Times,* Chapters I-III.
Biblical Selections—1 Samuel 9, 10; 1 Kings 18.

---

[42] See Exodus 4. 15, where Aaron is designated as a prophet to Moses, as the latter was a prophet to God.
[43] See Amos 3. 7.

CHAPTER XXII

THE REFORMER

AMOS was the pioneer of the eighth-century prophets and their successors, numbering all told sixteen, whose contribution in the sphere of religion and ethics was unparalleled in pre-Christian times, if indeed it was equaled in any age. He was the first to record the sermons he preached, for from his predecessors there remain only fragmentary sayings. He was the first to see Israel in relation to a world power. True, he saw chiefly the nations on the horizon line of his country—Phoenicia, Philistia, Edom, Moab, and Syria—but he looked beyond toward Assyria,[1] whose rising power of empire he envisaged. But he was unique in that he was the first to insist upon the moral character of God, who so far from being capricious, or whimsical, or inconstant, acted consistently with his own nature.

AMOS THE MAN

We know nothing of the prophet's family or of his early life. When we first meet him he is a herdsman of Tekoa,[2] a small village six miles south of Bethlehem. He has been termed by some modern writers a "rustic," or peasant, but he was more than a mere countryman, if his words are to be taken as a criterion. Who can fail to note their purity and power? More perhaps than any prophetic writing of the time they convey to us the feeling of impassioned oratory in written form. "Nowhere in the Old Testament," declared a great Hebrew scholar, "is there an example of stronger or purer literary style."[3] Moreover, he has a remarkable knowledge of contiguous nations,[4] of past and present history,[5] and of social conditions among his own people. He is

[1] 5. 27.
[2] 1. 1.
[3] William R. Harper, in I. C. C. Hosea-Amos, p. 106. Charles Scribner's Sons.
[4] 1. 3f.; 9. 7.
[5] 5. 25; 8. 9; 4. 7-10.

familiar with the location of countries and their physical characteristics.[6] He knows the constellations, naming Orion and the cluster of the Pleiades ;[7] nor does that which is close at hand escape his scrutiny.[8] He has desert eyes for the far and near. He combines spiritual insight with knowledge, and reasons from cause to effect.[9] His logic at times is unanswerable. A countryman? Yes, but in the highest sense of the word, an educated man.

How shall we explain his ability and account for his knowledge? A late Jewish writing represents him as a well-to-do wool trader, whose journeys to northern markets and to Jerusalem gave him ample facilities for current information.[10] The conjecture is plausible but seems inadequate to explain his ability. Moreover, it is unsupported by anything in his book.

His prophecy was addressed to the Northern Kingdom and disturbed the ritualists of Bethel, who resented his presence at the shrine as an intrusion.[11] Perhaps this was a handicap, that he, a southerner, should appear in the north, denouncing transgressions and predicting doom for a people who felt themselves religiously and politically separate from Judah, and superior. Whether his message affected the nation is doubtful. The complacency with which Israel viewed its material wealth, its religious rites, and the future was too complete to be more than momentarily disturbed.

The Prophet's Times

Our sources for the political and religious history of the time in which Amos lived are the book of Second Kings, and the nearly contemporary prophets, Hosea and Isaiah. In addition we have Assyrian annals, and some important disclosures from the excavations at Samaria. Jeroboam II, who was king during this most flourishing period of the Northern Kingdom, enlarged the palaces of his predecessors,

[6] 8. 8.
[7] 5. 8. Compare Job 38. 31.
[8] 3. 12a; 4. 7; 5. 19.
[9] 3. 1-8.
[10] I. C. C. Hosea-Amos, pp. 104, 105. Charles Scribner's Sons.
[11] 7. 10-14.

and it is likely that some of the findings of the Harvard
expedition belong to his time.[12]

In order to understand the prosperity of Samaria, we need
to go back in history to the plundering of Damascus in 841
B. C. The Assyrians, who were instrumental in this, returned
satisfied to their own capital, having exacted a very heavy
tribute. In 805 they came again and utterly devastated the
Syrian city. Thus Israel was rid at one blow of their
antagonist in war and chief rival in trade. They might have
felt some apprehension lest what had happened to Damascus
would fall upon Samaria, but fortunately during the first
half of the eighth century a series of petty, ineffective kings
ruled Assyria, freeing them from that source of evil. The
editor of the annals of this period in Israel tells us that Jeroboam II extended the borders of the country from Hamath
in the far north to the Dead Sea and the desert, an extent of
country that recalls the palmy days of Solomon. However,
there is no record of military campaigns, and the passage
should be broadly interpreted as a conquest of trade. It is
not unlikely that Damascus' lucrative commerce was diverted
to Samaria.

The material prosperity of Israel intoxicated its rulers and
men of wealth, who had visions of even greater riches; nor
did the small landowner escape the contagion, but mortgaged
his plot of ground with little thought for the day of payment. Outwardly it was an era of magnificence; in reality,
the period was one of rapid deterioration in which extravagance,[13] unbridled licentiousness,[14] corruption of the courts,[15]
the oppression of the poor,[16] and labor by slaves took the
place of nomadic simplicity. No nation can remain half
slave, half free. The selling of freeborn Israelites into bondage for the discharge of debts was the undoing of Israel, as
it has been of more powerful nations.[17]

Little could be expected from the religion of the day. It
had become completely formalized, its elaborate ceremonials

[12] See Chap. XII.
[13] 3. 12, 15; 6. 3-6.
[14] 2. 7; 7. 17.
[15] 5. 7, 12, 15.
[16] 2. 6; 5. 11.
[17] See T. H. Robinson, *History of Israel,* Vol. I, p. 363. Oxford Press.

concealing its true state.[18] The ritualists were in the saddle
and had much to say of a glorious future to be ushered in by
the "day of Yahweh."[19] Asceticism represented by the Rechabites and those who called themselves Nazarites was too far
removed from the sphere of daily life and ordinary interests
to make an effective protest. Into a society crazed by its
dream of wealth and morally derelict Amos was ushered.

He has been accused of a want of sympathy, always an
essential quality in an effective ministry. There is some
truth in the criticism, but it must be remembered that his
lack of compassion was due not to detachment, for he felt
himself one with all Israel, but to his personality, which was
a product of many factors and, not the least, a desert environment. How otherwise could he have obtained the
perspective by which he viewed the Northern Kingdom in
its relation to the present and the future?

While some of his discourses convey to us a sense of
inevitable doom,[20] it was this element in his preaching which
gained the attention of his hearers. That the priest Amaziah
should have regarded him as a dangerous fanatic, and his
expulsion from the country necessary, was a tribute to his
power.[21] At times one discerns in his utterances pathos, compassion, even hope. He knows the conditional nature of
prophecy and writes, pending a reform, the words, "It may
be that Yahweh, the God of hosts, will be gracious unto the
remnant of Joseph."[22]

It was Amos' destiny, as it has been the lot of reformers
generally, to be ahead of his age, his words to be unheeded,
and his predictions later to meet a complete and terrific fulfillment. Twenty-five years after his ministry closed the
Assyrians came and Samaria was utterly devastated, its ruin
so complete that it never recovered.[23] Under the circumstances his prophetic utterances do not seem to have been
unduly severe. In the following chapter we shall see whether
a prophet of different temperament and from a different
approach is more successful.

[18] 4. 4-6; 5. 21-27.
[19] 5. 18-20.
[20] 5. 27; 9. 1-8a.

[21] 7. 12, 13.
[22] See 5. 14, 15.
[23] C. 722 B. C.

THE PERMANENT QUALITY OF AMOS' REFORMS

Much that Amos wrote is applicable to any age, particularly to periods characterized by excessive values placed upon material prosperity and by a disregard of social justice. The years which immediately followed the Great War witnessed a slump in morals and indicated trends of thought which brought uneasiness to serious and discerning minds. The author recalls a sermon of the time preached to a fashionable audience in a metropolitan church with the title "Amos up to date," in which the speaker[24] set forth the principles enunciated by the prophet, which he applied to the present generation.

THE QUALITY OF THE WRITING

To the reader chiefly interested in the book as literature, there is much that is noteworthy, the writer's effective use of metaphor,[25] the choice of rugged but pure forms of speech[26] and the ample use of parallelism or accentual rhythm common to Hebrew poetry.[27] Attention has been frequently drawn to the resemblance of the stanzas in chapters one and two to Mark Antony's funeral oration in Shakespeare's *Julius Caesar*. The biting sarcasm with which he addresses the dissolute women of Israel[28] and the irony in his utterances to the ritualists[29] are as effective in their written form as when originally spoken.

HOW THE BOOK WAS WRITTEN

The plan of the book gives us only brief hints as to the sequence of writing. It reverses the chronological order, for the initiatory visions which determined his career come at the close.[30] The body of the prophecy is made up of addresses delivered presumably in Bethel.[31] Then came the interrup-

[24] Malcolm James Macleod.
[25] 2. 6, Selling the needy for a pair of shoes; 2. 13, As a wagon groans which is loaded with sheaves; 4. 11, A brand snatched from the burning; 5. 24, Let justice roll down like waters, and righteousness as an overflowing stream.
[26] 4. 6, 10.
[27] 3. 1-8.
[28] 4. 1-3.
[29] 4. 4, 5.
[30] Chaps. 7-9.
[31] Chaps. 3-6.

tion caused by his break with the priestly party,[32] followed by his forced exile when he most likely returned to Jerusalem, where he put into writing his addresses, prefacing them with the material contained in chapters one and two.

THE CONTENT

The appended analysis is recommended as giving the essential content of the prophecy:

I. Chapters 1, 2

The doom upon the nations from which Israel will not be exempt.

II. Chapters 3-6

Fragments of sermons preached against Israel in which the prophet specifically points out the social sins of the nation; its empty ritual, its impending doom. 3. 1-4. 3; 4. 4-13; 5. 1-17; 5. 18-27; 6. 1-14.

III. Chapters 7-9. 8a

A series of five visions indicating the corruption of Israel and the judgment to follow. A parenthetical statement (7. 10-14) shows priest arrayed against prophet.

IV. Chapters 9. 8b-15

Ultimate restoration of Judah; added by a late writer.

SUPPLEMENTARY READING

E. C. Baldwin, *The Prophets,* Chapter III.
J. A. Bewer, *Literature of the Old Testament,* Chapter VII, pp. 87-93.
J. P. Peters, *The Religion of the Hebrews,* Chapter XIII.
Henry P. Smith, *Religion of Israel,* Chapter VII.
J. M. P. Smith, *The Prophets and Their Times,* Chapter IV to p. 54.
Wood and Grant, *The Bible as Literature,* Chapter III.
Biblical Selections, Amos 2. 6-6. 14; 7. 10-17.

[32] 7. 10-14.

CHAPTER XXIII

THE PROPHET OF DIVINE COMPASSION

HOSEA was a prophet of the Northern Kingdom. He was a resident, not like Amos a visitor in the land. Their king was his king, as he tells us,[1] and the people his people. He was so identified with their interests that he was involved in their misfortunes. All this is significant in the interpretation of his message.

There are many causes leading to the divine call of a prophet, a vision of God,[2] a threatening peril, an indignant sense of the prevailing social injustice, a deep inwrought conviction from childhood to maturity that he the prophet has been summoned to his task.[3] In the case of Hosea, it was a tragic misfortune in his household which was the occasion of his ministry. The account is found in the first and third chapters of his book.

While there have been various interpretations of Hosea's enigmatical language,[4] their probable explanation is a reference to an actual marriage which took place with a young woman at the time unsullied by the corrupt social institutions which flourished in northern Israel. Later she was swept into the vortex of the licentious rites of the fertility cult, an experience common to many of her sex. She was called Gomer, which may not have been her real name. That he should employ names of allegorical significance for actual personages[5] and conceal rather than publish the account of his misfortune indicates a reticence which can easily be understood. It became apparent to Hosea that the children born of her, a son and daughter, were not his own.[6] He seems to have put her away, as he had the right to do under Hebrew law, or she went of her own accord. When he met her again, she was in the slave market having drifted

---

[1] 7. 5.
[2] Isaiah 6. 1f.
[3] Jeremiah 1. 4-6.
[4] 1. 2f.; 3. 1-3.
[5] Diblaim in 1. 3; also 1. 6, 9.
[6] 1. 6-9.

from one lover to another until now no one wanted her.
Hosea, by divine direction, so he tells us, when he related
the story, purchased her. "So I bought her to me for
fifteen pieces of silver and an homer and a half of barley
and I said unto her, 'Thou shalt abide for me many days.
Thou shalt not play the harlot and thou shalt not be any
man's wife, so will I also be toward thee.' "[7]

The student who is puzzled at the language of the first
chapter need not take it literally, as if the prophet had actually been commanded to take a prostitute as a wife, nor
need he fall back upon allegory, as the earlier commentators
did. He must remember that Hosea is writing years after
Gomer's unfaithfulness. Because the misfortune had been
the means of making him a prophet, he regarded it as a part
of a divine plan. He was like a captain sailing with sealed
orders. Dean Plumptre has given voice to this thought in
his poem "Gomer."

> "Thro' all the mystery of my years
> There runs a purpose which forbids the wail
> Of passionate despair. I have not lived
> At random, as a soul whom God forsakes,
> But evermore his Spirit led me on,
> Prompted each purpose, taught my lips to speak,
> Stirred up within me that deep love, and now
> Reveals the inner secret."

Hosea's experience was not uncommon. The license of
the agricultural festivals, when celebrated as the Canaanites
had observed them, must have been as destructive of family
relations as it was of nomadic religion. An air of sanctity
was given the rites, since they were paid to the gods of the
land. By this time the syncretizing process had proceeded
so far that Yahweh and Baal were identified in function
although the names were usually distinguished, but not
always. Hebrew words were compounded with Baal in the
case of proper nouns. We find Saul calling one of his sons
Meribaal, and there were other instances of the kind. This
did not mean that Baal worship had succeeded that of

[7] 3. 1-3.

Yahweh, but that the latter was considered as baal, or lord. Elijah had feared the introduction of Phoenician worship by an act of Jezebel, but far more insidious and harmful were the encroachments of the fertility cult upon nomadic religion.

The unique feature of Hosea's prophetic mission was his claim to an identification of suffering with Yahweh.[8] The disloyalty of Gomer is the counterpart of the faithlessness of Israel to God.[9] Later the compassion of the prophet for Gomer is made the measure of the much greater love of God for the nation.[10] The analogy is developed in chapter two, which may be regarded as a prologue to the poem, chapters four to fourteen.

THE CONSTRUCTION OF THE BOOK

The first stage in Hosea's prophetic work was a series of oral discourses or sermons delivered in one of the cities, perhaps the capital of the Northern Kingdom. Fragments of his sermons are preserved in his book, chapters four to fourteen. When these were edited, they were changed in form and were prefaced by the material found in the first three chapters, where he tells us indirectly of his marriage.[11] It is unfortunate that the translations of Hosea in ordinary use should give us the impression that the writing is prose in form and sermonic in content.[12] The body of the work is lyric poetry, betraying, as Professor Bewer has said, "a restlessness of spirit and ever-present sadness."[13] The prose is confined to the narrative portions in chapters one and three. Instead of a verbatim account of sermons, he has translated them into poetry of purity and power.

Hosea, like his great contemporary, was a reformer. He opposed with all the strength of his impetuous nature the system that had devastated his home and would destroy others. He particularizes sensuality, drunkenness,[14] and ritual religion.[15] He feels that men sin not willfully but

---

[8] I. 6-8.
[9] 2. 4, 5.
[10] 2. 14-17.
[11] See *supra*.

[12] King James and Revised Version.
[13] *Old Testament Literature:* "Hosea."
[14] 4. 1-4.
[15] 4. 2; 6. 6; 6. 9; 14. 2.

through ignorance. "My people are destroyed for lack of knowledge."[16] In this he betrays a sensitive appreciation of human nature, which is lacking in many reformers. Again, he has all the tenderness of a great evangelistic preacher.

"When Israel was a child, I came to love him,
And from Egypt I called him.
The more I called them,
The more they went away from me;
They sacrificed to the Baals,
And made offerings to idols.

"But it was I who taught Ephraim to walk;
I took them up in my arms;
But they did not know that I cared for them.
With human lines I led them,
With loving cords;
And I became for them like him who lifts the yoke from
    their jaws;
And I bent toward them and fed them."[17]

Amos and Hosea present a striking contrast. Amos was a stern moralist, single-minded and logical in his deductions. With clear eyes he saw as if already present the judgment of God falling upon a sunken and dissolute nation. Hosea, to the contrary, proclaims a compassionate God and assigns the cause of moral failure to ignorance, but is not less forceful. He is never indulgent, never excuses, never compromises. At times he can be as severe in his denunciation as any prophet, but there has been revealed to him through his misfortune an aspect of the divine nature which Amos never viewed. Hosea's character is as complex as that of Amos was simple. This is due to the antithesis between a sense of wrongdoing and his deeply affectionate and religious nature.[18]

In each man the background interprets the portrait. No

---

[16] 4. 6.
[17] 11. 1-4. O. T., Amer. Tr. J. M. P. Smith, Ed.; University of Chicago Press.
[18] 6. 4.

experience so completely changes the character of a man as
suffering, and afterward forgiving the person who has caused
the sorrow. To hate is human; to forgive, divine. In forgiving one lifts himself to a higher plane of understanding.
He becomes like God, receiving from such experience far
more than he bestows.

Did Hosea believe in the saving repentance of his people?
It is difficult to say. He writes:

> "The prophet is distracted,
> The man of the spirit is crazed,
> Because of your great guilt."[19]

But he feels that their repentance, if it comes, will be superficial.

> "What shall I do with you, O Ephraim?
> What shall I do with you, O Judah?
> For your piety is like a morning cloud,
> And like the dew that goes early away."[20]

In his compassion he attributes the sins of Israel to their
want of knowledge, meaning by knowledge intimate intercourse with God. He is confident that this relationship may
be resumed if the people will change their manner of life.

> "Come, let us return unto the Lord;
> For he has torn, and he will heal us,
> He smote, and he will bind us up.
>
> .   .   .   .
>
> "Let us know, let us press on to know the Lord;
> As soon as we seek him, we shall find him . . .
> He will come to us like the winter-rain,
> Like the spring rain that waters the land."[21]

In the fourteenth chapter, which most authorities attribute
to Hosea, we have a dialogue in which the speakers are
Israel, the prophet, and Jehovah. With a little care the stu-

---

[19] 9. 7, O. T., Amer. Tr. J. M. P. Smith, Ed.; U. of C. Press.
[20] 6. 4. *Ibid.*
[21] 6. 1-3. *Ibid.*

dent will be able to assign to each the words which properly
belong to him. Perhaps the most beautiful sentence in the
passage and the keynote of this book of lyrical and impassioned poetry is the fourth verse:

"I will heal their backsliding;
I will love them freely;
For my anger is turned away from them."

The following analysis of the book will enable the reader
to grasp the essential details and the progress of the thought:

I. Hosea's own story of misfortune, chapters 1-3 (chapter
2 is parenthetical).

II. Fragments of his oral discourses put in poetical form,
chapters 4-14.
(1) A morally degenerate people, chapters 4. 1-7. 7.
(2) The folly of political alliances, chapters 7. 8-10. 15.
(3) The love of God in calling Israel, chapter 11. 1-11.
(4) Israel ungrateful, chapters 11. 12-12. 14.
(5) Idolatry, the cause of her disaster, chapter 13.
1-16.
(6) Israel's ultimate salvation, chapter 14.

Can we find in the writing evidence of the time or duration
of his ministry? He was already preaching in 743 B. C. while
Jeroboam was still king. In his prediction of the downfall of
the dynasty of Jehu (1. 4) this is implied. Inasmuch as he
does not mention the Syro-Ephraimitish war against Judah,
as we certainly should expect him to do, if he were prophesying at the time, we may conclude that his ministry terminated in 734-733 B. C. or sooner.

The events recorded in chapter one do not require more
than a few years for their consummation, and we may suppose them to have taken place between 750 B. C. and his discovery of Gomer's unfaithfulness three or four years later,
after the birth of his first born. In the meantime he may
have followed the occupation of a priest. There is nothing
against this supposition, and in favor of it is his great interest in cult, his sensitiveness to its perversion, and the meta-

phors drawn from the sacrificial offerings (14. 2). As a priest he gained his intimate knowledge of the debasement of the priesthood and of Canaanitish practices. He may be compared with Luther, who in his early days was a priest of Rome.

In 743 Jeroboam died. A period of anarchy followed during the next six years, and Hosea, first involved in the misfortune in his own house, found himself later implicated in the ruin of the nation. Amos saw the Assyrian peril from a considerable distance. Hosea saw it close at hand and felt it more poignantly. Amos saw farther, Hosea deeper. Amos with indignation uttered his prophecies, while Hosea spoke with the deep concern of one who himself shares in the coming disaster.

SUPPLEMENTARY READING

E. C. Baldwin, *The Prophets,* Chapter IV.

J. A. Bewer, *Literature of the Old Testament,* Chapter VII, pp. 94-99.

William R. Harper, *I. C. C. Introduction to Hosea.*

J. M. P. Smith, *The Prophets and Their Times,* Chapter IV, pp. 55-65.

Biblical Selections—Chapters 1, 3 for narrative; Chapters 2, 4, 6, 11, 14 for discourse.

CHAPTER XXIV

THE PROPHET AS A COUNSELOR

BEFORE considering the life and work of Israel's greatest prophet, we shall do well to examine the content of the book attributed to him. Even a superficial survey will make clear that not all the writing is Isaiah's.

The book falls naturally into four parts. The first section, chapters one to thirty-five, contains his prophetic discourses. They are varied in content, including pungent sermons on reform, poems of great beauty, the account of the prophet's vision in the Temple, his interviews with kings, and the woes which he pronounces against the nations. The social conditions there portrayed, the kings named, the allusions to history belong to the eighth century before Christ, and the author, as we are informed in the opening chapter, was Isaiah, the son of Amos. The second section, chapters thirty-six to thirty-nine, is in the nature of an appendix. It is a historical excerpt from the book of Second Kings, and was probably added to Isaiah's book by an editor. It does, however, pertain to him, and is properly attached to his prophecies. This cannot be said of the next added section, chapters forty to fifty-five. There is all but unanimous agreement among scholars that it is the writing of a prophet of a later age. It presupposes the social and political conditions that prevailed in the sixth century, and not in the eighth. The Jews addressed are not in Jerusalem but in Babylon, and the threat of an Assyrian peril that like a dark cloud hung over the nation of Isaiah's day has given place to the promise of a deliverer, Cyrus, who at the very time when the prophet wrote was about to follow up his successes in southern Babylonia by entering the capital city (538 B. C.). The fourth part, chapter fifty-six to the end of the book, assumes that the Jews have returned from the exile. It was perhaps written about one hundred years after the third section was composed. The book of Isaiah, therefore, in its present form is of composite authorship, its writers living in different times and under widely different conditions. At the moment we are only interested in the first two sections, chapters one to thirty-nine, which pertain to Isaiah, son of Amos, greatest of the eighth-century prophets.

The arrangement of the material in the first section is probably not Isaiah's, but an editor's work. One feels that Isaiah would have placed his inaugural vision in the beginning instead of where it now stands.[1] Moreover, the predictions of the fall of Babylon[2] and of the return of the exiles[3] are evidently due to a postexilic editor, who should have assigned these prophecies to the Deutero Isaiah. However, we need not regard section one as "a prophetic miscellany" without literary unity. It is far from that.

ISAIAH CALLED TO BE A PROPHET

We know almost nothing of Isaiah's life before he became a prophet. He tells us that the vision which determined his career occurred in the year that King Uzziah died. This was 740 B. C., or, according to some authorities, 738 B. C. We may assume that he was twenty-five or thirty years old at that time. His home was in Jerusalem, and he had free access to kings, whether in virtue of the fact that he was a prophet or nobly born, we cannot say. His prophetic work seemed to have terminated in 701. A Jewish writing not earlier than the first century before Christ relates that he met a violent death at the hands of Manasseh. He "was sawn asunder by a wooden saw"—a refinement in cruelty not beyond the imagination of that arch persecutor of the prophets.[4]

In the sixth chapter of our book we have an account of the prophet's inaugural vision. The death of Uzziah by a loathsome disease, universally regarded as a punishment sent by God,[5] brought sorrow and dismay to Isaiah. He had gone to the Temple, that refuge of sorrowing souls, seeking in its

---

[1] Chap. 6.
[2] 14. 4-27.
[3] 34. 11 to 35. 10.
[4] The authenticity of the tradition is questioned.
[5] 2 Chronicles 26. 16-21.

sacred precincts for comfort. It is interesting to note that
the elements in the vision which followed are already present
in the prophet's conscious thought or unconscious experience.   That God should be represented as a king seated
upon a throne, his ample robes falling from him until they
covered the floor, seemed natural, though the effect is heightened in the vision.   Considerable mystery is attached to the
origin and meaning of the seraphim.   The word conveys the
idea of radiance.   Their function was to guard the majesty
of God and to prevent men from coming too near the
ineffable and holy Presence.   Isaiah's reaction to their
antiphonal chant and to the earthquake which shook the
Temple was to overwhelm him with the sense of the holiness of God as a moral quality, a holiness not only pertaining to the divine, but demanded of men.   It is doubtful if
before this time the word had a moral import.   "Holy" was
descriptive of buildings, clothing, trees, sacrificial offerings,
or of persons—priests, kings, and even the prostitutes who
frequented the shrines and temples.

As a corollary of the holiness of God, we have Isaiah's
perception of his own unworthiness.   "Woe is me! for I am
undone; because I am a man of unclean lips and I dwell in
the midst of a people of unclean lips."   He feels himself
incapable of addressing the august Being in whose presence
he stands.   Then flew one of the "shining ones" with a burning coal from off the incense altar, and with it he touched
the lips of the prophet.   There seems to have been in this
act a double significance, the cleansing away of impurity by
burning and the bestowment of the gift of prophecy.

The prophet receives his commission, which is the apparently hopeless task of speaking to a people who cannot hear
and of revealing to them visions which they cannot see.   Is
the language of Isaiah retrospective?   Or did Yahweh at
the time of the prophet's commission reveal the hopeless
nature of his task?   The question must remain unanswered,
though it is in keeping with our modern viewpoint to regard
verses nine to twelve as written by Isaiah after some years
of fruitless effort.

The account closes with the prophet's unshaken conviction

that whatever happens, a part of Israel will remain loyal, and from this tenth shall rise a new or restored nation.

Even from this cursory review of the vision, it may be gathered that it contains most of the ideas of Isaiah's prophetic teaching in germ.

THE PROPHET AS A REFORMER

Isaiah's early sermons reveal him as a reformer. In his scathing rebuke of those who oppress the weak, and in his satiric comment upon women of fashion, one catches the echo of Amos.[6] In common with other eighth-century prophets, he recognizes the futility of ritual apart from moral conduct.[7] It is to be observed, however, by those who complain of Isaiah's lack of originality, that he goes farther in his denunciations and that he uses greater art in expression. The figures he employs are heightened. In other words, there are higher lights with deeper shadows. Framing as it were the social message in chapters two to four are two passages of great beauty describing the ideal city, 2. 2-4 and 4. 2-6. It is part of the art of Isaiah to bring together here and elsewhere the striking contrast between the ideal and the real. The reader should observe the comparison between leaderless men seeking a ruler in 3. 6 and homeless women seeking a husband in 4. 1.

THE PROPHET AS A COUNSELOR

Three political crises occurred in Isaiah's life. First was the threatened ruin of Jerusalem in the Syro-Ephraimitish War, when Israel and Syria attacked the city to compel Judah to enter the coalition against Assyria. Ahaz had followed the advice of the prophet in keeping out of an entangling alliance, but brought consternation to Isaiah when he bought with a great sum of money the interference of the Assyrian ruler. Isaiah correctly reasoned that Assyria would find it to its own advantage to destroy the coalition and that it was unnecessary for Judah to pay its way to freedom. Moreover, the prophet distrusted any alliance with a

[6] 3. 16-26; compare Amos 4. 1-3.
[7] 1. 10-17.

foreign power, feeling that it compromised Jerusalem and paved the way to the acceptance of foreign gods.[8]

The second crisis was the fall of Samaria in 722 B. C. Isaiah must have contemplated the disaster with mixed feelings. He could not believe that Sargon's God was superior to the God of Israel. It was Yahweh who permitted, nay brought the disaster as a punishment for Samaria's guilt.[9]

"Woe to the proud crown of the drunkards of Ephraim
And the fading flower of his glorious beauty."

But this is to be a warning to Judah, for Jerusalem will not go unpunished for similar transgressions.[10]

Did Isaiah believe, as many writers declare, in the inviolability of the city and its Temple? It is difficult to say, since he frequently speaks of the threatening advance of Assyria, although elsewhere he proclaims his belief in the continuance of the city as a habitation for its people. He could imagine what occurred long afterward (597 B. C.) when Jerusalem surrendered to its invaders, when its principal people were carried away captive; but what happened at the second surrender, the destruction of the city, the razing of its walls, the burning of its buildings, he does not contemplate. Jerusalem was the city of the great King and the Temple his dwelling place. How could both be destroyed![11]

The most dramatic incident in Isaiah's career came at the close of his ministry. In the year 701 B. C. the Assyrian king sent a military force against the small states in Western Asia. First Phoenicia, then Philistia fell. Their allies, an Arabian or Egyptian army, were routed in the south. Forty-six garrison cities of Judea surrendered. Apparently two attempts were made to capture Jerusalem. In the first instance the Assyrians were diverted by the payment of a heavy tribute, to pay which Hezekiah even stripped the Temple of its gold.[12] Later in the year a second Assyrian army advanced, demanding unconditional surrender.[13] While the impregnable situation of Jerusalem enabled the Hebrews

---

[8] Cf. 2 Kings 16. 1of.
[9] 28. 1-6.
[10] 28. 7-22.
[11] 4. 3-6.
[12] 2 Kings 18. 13-16.
[13] 2 Kings 18. 17f.

to hold out, they faced a shortage of provisions, and it seemed to be only a question of time before the city would have to capitulate. The morale of the people was running low, their condition desperate, and the king at his wits end. At this juncture the prophet came forward with his assuring words. The Temple, he declared, was inviolable and the city could not fall. His prediction was fulfilled. The Assyrian army suddenly withdrew. Why we shall never know because of the legendary encrustations[14] which adorn the account, but it is probable that an outbreak of cholera or other infectious disease spread with such rapidity in the Assyrian army that the commander in alarm withdrew his forces. Jerusalem was again spared, destined to stand for another hundred years.

MICAH

Micah was a contemporary of Isaiah but does not seem to have begun his prophetic career until Samaria fell. He is the last, therefore, in chronological order of the eighth-century prophets.

He was an inhabitant of the Shepelah. The unimportant village associated with his name was Mareshah. Accustomed to rural simplicity, actuated by the stern morality of the nomad, when chance or necessity took him to the city he looked with reproving eyes upon the vices there prevalent. The social injustice which Amos had denounced in the Northern Kingdom was part and parcel of Judah, especially its capital. He was impressed with the futility of sacrifice and ritual on the part of a morally corrupt priesthood. He is extreme in his denunciation predicting that:

> "Zion shall be plowed like a field,
> Jerusalem shall become ruins."[15]

He is credited with the prophecy, that out of an unimportant city of Judah, Bethlehem, shall come a ruler of Israel, whose origins are of old, from ancient days.[16]

---

[14] Cf. 2 Kings 19. 35; also Herodotus's account.
[15] 3. 12.
[16] 5. 2.

While the content of his book is small, he has found room
for the inclusion of a conception of religion that sums up all
the best that the eighth-century prophets had taught.[17]   One
must read this passage as if it were dialogue in which we
have for speakers, the prophet and man.

Man—   Wherewith shall I come before the Lord
            And bow myself before God most high?
            Shall I come before him with burnt-offerings,
            With calves a year old?

Prophet—Will the Lord be pleased with thousands of rams,
            With myriad rivers of oil?

Man—   Shall I give my first born for my transgression,
            The fruit of my body for the sin of my soul?

Prophet—He hath showed thee, O Man, what is good:
            And what doth the Lord require of thee
            But to do justly, and to love mercy
            And to walk humbly with thy God?

SUPPLEMENTARY READING

E. C. Baldwin, *The Prophets,* Chapters V, VI.
J. A. Bewer, *Literature of the Old Testament,* Chapter VIII.
S. R. Driver, *Introduction to the Literature of the Old Testa-
ment,* Chapter III (205-218).
John P. Peters, *The Religion of the Hebrews,* Chapters XIV,
XV.
George Adams Smith, *Expositors Bible, Book of the Twelve,
Micah.*
H. P. Smith, *Religion of Israel,* Chapter VIII.
J. M. P. Smith, *The Prophets and Their Times,* Chapters V, VI.
Biblical Selections: Isaiah's Call, 6. 1f.; As a Reformer, 3. 1ff.;
As a Counselor, 7. 3-17; 37. 21-38; Summary of His Teach-
ing, Chapter 1; His Confident Hope, 4. 2-6; 9. 6f.; 11. 1f.;
32. 1f.; 33. 17f.; Keynote of His Message, 26. 3-4; 7. 9;
Micah's Prediction of the Fall of Jerusalem, 3. 9-12; of the
Messiah, 5. 2; God's Requirement of Man, 6. 6-8 (one of the
most celebrated passages in the Old Testament).

---
[17] 6. 6-8.

CHAPTER XXV

IN THE DAYS OF JEREMIAH

JEREMIAH'S life and times are told in the book which bears his name. One experiences no difficulty in detecting the thread of narrative which runs through its pages, describing the relation of his colorful life to momentous events. He lived during the decline and fall of the Judean state and his prophecy may be regarded as its swan song.

His words are self-revealing. His sensitiveness to circumstance is expressed in laments, complaints, protests; he is subject to bursts of indignation and to despairing moods. The willingness of Isaiah to receive a divine commission finds no counterpart in Jeremiah, who reluctantly accepts the rôle of prophet. He obeys because he must. He pleads his inexperience and feels the hopelessness of the undertaking. He is certain that the nation is in no mood to hear him.[1] He might have said with Hamlet:

> "The time is out of joint: O cursed spite,
> That ever I was born to set it right!"

The event, as it happened, justified his prediction. He found himself arrayed against his fellow townsmen, against prophet and priest, against princes and rulers. He never married, so no children perpetuated his name.[2] He died in exile, disillusioned by his countrymen and disappointed in his expectations, leaving to posterity to pronounce the verdict of success or failure.

No prophet of the Old Testament lived through such stirring times. First from Anathoth, his native village, and later from Jerusalem, he watched the procession of important events which shook not only the little kingdom of Judah but far distant empires—the threat of a Scythian invasion,

---

[1] 20. 7f.
[2] 16. 1, 2.

the discovery of the book of Deuteronomy in the Temple
archives, the fall of Nineveh, bringing to an end the great
Assyrian Empire; the tragic death of Josiah, Judah's noble
king; the decisive battle of Carchemish, which broke Egypt's
power in Asia and established the Chaldean; the siege of
Jerusalem and the surrender of the elite of her population.
After that the worse happened. Jerusalem was besieged a
second time and destroyed. Only the smoking ruins of her
Temple and palaces remained to testify to the power of a
relentless foe. Some of the villages of Judea were spared,
and the rural inhabitants generally speaking escaped the
second exile. Under the shadow of these events Jeremiah
lived. They explain his personality, they interpret his book.

THE SCYTHIAN INVASION

The external circumstance that led to the prophet's call was
the threatened invasion of a people from the north.[3] Near
the beginning of Jeremiah's ministry a fierce and warlike
race, having kinship with those who later ravaged Europe,
left their home east of the Caspian Sea and made inroads
upon the fertile crescent. Herodotus tells us that they were
twenty-eight years in Western Asia and would have attacked
Egypt had they not been turned back by the promise of rich
gifts. The Greek historian is an uncertain authority for
this particular epoch and has given us little real evidence.
But it seems fairly certain that the Scythians first attacked
Media, were bought off, and then as mercenaries aided both
Medes and Babylonians to conquer Nineveh. This happened several years after Jeremiah began his ministry.
When they first appeared on the horizon they were an unknown foe and described only in general terms, "a people
from the north," fierce and implacable, riding swift horses,
unerring marksmen, who by pillaging and burning terrorized
the villages and towns of western Asia.

That Jeremiah meant the Scythians, and not another people, seems probable from the vision of the caldron in the
north,[4] the fiery contents of which were to be poured out on

[3] 1. 14; 4. 19-26.
[4] 1. 13.

the south, and also from the poems in chapter 4, the language of which seems to point in this direction.

"My anguish, my anguish, I am pained at my very heart,
My heart is disquieted within me, I cannot hold my peace;
Because thou hast heard, O my soul, the sound of the
    trumpet,
The alarm of war.

"Destruction upon destruction is cried,
For the whole land is spoiled:
Suddenly are my tents destroyed, and my curtains in a
    moment.
How long shall I see the standard and hear the sound of
    the trumpet?

.   .   .   .

"I beheld, and, lo, there was no man, and all the birds of the
    heavens were fled.
I beheld, and, lo, the fruitful field was a wilderness,
And all cities thereof were broken down."[5]

It is difficult to imagine a scene more desolate than the poet has depicted. But the Scythians did not come. Judah for the time being was secured and Jeremiah was discredited as a prophet. What he himself thought about it we may perhaps discern in the words with which he replies to the taunts of his enemies.

"Lo, they continue saying to me,
Where is the word of the Lord?
    Pray let it come!

"Yet I never urged thee to bring trouble upon them,
Nor longed for the fatal day—
    Thou knowest!"[6]

He probably regarded prophecy as conditional. Its fulfillment might be turned aside either by the repentance of the

[5] 4. 19-21, 26.
[6] Compare 17. 15, 16. Old Test., Amer. Tr. J. M. P. Smith, Ed.; University of Chicago Press.

people or because of the compassion of God. In uttering a
prediction a prophet ran a risk; his words might not be
fulfilled, his credit be jeopardized, himself be ridiculed as a
false seer. The meaning of what Jeremiah saw in the potter's
house illustrates this:

"And when the vessel that he made of the clay was marred
in the hand of the potter, he made it again another vessel,
as seemed good to the potter to make it. . . . Behold, as
the clay in the potter's hand, so are ye in my hand, O house
of Israel. . . . If that nation concerning which I have
spoken turn from their evil, I will repent of the evil that I
thought to do unto them."[7]

As a matter of fact, several important predictions of Jeremiah did not fall out as he foretold, or else were only
partially fulfilled. In some instances the punishment was
modified. Apparently, the prophet was altogether mistaken
in his prediction relating to the exiles in Egypt who became a
numerous, influential, and religious people. There is no
hard-and-fast rule by which a prophet's word concerning the
future must come to pass. If the prophet is infallible, why
preach repentance or believe in the freedom of human choice?

THE DISCOVERY OF THE BOOK OF DEUTERONOMY

During the long and evil reign of Manasseh the prophets
were repressed if not actually persecuted.[8] However, they
formed a brotherhood, and from the group emanated a code
of laws aimed against the prevailing immoral practices. The
laws purported to come from Moses and the writing which
contained them has been called "a pious literary forgery,"
which seems unfair since the prophets had caught the spirit
reflected in the early codes and embodied many ancient
decrees. The publication of the book was withheld during
Manasseh's reign and the priests who had shared in its compilation deposited it in the Temple archives. Here it remained until the reign of Josiah, the young and promising
king of Judah, who made its reception possible.[9]

[7] 18. 4, 6, 8.
[8] 2 Kings 21. 16.
[9] 2 Kings 22. 8ff.

There can be no reasonable doubt concerning its identity. It was part of our book of Deuteronomy. It forbade the evils practiced in Manasseh's reign, and positively it stressed three things—moral reform, a central sanctuary, and ritual. It should have pleased both prophet and priest, and it did. When "discovered," it was brought to the king and read to him, to the nobles and to the people, three times in a single day. Wholeheartedly the young king began his work of reform. The Temple, which was regarded as the central sanctuary, was rehabilitated. All other shrines were destroyed; the sacrificial cult and the feast days were observed with new enthusiasm.

Now, what was Jeremiah's relation to all this? He seems to have had no part in the reform. His book contains at the most two references to the Deuteronomic Code, the earlier being favorable and the latter quite the reverse.[10] There have been several explanations of Jeremiah's silence —some critics would say hostility—concerning the new code.

It is suggested that Jeremiah, as a discredited prophet, was given no part in the reform movement; that he was out of sympathy with a code which emphasized the religion of the Temple; that he suspected the book to be a literary forgery, and to this refers in the words:

> "How can you say, 'We are wise
> And the law of the Lord is with us?'
> When lo! the lying pen of the scribes
> Has turned it into a lie!"[11]

But the best explanation seems to be that Jeremiah, at first hopeful as to the outcome of moral reforms, with which he was surely in sympathy, felt in the end that these were purely external and therefore short-lived. Some such experience all of us have had who have passed through some sensational religious revival in which the emotions were quickened but conduct remained unchanged.

---

[10] Compare 11. 1-8 with 8. 8.
[11] 8. 8. Old Test., Amer. Tr. Ed. J. M. P. Smith. University of Chicago Press.

Jeremiah's Proposed Reforms

Jeremiah's idea of moral reform stands in striking contrast to the external measures adopted by other religious leaders. In his early sermons, which probably belong to the time when the Deuteronomic Code was being enforced, we find trenchant sayings, strikingly original metaphors, and descriptions vivid and colorful. He may not have felt more keenly than earlier prophets the moral failure of the nation, but he has an original way of expressing himself. He addresses "a backsliding people," who have "forsaken the fountain of living waters to hew for themselves cisterns, broken cisterns, that can hold no water."[12] He despairs of their repentance because it is unreal.

> "Though you wash yourself with lye
>   And use much soap,
>   Your guilt stands marked in my sight."[13]

> "Thou art a swift dromedary traversing her ways,
>   A wild ass trained to the desert,
>   Snuffing the wind in her passion. . . .
>   Who can restrain her lust?
>   None that seek her need weary themselves;
>   In her month they shall find her."[14]

> "You have a harlot's forehead
>   And will not blush for shame."[15]

He pictures himself going through the streets of Jerusalem and searching her open places to see if he could find one man who does justly and aims at honesty. He finds none, and then he concludes:

> "Surely these are the poor folk
>   Who are without sense.

> "I will go to the great men
>   And will speak with them.

[12] 2. 13.
[13] 2. 22.
[14] 2. 23, 24.
[15] 3. 3.

"But these with one accord have broken the yoke
  And burst the bonds."[16]

What kind of a yoke Jeremiah had in mind is found in a famous passage often quoted:

"Stand ye in the ways and see
  And ask for the old paths,
  Where is the good way, and walk therein,
  And ye shall find rest for your souls."[17]

One should compare these words with a similar form of expression used by Jesus.[18]

But Jeremiah's proposed reforms were unheeded. Men find it easier to follow the priest than the prophet.

The fall of Nineveh took place in 612 B. C. Without doubt Jeremiah was informed and reflected upon the act of providence that made the Chaldeans masters in the East. But he passes the event by in silence.

The disaster which befell the nation at Megiddo in the death of Josiah, called forth no word from the prophet save the injunction not to mourn. The young prince Jehoahaz had come to the throne only to be deposed by the Egyptian king. It is doubtful if he reigned even three months before he was sent into exile. For some reason the funeral rites for Josiah had been postponed or protracted and were being celebrated at this very time. In the midst of the weeping people Jeremiah appeared with this dirge:

"Weep ye not for the dead.
  Neither bemoan him:
  But weep sore for him that goeth away,
  For he shall return no more,
  Nor see his native land."[19]

There is a hint in the last couplet that there would be no throne, nor royal house in Jerusalem to which Jehoahaz could return.

Three years later occurred the battle of Carchemish, to

[16] 5. 4, 5.
[17] 6. 16.

[18] Matthew 11. 28-30.
[19] 22. 10.

which the prophet makes no allusion though its significance was not missed. Judah was no longer a vassal of Egypt, but the Chaldeans were their masters who were bound to follow up their successes on the western coast by exacting heavy tribute from the Hebrew state, while Judah, under the ill-advised leadership of Jehoiakim, would rebel. A Chaldean invasion seemed inevitable. Jeremiah determined to act. His prophecies, which had been put in written form by his secretary, Baruch, were read to the people and to the princes; then they were carried to the king. The latter, disturbed by the Cassandralike predictions, destroyed the roll on which they were written. This led to the preparation of another roll with added words. Jeremiah was now embroiled in politics. Through certain fortunate friendships in the court he was able to maintain the stand he had taken.

His political policy may be summed up in one word—submission. The city, he felt, could not escape its destiny. Let the rulers meet it with dignity, apart from foreign alliances and with no effort to escape. This was his consistent policy for twenty years preceding the first surrender of the city and during the troubled years that followed. To us such a policy seems sane and his counsels to people and king wise. But his contemporaries felt different. They called him mad, a pro-Babylonian, and accused him of treason. They arrested him, threw him into a dungeon of mire, heaped upon him every indignity. The mental suffering was greater than the physical injuries he received, as is always the case when the outrageous arrows of fortune fall upon a shy and sensitive spirit. Like Job he deplores the day of his birth:

"Woe is me, my mother, that thou hast borne me,
A man of strife and a man of contention to the whole earth.
Why is my pain perpetual
And my wound incurable
Which refuseth to be healed?
Wilt thou be to me as a deceitful brook,
As waters that fail?"[20]

The last lines express his utter discouragement.

[20] 15. 10, 18. Compare Job 3. 3f.

But Jeremiah is not to be judged by his occasional utterances of despair, the outburst of a sorely tried spirit, chagrined by a situation which appeared to be beyond remedy.

The prophet was in Jerusalem during the siege, some of the time under arrest because of his "defeatist" policy. For two and one half years the people valiantly held out. Doubtless an early surrender, advocated by Jeremiah, would have been wise, but one cannot withhold admiration for a people desperately defending their city, their homes, and Temple. Finally starved out, they capitulated and Jerusalem was reduced to ashes.

According to an incident, preserved in chapter forty,[21] Jeremiah's identity was not at first recognized. He was arrested and put in shackles and led away with other captives. At the border he was made known to the captain of the convoy, and the choice was given him between proceeding as a free man under escort to Babylon, or of returning to the peasantry of Judah. He cast in his lot with the latter. Gedaliah, an enlightened and gifted Hebrew, had been appointed governor of Judea, and had set up a temporary capital in Mispah. To this center Jeremiah came.[22]

The prophet might well conclude as he contemplated the ruin of Jerusalem, the exile of its inhabitants and the small remnant of Judah, that for him and for his people:

"The harvest is past, the summer is ended and we are not saved."[23]

That is to say, the flower and fruitage of life is over. As it happened he was entering upon an Indian summer, the one serene period in his troubled life.

In Gedaliah he found a man of outstanding ability and character, who had been sympathetic with his policy and, like Jeremiah, would have shortened the siege of Jerusalem by an early surrender. Like the prophet, he believed that now the hope of the peasantry lay in peaceful submission, in the cultivation of land, and the payment of tribute to their

[21] 40. 1-5.
[22] 40. 6.
[23] 8. 20.

Chaldean overlords. Gradually peace and prosperity returned to the people of Judah. Fertile valleys and terraced
hills rewarded the efforts of those who sought to turn a
war-stricken land into Eden.[24]

It was too good to last. There followed in quick succession an uprising of discontented leaders with their followers,
the murder of Gedaliah, and the abandonment of the land
for a self-imposed exile in Egypt. Jeremiah and his faithful
secretary are dragged with them to the land of the Pharaohs,
thus giving a semblance of religion to their defection.[25]

Two incidents relating to Jeremiah have been preserved
by Baruch—a prediction of the prophet made in front of the
palace at Daphne that Egypt should be invaded, and the
other, the protest in Pathros against the wives of the exiles,
who were offering sacrifice to the queen of heaven.[26] To the
denunciation of the prophet, the women replied that the
source of all their misfortunes had been the neglect of the
service of the goddess. It need not surprise us that Jeremiah
felt that the outlook of the exiles was hopeless, idolatry succeeding idolatry on the part of a people whose punishment
had taught them nothing.[27]

Did Jeremiah feel that he had failed in achieving his life's
purpose? His counsel, as we have seen, was invariably
rejected. He must have felt the hostility not alone of people
but of circumstance. But through his writing, like a vein of
pure gold, runs the hope of Israel's ultimate restoration. This
unalterable conviction must have sustained him. Posterity,
if not his contemporaries, would justify him. And it has
done so. He is referred to as "the prophet" by the Jews in
Christ's day. Moderns, both Jews and Christians, regard him
as the greatest prophet of Old-Testament times, whose unique
contribution is in the field of personal religion. He was the
first to see the importance of an intimate relationship between
God and man. In contrast to the covenant code of Deuteronomy, so highly esteemed by the prophets and priests of

[24] 40. 10-12.
[25] 41. 1f.; 43. 6, 7.
[26] See 44. 17, a reference to Ashtoreth or Anath. The name is Semitic.
[27] 44. 25f.

his time, Jeremiah predicted the enactment of a new covenant supplanting the old:

"Behold! the days come when I will make a new covenant with the house of Israel and with the house of Judah, not like the covenant made with your fathers when I led them out of Egypt—but this covenant, 'I will put my law within them and I will write it on their hearts.' "[28]

That is to say, life is to be governed by inward principles and the individual held morally responsible.

SUPPLEMENTARY READING

J. A. Bewer, *Literature of the Old Testament*, Chapter XI.

John P. Peters, *The Religion of the Hebrews*, Chapters XVI, XVII

George Adams Smith, *Jeremiah.*

Henry P. Smith, *Religion of Israel*, Chapter IX.

J. M. P. Smith, *The Prophets and Their Times*, Chapter VII, p. 110f.; Chapter IX.

Wood and Grant, *The Bible as Literature*, Chapter VII.

Biblical Selections: 1. 4-10, Prophet's call; 20. 1-3, His arrest; 36. 4-32, Writings destroyed; 37. 11f., Again arrested and thrown into a dungeon; 39. 11-14, Chaldean offer of amnesty; 40. 6f., With a remnant of Israel in Palestine; 43. 6ff., The prophet in Egypt; 51. 59-64, Last words.

[28] 31. 31-34.

CHAPTER XXVI

THE VISIONS OF EZEKIEL

WHEN Jerusalem first surrendered to the Chaldeans (597 B. C.) many of its leading citizens were sent captive to Babylon. Among them was a young priest of the house of Zadok, Ezekiel.

He seems to have been a man of assured social position and owning his own house.[1] He was married, and touchingly referred to his wife at the time of her death as one who had been "the delight of his eyes."[2] Having lost his priestly office on account of the exile, he spent his time in reflecting upon the vicissitudes of his country, its corrupt morals, and the fatality that had overtaken Jerusalem.

In the fifth year of his captivity occurred the inaugural vision by which he became a prophet. During the remainder of his life he exercised the prophetic function, but the priest in him overshadowed the prophet. There are several examples of this in his writing which we may cite: the reference in the fourth chapter to an unpleasant symbolic act from which a modern would have turned away in disgust, but which he avoided lest it render him ceremonially unclean.[3] The repeated use of the expression, "they profaned my sabbaths," represents the priestly point of view, while the vision of a restored Jerusalem is seen through the eyes of the sacerdotalist.

We must also in our interpretation of the prophet view him as a mystic. In a very true sense his book is a piece of imaginative writing. No one can fail to see the prominent place given to visions, to symbolic acts, and to a restored Jerusalem.

It may be well at this point to inquire concerning the nature of a vision. It is not a revelation of something previously

[1] 8. 1.
[2] 24. 16—The year of her death was 586 B. C.
[3] 4. 14.

unknown. It is not objective, but lies within the mind of the
observer. It may be regarded as a spiritual illumination, or
simply as the concentration or focus of thoughts that have
been in the mind of the recipient. The time element is unimportant, a period of many days being compressed into a few
seconds.[4] It is always a present moment in the consciousness
of the beholder, but every element in the vision pertains to
the past. If we can regard the visions of Ezekiel in some
such way, and interpret the expression, "the hand of the Lord
was upon me," as denoting a trance, the narrative at once
becomes intelligible.

An additional observation seems necessary. The vision as
related in the book may not be the vision as the prophet first
perceived it. The difficulty of visualizing what Ezekiel
describes in chapter one is on account of its complex nature.[5]
It is a spectacle or a pageant which could not be embraced in
a single glance by the prophet or his readers any more than
Holman Hunt could have perceived in a mental image all the
detail in his painting, "The Light of the World."

The original visual image of the prophet was lost, buried
as it were under accretions, for the theologian in Ezekiel had
dwelt upon the scene, gradually adding details which gave it
greater significance but which contributed to its complexity.
It is interesting that Raphael in his Vision of Ezekiel has
eliminated the detail and given a scene which can be comprehended in a single glance. The early church, ever on the
watch for symbolism, and finding it in the prophet's inaugural
vision, employed the same discriminating power, perceiving
only the Divine Being upborne by the four figures of the
angel, the lion, the ox, and the eagle—the respective symbols,
they thought, of the four Gospels.

In contrast to Ezekiel's difficult and obscure account of his
prophetic call, one should study Isaiah's inaugural vision,[6]
distinguished alike for majesty and simplicity. In the one
case we have an impression gained in a glance, and in the
other a vision plus the reflections of the prophet.

---

[4] 4. 4-6.
[5] 1. 4-28.
[6] Isaiah 6. 1f.

A Vision of Jerusalem

In chapters eight to ten we find the account of the prophet's visit to Jerusalem. The language makes it clear that this transference of himself from Babylon to Jerusalem was not actual but imaginary. While in a trance he sees himself transported through the air and deposited by the north gate of the Temple.

"And a spirit lifted me up between earth and heaven, and brought me in visions of God to Jerusalem 'to the door of the north gate.' "[7]

By a series of vivid pictures he describes the profanation of the sanctuary by idolatry. Near the entrance stood an idol, probably the image of the Babylonian goddess Ishtar.[8] Ezekiel does not identify the deity save to say that it was an image which aroused his resentment or jealousy. Within the Temple proper upon the walls were engraved representations —"reptiles and beasts, and all the idols of Israel,"—while before them were the seventy elders swinging their censers.[9]

Again he came to the northern gate, and here he found women lamenting for Tammuz, the Babylonian god of fertility, whose death, symbolical of the decay of vegetation, these women of Israel mourned.[10] And, finally, within an inner court, he saw twenty-five men whose backs were turned to the Temple, that they might worship the rising sun.[11] It was because of these idolatrous practices that Jehovah had forsaken his Temple to dwell in the mountains of the north.[12] The time was ripe, thought Ezekiel, for the destruction of the city and its sanctuary.

It may be inquired, since the journey was a vision and imaginary, if the Temple practices were imaginary also. Not, if we remember what occurred in Manasseh's reign and was repeated when Jehoiakim ruled, a period of reaction to the reforming zeal of Josiah. Certainly, Jeremiah's witness is conclusive, and we may well believe that Ezekiel previous to exile as a priest in the Temple had plenty of first-hand knowl-

[7] 8. 3.
[8] Compare 2 Kings 21. 3, 7.
[9] 8. 10, 11.
[10] 8. 14.
[11] 8. 16.
[12] See 1. 4 and 9. 2-3.

edge of idolatrous practices. The horror of the young priest
can well be understood, and his prediction that cleansing could
only come by burning was natural.[13]

The Vision of the Valley of Dry Bones

The student of the book of Ezekiel will observe that the
prophecy falls into three well-defined divisions: utterances
against Jerusalem (1-24), the oracles against foreign nations
(25-32), and the promises relating to the restoration of Israel
(33-48). In the third division he shows with meticulous care
the steps leading to his major prediction, a restored Jerusalem.
He asserts that Israel will return though it means "life from
the dead." The vision which he relates is for the sake of a
despondent people who say, "Our bones are dried up, our
hope is lost."[14]

The vision vividly described is seen by the prophet while in
a trance. He is taken to a valley where God had appeared to
him at the first. Scattered on the surface of the great plain
are the bones of an innumerable host, and over these he is
commanded to prophesy. As he speaks bones unite with
bones, flesh clothes them and the wind of God blows upon
them. "They lived, and stood upon their feet, an exceeding
great army."[15]

It must be understood that the prophet was not predicting
the resurrection of the dead, a dogma not developed until a
much later day, but the moral resurrection of his people which
was essential, if Jerusalem was once again to be inhabited.

Vision of Jerusalem Restored

In chapters forty to forty-eight we come to his last recorded
vision. A considerable period of time had elapsed between
the prophecies uttered in chapter thirty-nine and those which
follow. The prophet tells us that it is the twenty-fifth year
of his captivity (572 B. C.) when these visions occurred.
Here more than in any previous experience the succession of
prophetic pictures shows the marks of a carefully thought-out

[13] 24. 1-14.
[14] 37. 11.
[15] 37. 1-10.

plan. One is tempted to conclude that he is employing the vision as a literary device by which he can make his prophecy concrete.

His predictions include a rebuilt Temple, a holy priesthood, a revivified land, and the division of the territory among the twelve tribes now restored.

The provisions made for governing the new state, particularly those relating to the Temple, the priesthood and the sacrificial cult, are of great interest to us, because they reveal Ezekiel's point of view. Here, he is not a prophet but a priest, emphasizing sacrifice as essential to an approach to God.

As we have already seen, the eighth-century prophets and Jeremiah have repudiated sacrifice. There is no other inference to be drawn from their language, unless we do violence to its meaning. Professor C. B. Gray does not put the case too strongly when he says: "It is not the institution but the repudiation of sacrifice that distinguishes the religion of Israel."[16] Here are some of the well-known passages, most of which separately have been called to our attention, but they receive additional confirmation when considered together.

Amos declares as an oracle: "I hate, I despise your sacrificial feasts. . . . Yea, though thou offer me your burnt offerings and meal offerings, I will not accept them; . . . but let justice roll down as waters and righteousness as an overflowing stream."[17]

Hosea's attitude is seen in the oft-quoted statement: "I desire mercy and not sacrifice; and the knowledge of God more than burnt offerings."[18]

Isaiah is more severe: "To what purpose is the multitude of your sacrifices, saith the Lord. I have had enough of the burnt offering of rams, . . . and I delight not in the blood of bullocks or of lambs or of he-goats. . . . Your new moons and your appointed feasts my soul hateth; they are a trouble unto me."[19]

Micah's definition of religion gains, force from the contrast afforded by a futile ritual. Speaking for Israel the prophet says: "Wherewith shall I come before the Lord, and

[16] I. C. C., Isaiah, p. 17.
[17] Amos 5. 21, 22, 24.
[18] Hosea 6. 6.
[19] Isaiah 1. 11, 14.

bow myself before the high God? Shall I come before him with burnt offerings? Will the Lord be pleased with thousands of rams or ten thousands of rivers of oil? Shall I give my first born, the fruit of my body, for the sin of my soul? He hath shewed thee, O man, what is good; *and what doth the Lord require of thee but to do justly and to love mercy and to walk humbly with thy God?*"[20]

Jeremiah goes even further than the prophets cited, for he not only unites with them in repudiating sacrifice, but denies that divine sanction was ever given. "Thus saith the Lord of Hosts, the God of Israel: Add your burnt offerings unto your sacrifices and eat ye flesh. For I spake not unto your fathers, nor commanded them in the day that I brought them out of Egypt, concerning burnt offerings and sacrifices."[21] The first statement is to be regarded as ironical, and the second stigmatizes the sacrificial cult as a man-made ritual—which, indeed, it was.

To the student of religion constantly on the watch for new elements and rejuvenating forces to arrest decay, the work of Ezekiel to re-establish the sacrificial cult is a matter of great regret.

While some of the features of the new theocratic state remain only a prophet's dream, those relating to a rebuilt Temple and the re-establishment of sacrifice were carried out by the Jews who returned from Babylon. Legalism at that time became dominant. The message of the great prophets of the past was forgotten. Increased emphasis was laid upon ceremonials. A contemporary or follower of Ezekiel worked upon the Holiness Code, embodied in Leviticus 17-26, defining with minute distinction the difference between clean and unclean, frequently confusing moral issues with ceremonial requirements. In the time of Ezra we have the publication of the Priests' Code and later the work of the Priestly writers. Legalism remained triumphant throughout the course of Jewish history from the beginning of the second Temple until its destruction in 69 A. D. Ezekiel cannot be absolved from responsibility for this. He has well been called "the father of

---

[20] Micah 6. 6-8.
[21] Jeremiah 7. 21, 22.

Judaism," for the legalism he stressed became the dominant
feature of Jewish religion. The parasite that fed upon this
vigorous growth was Pharisaism.

It is true that Ezekiel pictured a Temple where sacrificial
gifts were brought by a spiritual people and offered to God
by a sanctified priesthood, but even so, his view of what God
required was a mistaken one, nor could he guarantee that
formalism, the invariable accompaniment of such ritual,
would not creep in.

That Ezekiel acted unknowingly in his endorsement of the
sacrificial cult we cannot believe. He knew what his predecessors, the prophets, had taught. The issue was clear; on the
one hand the repudiation of sacrifice, on the other, the establishment and endorsement of cult. As Christ and his followers stood arrayed against priest and Pharisee, an ethical and
spiritual religion opposed to legalism, so in Ezekiel's day are
two religious opinions, the one held by Jeremiah and the
eighth-century prophets, the other, the ritualism of priests
and Deuteronomists. Ezekiel was a Deuteronomist, believing
in a central sanctuary and the permanence of the sacrificial
cult. Doubtless, the prophet had in mind practical considerations, that only through sacrificial offerings could religion
be preserved, that the priests of the Temple should be supported, that the people of the land would not willingly suffer
the abandonment of what had always meant much to them,
the annual sacrificial feasts.

The reply to this is that a reasonable ritual in the Temple
worship and the synagogue would preserve the Jewish church
from disintegration. Present-day Judaism, as we know, survives having only the synagogue as its rallying point. Priests
could be supported by free-will offerings and the annual feasts
continue apart from sacrifice. The Jews returning to Jerusalem after the exile faced a glorious opportunity—that of
building upon the foundation of the prophets a spiritual
church. Instead, legalism triumphed and the stream of early
prophetic thought disappeared, not to emerge until Christ
taught his new ethic and replaced the letter of the law with
the spirit.

There are other strictures upon Ezekiel's prophetic work.

He was narrowly exclusive in his ethical views, in his conception of God and the religion of the future.   In his ethic he
seems to have forgotten character and stressed only the wrong
or right of deeds.   For a single act of wickedness a sinner
will die; for a single righteous act the righteous man will
live.[22]   Undoubtedly, this influenced his view of Israel's past.
Few writers have so misinterpreted history.   One gains the
impression from his writing that he believed Israel had gone
wrong from the beginning, that the history of the nation was
a record of only evil continually, finding its climax in the
moral corruption that preceded the destruction of Jerusalem
(chapters 16 and 23).

It has been said that while Ezekiel did not believe in a
universal religion, he did accept a universal God.[23]   That is
only partly true, since he places the throne of God in Jerusalem, which is henceforth to be called by a name which means
"God is there."[24]

In his picture of the future he contemplates only the blessedness of Israel.   Nations war against the theocratic state
only to be utterly destroyed, but none share in the glory of
the people whom God exalts.[25]

. All this in the interest of a true evaluation of the prophet
and his message I think we must concede.   On the other
hand, Ezekiel deserves high praise for his moral earnestness,
his courage and persistence in the face of opposition, and
especially for his contribution to Old-Testament literature of
a book which contains much of permanent value.

SUPPLEMENTARY READING

E. C. Baldwin, *The Prophets,* Chapter XII.
John P. Peters, *The Religion of the Hebrews,* Chapters XVIII,
XIX.
Henry P. Smith, *Religion of Israel,* Chapter IX.
J. M. P. Smith, *The Prophets and Their Times,* Chapter X.
Wood and Grant, *The Bible as Literature,* Chapter VIII.

---

[22] 33. 10-16.
[23] J. A. Bewer, *Literature of Old Testament,* "Ezekiel."   Columbia
Press.
[24] 37. 27, 28.
[25] Chap. 39.

Biblical Selections: Chapters 1-3, The Inaugural Vision; chapter
8, The Idolatrous Cults of Jerusalem; 16. 1-22, The Foundling;
chapter 27, The Merchant Ship, chapter 37, The Valley of
Dry Bones; chapter 47, The Fertilizing River.

CHAPTER XXVII

THE UNKNOWN PROPHET

TWENTY-FIVE years after Ezekiel had concluded his prophetic work by painting a glowing picture of a restored Jerusalem, another voice is heard in Babylon. We do not know the name of this prophet. He has been called the Deutero Isaiah because his prophetic utterances have been attached to the writing of the first Isaiah. But no title is satisfactory. He must remain to posterity as the "Great Unknown." Scholars are all but unanimous in assigning to him Isaiah, chapters forty to fifty-five, a section which presupposes conditions prevalent in western Asia in the sixth century. Cyrus, a Persian prince, at this time was at the height of his military career. He had conquered Media, followed his success by a series of victories over western states, among them Lydia, whose ruler Croesus was famous for his fabulous wealth, and next turned to the south, defeating Nabonidus, the king of Babylon.

No one watched with more interest the military successes of Cyrus than the Unknown Prophet, who hailed him as the deliverer of the Jews in Babylon.

The call of the prophet to his task is implied rather than directly related. In the opening chapter of his prophetic utterances, we hear the voice of Yahweh summoning his messenger.[1]

"The voice of one that crieth,
    Prepare ye in the wilderness the way of the Lord;
    Make level in the desert the highway of our God."

. . . .

The opening line is repeated and is yet more urgent:
    "The voice of one saying, Cry"—

---

[1] 40. 3-8.

Then the response:

"What shall I cry? All flesh is grass,
And all its beauty is like the flower of the field.
The grass withers, the flower fades,
Because the breath of the Lord blows upon it."

But the objection is met in almost the very words of the reluctant messenger:

"Surely the people are grass,
The grass withers, the flower fades,
But the word of our God shall stand forever."

The task of the prophet is difficult. He is to inspire the faint-hearted with courage, to awaken a lethargic and indifferent people to the consciousness of their destiny, to proclaim as a reality the dream of deliverance.

Most of the exiles had been born in Babylon; those who had not been came as children to this country. They were satisfied with their material condition. For the most part they had prospered and had no intention of sacrificing their present security for a vague, unknown future. Probably a few nourished in their hearts the hope of national restoration, but the difficulties in realizing it were many. Doubtless they reasoned that if Cyrus entered Babylon and granted a general amnesty to the Jews, they would return to a Persian colony. They would not achieve independence but simply a change of masters. There was so much sanity in this view that the task of changing the mental attitude of the exiles would require superhuman power. To the accomplishment of this task, however difficult, the Unknown Prophet sets himself.

The ideas which are successively developed in chapters forty to fifty-five show us how the prophet sought to accomplish the seemingly impossible. It is to be noted that he emphasizes the spiritual resources of Israel and keeps spiritual ends in view. Thus he strikes a different note from the earlier prophet of the exile. The truths that the Unknown Prophet enunciates are universal, and the literary expression faultless. It is not without reason that Gladstone speaks of Isaiah 40 as the grandest chapter in the Old Testament. The flowing

style and the lyric beauty of the interpolated songs loaned
themselves to Handel's oratorio, which in its recitative parts
is a transcript of the prophet's words.

The prophet begins with the revelation of a compassionate
and forgiving God:

> "Comfort, O comfort my people,
>> Says your God,
> Speak to the heart of Jerusalem
>> And call to her . . .
> That her time of service is ended,
>> That her guilt is paid in full,
> That she has received of the Lord's hand
>> Double for all her sins."[2]

He reminds his people that the magnificence of Babylon, the
might of her armies, and all her beauty, is like the flower of
the field. All is ephemeral, but the word of God shall stand
forever.

In a flight of imagination he sees himself in Jerusalem,
standing with the watchers on mountain heights:

> "O thou that tellest good tidings to Zion,
>> Get thee up on a high mountain;
> O thou that tellest good tidings to Jerusalem,
>> Lift up thy voice with strength;
>> Lift it up, be not afraid;
> Say unto the cities of Judah,
>> Behold, your God!"[3]

The prophet is impressed with the goodness and gentleness
of God:

> "Behold his reward is with him
> And his recompense before him
> He shall feed his flock like a shepherd.
> He shall gather the lambs in his arms
> And carry them in his bosom,
> And shall gently lead those that have their young."[4]

---

[2] Verses 1, 2. Old Test. Amer. Tr. Ed. J. M. P. Smith. University
of Chicago Press.
[3] Verse 9.
[4] Verses 10, 11.

Then in contrast he proclaims his omnipotence:

"Who hath measured the waters in the hollow of his hand,
And meted out heaven with the span,
And comprehended the dust of the earth in a measure,
And weighed the mountains in scales
And the hills in a balance?"

.   .   .   .

"Lift up your eyes on high,
And see who hath created these,
That bringeth out their host by number:
He calleth them all by name;
By the greatness of his might
And the strength of his power
Not one is lacking."[5]

He ridicules the worship of images, identifying the gods of Babylon with their idols. What folly to worship pieces of wood overlaid with silver and gold! He prophesies the downfall of the false gods:

"Bel crouches, Nebo cowers;
Their idols are consigned to beasts;
They are laid as a load upon weary cattle.
.   .   .   themselves go into captivity."[6]

In never-to-be-forgotten words he declares the unity of God:

"And know that I am God, and there is none else;
The true God and none like me."[7]

In daring words he prophesies the downfall of Babylon, comparing the city to a humbled slave girl:

"Come down and sit in the dust,
O Virgin, daughter of Babylon;
Sit on the ground without a throne,
O daughter of the Chaldeans:
For no more shall you be called
Tender and delicate.

---

[5] Verses 12, 26.
[6] 46. 1, 2. Old Test. Amer. Tr. Ed. J. M. P. Smith. University of Chicago Press.
[7] 46. 9.

Take millstones and grind meal,
   Remove your veil,
Strip off the train, lay bare the leg,
   Pass through the rivers.
Thy nakedness shall be laid bare,
   Yea, thy shame shall be seen."[8]

The unconscious agent, who effects the redemption of Israel, is Cyrus. He is simply an instrument carrying out the divine plan. But eventually he comes to know that Israel's God is the sole Deity.

"Who saith of Cyrus, He is my shepherd
And shall fulfill all my pleasure.

·   ·   ·   ·   ·   ·   ·   ·   ·
Cyrus, whose right hand I have grasped
To subdue nations before him,

·   ·   ·   ·   ·   ·   ·   ·   ·
I will gird thee, though thou hast not known me,
That men may know from the rising of the sun
And from the west,
That there is none beside me;
I am the Lord and there is no other."[9]

The crowning glory of the Unknown Prophet is perceived in four poems on the servant of Yahweh.[10] The identification of the Servant has caused much speculation. It has been asked, Does the prophet refer to the nation, to a select group or to an individual? The tendency of modern criticism is to identify the Servant with the nation. But there are great difficulties in the way, especially when the last poem on the suffering Servant is thus interpreted. It taxes one's credulity to the utmost to be told that the nations of the world are to stand astounded before Israel, who has suffered vicariously for all the world. If this was the prophet's conception, it is a dream without fulfillment. Neither in the past, nor now, has Israel justified the prediction, nor nations shown repentance.

---

[8] 47. 1-3.
[9] 44. 28; 45. 1, 4-6.
[10] 42. 1-14; 49. 1-6; 50. 4-9 and 52. 13-53. 12.

The interpretation of "the Servant" as referring to a select group has met favor with some scholars. Undoubtedly, the prophet knew that his clarion call would be heeded by only a part of the exiles, and upon these he placed great reliance. But if all his glowing expectations were to be fulfilled in the group that rebuilt Jerusalem, he was doomed to disappointment. Among the returning exiles neither a group, nor individual, rises above mediocrity. Not once in the next four hundred years did an event occur or a personage come forward to justify his predictions. Israel's great leaders with few exceptions were on the other side of the watershed which we call the exile. The last great prophetic voice was that of Deutero-Isaiah himself.

Why may not the prophet have an individual in mind? A persecuted and righteous Jeremiah fulfills the detailed description of the Servant equally as well as the personified nation or group. But the writer is describing one who transcends his race and age, a figure both ideal and real; ideal in that he exhibits the noblest qualities of his race, actual in that he is a servant whose ministry as such can be predicted.[11] If the Old-Testament Messianic hope is a conception including not only the idea of a king in Zion, but a suffering Saviour, who was better fitted to conceive this than the author of the Servant poems, himself a sufferer and unknown?[12]

"Who hath believed our report?

. . . .

Surely he hath borne our griefs
And carried our sorrows,
Yet we esteemed him stricken,
Smitten by God and afflicted.
He was wounded for our transgressions,
He was bruised for our iniquities;
The chastisement of our peace was upon him,
And with his stripes we are healed."[13]

---

[11] 42. 1-4.
[12] One should distinguish the "Servant of Jehovah" in the poems from the title used elsewhere as a personification of the nation (42. 19, 43. 10), and of a spiritual group within the nation (41. 8-9; 44. 1, 2, 21; 45. 4; 48. 20).
[13] 53. 1, 4, 5.

We are not to regard the prophet's words as merely rapturous, a dream fulfilled after the lapse of centuries. There were immediate results. To him more than to any prophet of Israel we owe the conception of a monotheistic faith. To what extent he crystallized the growing conviction among the exiles that there was one God and only one, or whether the discipline of suffering and exile had burned out their idolatry, we cannot be certain. But the fact is patent that Israel did not return to idolatrous cults, but to the monotheism that the Unknown Prophet had proclaimed.

The prophet's noblest conception is the idea of a universal God and a universal religion. The misgivings we felt in contemplating Ezekiel's restored Jerusalem vanish. Israel's redemption was near at hand, but it was only a prelude to something infinitely greater, the salvation of the world.[14]

> "Look unto me, and be ye saved
>   All ends of the earth;
> For I am God and there is no other;
>   By myself have I sworn—
> The word is gone forth from my mouth,
>   In righteousness, and shall not return,
> That to me every knee shall bow,
>   Every tongue shall swear."[15]

SUPPLEMENTARY READING

E. C. Baldwin, *The Prophets,* Chapter XIII.

J. A. Bewer, *Literature of the Old Testament,* Chapter XIV.

S. R. Driver, *Introduction to the Literature of the Old Testament,* Chapter III, pp. 230-246.

John P. Peters, *The Religion of the Hebrews,* Chapters XX, XXI.

Henry P. Smith, *Religion of Israel,* Chapter XV.

J. M. P. Smith, *The Prophets and Their Times,* Chapter XI.

Biblical Selections: Chapters 40, 52, 55, and "The Servant" passages designated as 42. 1-4; 49. 1-6; 50. 4-9; 52. 13-53. 12.

[14] 51. 4, 5; 49. 6.
[15] 45. 22, 23.

PART IV

RELIGIOUS THOUGHT IN NEIGHBORING STATES

CHAPTER XXVIII

ZOROASTER AND HIS FOLLOWERS

TRANSITION. In this and the following chapters we turn to two non-Semitic races, the Persians and the Greeks, destined to influence the political fortunes, the social conditions, and, to a limited extent, the religious thought of the Jews. In the preceding section attention was drawn to the former, whose king, Cyrus the Great, had delivered the Jews and subjugated western Asia.

The country from which the conquering race came was known in ancient times as Iran (a name recently restored), and their people Iranians. It once had an area of a million square miles and extended from the Caspian Sea to the banks of the Indus, from the grassy slopes of Turkestan to the Persian Gulf. Such a territory exhibited, as one would suppose, great variations in topography and striking contrasts in climate. It included fertile valleys and mountain ranges, peaks some of which reached an elevation of thirteen thousand feet; sterile deserts and verdant river bottoms, malarial coast lands and salubrious plateaus.

In biblical history the inhabitants of Iran were known as Medes and Persians, but they were the same racial stock, distinguished only by political divisions which were later wiped out. Their linguistic affinities with Indo-European peoples is proved by the more than five hundred words which are the common property of this division of the human race, often designated as Aryan, although the word accurately designates the Persian and Indian branches, since it is derived from Iran.[1]

Where was the early home of the Aryan people before they separated? According to an early supposition, it was in Central Asia, and from this starting point there were migrations southward into Iran and India, while others moved westward

[1] Racial designations are invariably misleading.

267

appearing successively in Babylonia, Asia Minor, Syria, and Europe. In recent times the theory has been advanced that the early Aryan home was southwestern Europe on the grassy plateaus which were suited for the grazing of cattle. From this center there were frequent migrations east and south across Asia Minor, the Euphratean Plain to Iran and India. Later there were western migrations which in time reached the North Sea and the Atlantic coast. A more tenable view than either, acceptable because of its very inexactness, suggests that the early Aryans were groups in central Asia and southern Russia, who about the middle of the third millennium moved southward until they occupied the lands where we find them in historical times.[2] They were a nomadic race, traveling swiftly, for they used the horse, which they had domesticated. They were experts in metallurgy, fashioning superior weapons. These, their swift horses, and the great courage of their warriors made them invariably victors in war. They usually imposed their language upon the defeated, and formed of themselves a small ruling aristocracy in the captured city. In time they intermarried with their dependents and lost their racial purity.

While the Iranians were racially one there were political subdivisions and ethnic groups other than the Medes and Persians. But the latter were dominant, the Medes being the first to attain power and prestige. Before the time of Cyrus, we hear of a Median kingdom which claimed lordship over all Iran and made its influence felt in Assyria[3] and Babylonia. But this dominance was surrendered to Cyrus, who made Persia a great Asiatic Power.

ARYAN RELIGION

Our knowledge of early Aryan religion is derived from meager sources. Archaeology has shed some light, and inferences may be drawn from Zoroastrianism, for no personality is so commanding as to break entirely with the religion of

[2] Cf. A. T. Olmstead, *History of Palestine and Syria,* p. 115. Charles Scribner's Sons.
[3] Nineveh fell in 612 B. C., as the result of a joint attack of Medes and Babylonians, aided by Scythian mercenaries.

the past, nor did Zoroaster make the attempt.   On the contrary, he is careful to tell us in the Gathas that he sought to purify the religion of the land and not to destroy it.[4]

Otto Schrader, in the *Encyclopedia of Religion and Ethics,* has given us a comprehensive survey of the religion of ancient Iran, from which we gather that it was a nature religion, with great stress placed upon the worship of the sun, moon, and stars and the elements of fire, earth and water.   A feature of the early cult was ancestor worship.   The burial of their chief was attended with great pomp.   His body was prepared by being painted over with red ochre—the sign of life—and in the grave with him were placed his valued possessions. Over all was heaped a huge covering of earth.   The extension of such ceremonies after death led to ancestor or spirit worship.   The cultic practice of the Aryans included the worship of daemons or daevas.   This Zoroaster regarded as debasing, for the first step taken by his converts was to renounce the daevas.   Ethical standards were low in the early Aryan society, which may be characterized as cruel, inhuman, and morally corrupt.   The necessity of reformation was paramount when Zoroaster appeared.

LIFE OF ZOROASTER

We know little of Zoroaster save the allusions which come from his own lips and which have been preserved in the Gathas.   In addition we have late traditions as a possible source of knowledge.   While there has been a great deal of argument over the time of Zoroaster, we can accept without much hesitance the traditional date of 660 to 583 B. C.[5]   His birthplace seems to have been northwestern Iran.   His name and the names of members of his family are compounded with names of animals.   This, together with the emphasis in his writings on kindness to animals and the benefits of agriculture and husbandry, bears witness to his origin and early environment.   His call to a meditative life seems to have occurred when he was twenty years of age, but he does not become a

---

[4] Compare Matthew 5. 17.
[5] See George William Carter, *Zoroastrianism and Judaism,* p. 24. Richard G. Badger, Pub.

prophet with a mission to evangelize until he is thirty, when the first of the seven visions or revelations occurred. For twelve years his work was almost fruitless, for he had gained only one follower, his cousin.

THE PROPHET GAINS AN IMPORTANT CONVERT

Zoroaster, or Zarathustra, as he was called in the old Persian, persisted in his mission, leaving his home, where he had been unsuccessful, and journeying as far east as Bactria, where he converted the king, Vishtaspa, to his doctrine. One of the traditions connected with the conversion of the ruler tells us that the king's black horse was sick and that the prophet miraculously cured the animal, thus gaining the attention and the affection of the monarch. Whether this be true or not, there is no doubt about the king's conversion. He became the Constantine of the new faith, and the religion which Zoroaster addressed to individuals was proclaimed the faith of the nation.

ZOROASTER'S TEACHING

The sources of our knowledge of the religion of Zoroaster are found in the Avestan scriptures, a composite work compiled many years after the prophet's time. We can assign only the first part of the Avesta to Zoroaster. This division is called the Yasna and includes in metrical form the Gathas. For Zarathustra's own document we must consult Yasna 28-34, 43-46, 47-50, 51, 53.

Zoroaster's tenets were essentially ethical. He bade his followers to renounce cattle thievery, violence, and above all else lying, which he hated, believing it to be of the utmost importance to distinguish between falsehood and truth. On the positive side of conduct, he taught his followers to esteem good thoughts, good words, and good deeds. We perceive that the doctrine of Zoroaster was at first a thoroughgoing ethical dualism in which he stressed the wide gulf between evil and good.

Little emphasis was placed upon priestly ceremonies and cultic practices. The land had been priest-ridden, and now the pendulum was swinging to the other side. No provision was made for temples or sacrifices. Fire worship remained, but the cult was modified, Zoroaster believing fire to be a symbol. If any importance was attached to ceremonial purification, it was on account of its ethical significance. Superstitious care was observed that the three primal elements, earth, fire, and water, be uncontaminated.

Zoroaster was a practical monotheist. As we have seen, he renounced devil worship. In the Gathas he named Ahura Mazda as supreme Deity, beside whom there was no god. His name meant "wisdom" and his attributes were more than abstract qualities. They were so actual to Zoroaster that he personified them. Collectively they were known as the Amesha Spentas, or the Immortal Beneficent Ones. They appear in the following order: Good, Mind, Right, Sovereignty, Devotion,[6] Welfare, Immortality. Apparently, some of these were originally human qualities but in time became divine attributes. In the development of Zoroastrianism the personified attributes become spirits and finally archangels. Zoroaster's conception of God is quite beautifully summed up in this quotation:[7]

"Who appointed the power of the sun and the stars?
Who is it by whose power the moon waxes and wanes?
Who founded the earth beneath and the heavens above in such
    wise that they do not fall?
Who created water and plants?
Who gave the wind and clouds their speed?
Who in his goodness made light and darkness, sleep and wake-
    fulness?
Who made morning, noon, and night to remind the wise man
    of his duty?"

Zoroastrianism is distinguished by its ethical dualism, that is, it is relative not absolute. The prophet regards evil as existent from the beginning, tracing it back to a primeval, wicked spirit, but leaves the question of origin undecided.[8] He speaks with finality concerning the future. The long con-

[6] Or humble piety.
[7] Citation from Carl Clemen, *Religions of the World*, p. 143. Harcourt, Brace and Company, Inc.
[8] So Jewish and Christian theologians.

flict between right and wrong, in which the arch participants are Ahura Mazda and Angra Mainu,[9] will be concluded by the victory of righteousness.   This, it will be observed, is moral, not metaphysical dualism.   It is a practical, optimistic view of the end of human society.

Zoroaster reasoned that the conquest of evil could only be effected through its utter destruction, a view which paved the way for his doctrine of retribution, which resembled closely that of medieval theology.   One of his most striking metaphors is that of the bridge which crosses the abyss of hell.   This bridge is wide for the righteous and keeps growing wider, while for the wicked it narrows until finally it becomes a razor's edge on which it is impossible for them to stand. In hell the wicked are crowded so closely together that hair touches hair, yet each is conscious of his isolation.   At the conclusion of a single day the prisoner asks how many years of the nine thousand of his captivity have already passed. Undoubtedly, some of these cruel predictions bearing on the future state of the wicked are refinements of a later theological age and are not to be credited to Zoroaster.   However, we must concede that the prophet was intolerant and that his moral code was so strict that it made conformity next to impossible.   Even the sympathetic critic of Zoroastrianism is obliged to view it as a hopeless faith, because it taught men to save themselves, when they were powerless to do so.

LATER ZOROASTRIANISM

The history of Zoroaster's religion in the centuries that followed the prophet's death may be briefly summarized. When Macedonia conquered Persia, Zoroastrianism received all but a deathblow.   It is said that Alexander destroyed an original copy of the Gathas.   Whether this be a fact or not, it is certain that the program of Greek culture which the conqueror imposed upon Asia would not suffer a previous state religion to be potent.   The period that followed has been called "the dark ages" of Zoroastrianism.   It came to an end in the third century A. D., with the rise of a powerful dynasty, the Sassanids, who ruled from 226 A. D. to 641 A. D.   Then

[9] Another name for the evil spirit is Ahriman.

again Zoroaster's religion became a state affair, and the patronage of the kings of the ruling dynasty contributed much to the propagation of the religion, which was carried as far afield as China. In 637 A. D. we have the Moslem subjugation of Persia. Many of the Zoroastrians succumbed. Others preferred death rather than to yield. The greater part fled to India, finding safety in exile. Here they and their descendants remained. Today their faith numbers ninety thousand adherents, known as Parsi. A feature of their worship, which impresses the modern traveler, is the zealous care paid to the sacred fire, which under no circumstances must go out. Always in attendance are priests, who preserve the symbol of their ancient faith and the eternal God whom they serve. Not less interesting are the circular towers of silence, the resting place of their dead, whose remains are placed between earth and sky, lest they defile the primal elements of earth and water. Always hovering over the towers are vultures waiting for their prey.

In addition to the adherents of the prophet in India, there are about ten thousand Zoroastrians in Persia. Zoroastrianism is therefore a living faith among the religions of mankind, though its days of influence have long since passed.

Zarathustra's egoism appealed to Nietzsche, who describes him as superman. Doubtless to some he has appeared to be a sort of heaven-storming person, Promethean in his fire-snatching, nobly impudent in the manner in which he buttonholes the Almighty and interrogates the sky.[10] It is more likely that the eschatology of later Judaism was evolved from such a seer than from the prophets of Israel and Judah. Probably Von Gall[11] goes too far when he says, contrary to Gunkle and Gressman, that pre-exilic Israel had no eschatological ideas, but admittedly the Hebrew conception of the future was vague and shadowy. The prophetic voices of Israel were contented with moderate statements, and the scene of Israel's glorious future state was laid on earth. There was no dogma of the resurrection of the body, no

---

[10] Citation from George William Carter's *Zoroastrianism and Judaism,* pp. 10, 11. Richard G. Badger, publisher.
[11] See his *Kingdom of God.*

scheme of rewards and punishment after death, following a general Judgment. Judgment there was, but it fell upon a nation having a corporate existence, and destined through discipline and purification to endure as an earthly power. During the two centuries of Persian rule the Jews were in contact with Zoroastrianism, the leading ideas of which must have been congenial to them, namely, a belief in one supreme God, ethical dualism, the doctrine of a coming Saviour, and a lofty code of morals. These tenets were as familiar to Jews as they were to Persians. That the contagion of the apocalyptic ideas would spread in Jewish circles was to be expected. Moreover, the tumult of civil dissensions, the fear of what the future might reveal, loaned color to the expectation. That the spiritual in Israel during the days of Maccabean decadence and dissolution lost faith in any triumph, other than that secured by a direct intervention of God, we very well know. Doubtless, then, they turned to the eschatologists.

In recent years scholars have reverted to the comparative study of Jewish and Persian apocalyptic writing. Numbered among them are the names of Cheyne,[12] Kohut, Lagarde, Meyer, Mills, Moulton,[13] Stave, Scheftelowitz, and Von Gall. Oesterley, in his latest book, sums up a general opinion when he writes, "It is certain that Jewish eschatology is saturated with Persian elements."[14]

The references in the Old Testament and the Apocrypha to Persian contact with Jews are plentiful.[15] While they do not establish the claim that Jewish thought was influenced by Zoroastrianism, they are valuable in indicating the friendly, even intimate, relation between the two races. The Jew and the Persian were living in the same world, trading, intermarrying, and exchanging ideas. So far as there was borrowing, the Jew was the debtor, for the tenets of Zoroaster

---

[12] See *Expository Times*, Vol. II, Nos. 9, 10, 11.
[13] *Ibid.*, Vol. IX, pp. 352-58.
[14] *History of Israel*, Vol. II, p. 168. Oxford Press.
[15] Isaiah 45. 1-3, 13; 44. 28; 41. 2. Daniel 6. 8-12. 2 Kings 17. 6; 18. 11. Ezra 6. 2-5. Esther 1. 19; 6. 1; 10. 2. An apocryphal New-Testament writing states that the magi who visited the child Jesus were Persians and came in obedience to the prophecy of Zoroaster. Apoc. N. T. Infancy 3. 7; compare Matthew 2. 1-2. See also Book of Tobit.

had been formulated before there was any contact between the two states.

SUPPLEMENTARY READING

Edwyn Robert Bevan, *Jerusalem Under the High Priests,* Chapter I.

George William Carter, *Zoroastrianism and Judaism.*

A. V. W. Jackson, *Zoroastrian Studies.*

George F. Moore, *History of Religions,* Vol. I, Chapters XV, XVI.

James Hope Moulton, *Treasure of the Magi.*

W. E. O. Oesterley, *History of Israel,* Vol. II, Chapter XII.

Carl Clemen, *Religions of the World,* 5, *Persian.*

Encyclopedia Britannica, article on "Zoroaster."

Hastings' *Encyclopedia of Religion and Ethics,* article on "Zoroastrianism."

CHAPTER XXIX

HOMERIC RELIGION[1]

TRANSITION. The political ferment in Palestine, coincident with prophetical activity and influencing it, continued until the fall of Jerusalem in 586. The prophets of the exile, Ezekiel and the Deutero-Isaiah, represent their nation in the ebbing tide of its fortunes. If they foresaw the future of their country in the terms of a glorified church rather than a political entity, we need not be surprised. The unrest of the Judean state, its decline and fall were shared by every country in western Asia. In the end there was only one Asiatic power. All lines converged in Persia.

The empire which Cyrus left to his successors was greater in extent and more powerful than any hitherto. It was not content with being an Asiatic power. It threatened Egypt and turned longing eyes toward Europe. A conflict between Persia and Greece was inevitable. The outcome is well known. Egypt fell,[2] but Greece was victorious[3] and in the end penetrated Asia politically and culturally. The political domination was relatively brief but Greek cultural influences continued through several centuries affecting Palestine and every state in western Asia. This will become increasingly evident as we proceed.

Several questions arise which demand careful consideration. What was the nature of Greek culture, to what extent was it religious, how deeply did it penetrate the social structure of the states effected?

HISTORICAL BASIS OF HOMERIC WRITINGS

Until recent years all that we knew of the early Greeks we learned from Homer who three centuries afterward celebrated their exploits. It was thought that the Trojan War

---

[1] Ninth century B. C.
[2] In 515 B. C.
[3] 490-480 B. C.

276

was a myth and there was only a slight foundation for much that Homer wrote. But when the archaeologists uncovered Troy and towns in southern Greece where the treasures of Achaean civilization had lain undisturbed for millenniums, it was established beyond doubt that the *Iliad* contained historical material and that the Greek conflict with the Trojans was actual and not imaginary.

There has been much debate over the authorship of the epics, but we shall spare ourselves the inquiry by calling their author Homer as past generations have done. Undoubtedly, the myths, the folklore, and the songs were derived from many sources, and in their oral form had literary qualities, but this is not to admit that Homer was merely an editor; nor can we suppose that the author is the X of an algebraic formula. The design and workmanship of one creative artist prevails throughout. Concerning his personality, we know little. Whether, as tradition affirms, he was "the blind old man of Scio's rocky isle" may be doubted. He writes objectively, as an artist not a historian. Like Shakespeare, he borrowed widely and by his genius wrought into a harmonious whole his diverse selection. Herein lay his genius. He might have begun like the Mantuan bard upon whom his mantle fell: "Of men and gods I sing," for the stage is set for a society both human and divine.

Subject Matter of the "Iliad"

The subject of the *Iliad* is a short, critical episode extending over six weeks in the ninth year of the siege of Troy.

Chryseis, the beautiful daughter of a priest of Apollo, has been taken captive by the Greeks and is in the tent of Agamemnon. The king refuses ransom, and when the desperate father appeals to Apollo, the god sends a plague among the Greeks. This leads to a solemn assembly, convoked by Achilles, in which the decision is reached that Chryseis must be returned. The sullen king consents, but demands in her place, the no less lovely captive whom Achilles has taken, Briseis. Achilles is angry, retires to his tent, and refuses to fight. His mother, the sea goddess, persuades Zeus to avenge him by giving victory to the

Trojans. The wrath of Achilles and the dire results that follow Zeus's decision form the subject matter of the poem.

After his promise to Thetis, Zeus does not immediately intervene. In this delayed action, the poet finds opportunity to introduce the heroes and to tell us something of the gods who espouse the cause of Greeks or Trojans. We see the Greeks digging a trench and building a protecting wall against an expected attack. All this occupies about one fourth of the poem (Books II-VII). The author without wearying us has sketched in his background and held us in suspense as we wonder what Zeus is going to do. The latter finally acts by forbidding the Olympian deities to intervene. But can we expect the gods to remain neutral? Will Zeus in the end remain impartial? The answer is in the negative. The gods are bound to support their favorites, Greek or Trojan.

The Achaeans are now so hard pressed that Agamemnon swallows his pride and makes overtures to Achilles, but in vain. Odysseus and Diomede secretly break through the lines of the Greeks, capture a Trojan spy and learn from him of the arrival of a new Trojan ally, a Thracian chieftain who had brought to Troy beautiful white horses. These the Greek heroes steal. The episode is entertaining but does not prevent the Trojans from gaining an advantage. They reach the Greek ships and a Trojan victory seems inevitable. In the crisis, Achilles' bosom friend appeals to him, and while the hero remains obdurate, he makes the concession of loaning his armor to Patroclus—an unfortunate gift for because of it Patroclus meets death.

Achilles, furious at the outcome, forgets his long-standing grudge and seeks to avenge his fallen friend. Hephaestus forges for him new armor and with it a shield of remarkable design (Book XVIII). Achilles resumes the leadership of the Greek forces, gains a decisive victory and slays Hector, who had killed his friend. The *Iliad* concludes with the burial and funeral games of Patroclus and the visit of Priam to the Greek camp to ransom the body of Hector (Bks. XXIII, XXIV).

The poem is a tapestry in which the design as a whole engages us rather than a single point of interest. It is epic not dramatic, revealing to us the society of the Achaeans, in concepts which belong to Homer's own time.

Following the *Iliad* is the *Odyssey,* a fascinating tale of the adventures of Odysseus, whose return from Troy to his Ithaca kingdom constitutes the subject matter of the second epic, so familiar that it needs no retelling.

Homeric Religion

The presence of the supernatural in the *Iliad* does not invalidate the claim that the fall of Troy was historical. Moreover, the gods are more than a literary device to achieve the improbable or secure a happy ending. They were real personages to the men of Homer's time, though to what extent the poet reflects the current religious opinion is impossible to say. Perhaps as much as Shakespeare, the Elizabethan period. Homer, as Professor Glover reminds us, was not an ordinary man, and we can expect from him a synthesis, a completeness of view such as his contemporaries did not share. Herodotus writing four centuries later expresses the conviction that Homer and Hesiod created the gods, gave the divinities names, and assigned them functions (Herodotus 2, 53). By this he meant that Homer and Hesiod made the gods intelligible to the Greeks. But the excavations indicate that the gods of Hellas were older even than Mycenae or Troy.

The gods are regarded seriously, although at times they play comic rôles and the Olympian interludes perform the same function as the comic scenes in Shakespeare's tragedies.[4] It is probable that some of the scenes depicted in Zeus' troublesome family reflect the poet's irony. In general the character of Homeric religious thought is high compared to the primitive elements of Greek religion and far removed from the barbaric. His ideas are capable of moral and social development, but confessedly his works admit many perplexing inconsistencies. The gods are universal in the sense that they are present with the Greeks at home or abroad, in one country or another, but they are not omnipresent. In

---

[4] See J. B. Bury, *Cambridge Ancient History,* Vol. II, Chap. XVIII.

the opening pages of the *Iliad,* Zeus is away on a journey, nor is there divine intervention until he returns. Zeus is thought of as sovereign. He is father of gods and men, but not all powerful. He cannot prevent the death of Sarpedon whose loss he mourns. Homer makes Zeus say, "Lo, you now, how vainly mortal men do blame the gods! For of us they say comes evil, whereas they even of themselves through the blindness of their own hearts have sorrows beyond that which is ordained." In this approach to the solution of the problem of evil, Homer reminds us of Shakespeare who has one of his characters say, "The fault, dear Brutus, is not in our stars, but in ourselves that we are underlings."

Turning to the externals of religion in Homeric times, we have priests, shrines, oracles, and sacrifice, but the priest is of minor importance. As with the early Hebrews, the individual can approach deity without the intervention of priest. In the case of national worship the king is the religious head; that is, worship is royal not sacerdotal.

THE OLYMPIAN DEITIES

Zeus is depicted as the father of gods and men. The tie is moral not physical, as in the case of the Egyptians. Divine fatherhood among the Greeks was akin to the Hebrew conception. Zeus was sovereign but his power was conditioned. He might be outwitted by other gods. Over all the gods, Zeus included, is Fate, or Nemesis.

Hera, the sister and wife of Zeus, played often the rôle of jealous wife, and is, we suspect, somewhat of a shrew. But remembering the intrigues of Zeus with mortal women, what else could one expect?

Poseidon, brother of Zeus, is the god of the sea whose symbol is the trident, powerful alike on land and sea. He summons the storm and with his trident arouses the earthquake.

Apollo is the god of prophecy and the patron of all musicians and artists. He is the builder of cities and the framer of laws. He epitomizes civilization. Later he becomes a solar deity, but Homer knows him in no such aspect. As the god of prophecy his shrine is at Delphi.

Artemis, sister of Apollo, is the goddess of the hunt and leader of the nymphs. She is chaste as pictured by Homer, but elsewhere she is known as the goddess of the wilds, unwedded but not virginal.

Athena is the goddess of wisdom, the warrior maid and the chief power after Zeus. She is said at birth to have sprung "fully armed from the head of Zeus." Hers was the chief cult in Athens, and temples from ancient times were erected for her worship on the Acropolis.

Demeter was the earth mother, goddess of fertility, patroness of all who till the fields and cultivate the vineyards. With her is associated a daughter, Persephone, whose charm attracted Pluto.

Hermes was the messenger of the gods, the patron of shepherds, and the leader of the nymphs. The male organ of generation was his symbol as the deity of fertility and increase. He was worshiped under the name Phales, whence the term "phallic worship." The image of this god was a pillar or pile of stones usually erected at crossroads. He was the god of luck and a patron of "the gentlemen of the road."

Ares was the god of war, for whom Homer had small respect. He was thought to be Thracian in origin and is usually a butt for ridicule among the Olympian deities. With him was associated as a mistress Aphrodite, goddess of love. She also is out of favor with Homer, who regarded her as pro-Trojan in her sympathies. Her favorite seat of worship was the partly Oriental isle of Cyprus. Like Ares, she seems to be a foreigner and unable to assimilate Hellenic civilization.

GODS HUMAN AND DIVINE

To Homer the gods had a near and far side. Zeus is sovereign and men bow to his will as to a king. Apollo walks "like the night." Hera descends from her abode to help her suppliant as swiftly as the passage of thought. Again the gods are human and appropriately so, for this brings them near to man and his level. Zeus weeps for the misfortunes of those he loves; not infrequently he comes to their aid.

Prayers and sacrifices are offered to him, nor is it a necessary element of weakness that gods should be human or
endowed with human passions. It must be rememebered that
this was not an age of criticism. Religion was potent because
it was felt. It lost its power when its traditions were
examined, when critical insight took the place of emotion.

In the Homeric thought we have a fatalistic view of life,
fate being conceived as a destiny fixed at birth, for the thread
of life had already been spun. Hector to Andromache just
before the battle says, "My good wife, grieve not overmuch
for me in thy heart, for no man shall send me to Hades
contrary to my fate; and say that none be he coward or
brave has ever escaped a doom when once it comes." The
Homeric man recognized the agency of the gods in everything. When a thing happened, it was said to be "with god's
help." But by this he does not mean Providence; nor does
he know what god has acted, therefore he leaves him name-
less.

The Weakness of the Gods

The gods often act at cross purposes. Poseidon is on the
side of the Trojans; the Olympians side with the Greeks,
but they have their favorites and are actuated by different
and counter motives.

Much has been said about their immorality. We must
recall that in an age much earlier than Homer all the gods
were localized like the nymphs and water deities. The various traditions concerning Zeus, his love affairs with mortal
women, owe their origin to the localities from which the
stories were first current. These were syncretized by Homer
without regard to scandal or inconstancy. As has been said,
it was not a critical age. Indeed, it seemed desirable that a
god should have the power to act upon impulse. Brought
down to the level of human life it seemed inevitable that
divinities should be endowed with passions and infirmities of
men. Later they will become responsible, because human
and liable to the laws that govern human conduct. Hence we
find Zeus warning Aegisthus that he shall not go unpunished
for his adultery and murder.

The Ethical Standards of the "Iliad"

The *Iliad* abounds in moral sentiments. A counterpart to some of the commands in the Decalogue may be found, and to these we can add a command enjoining hospitality. Achilles is heard saying, "I hate more than the gates of Hades the man who devises one thing in his heart and appears another." And, as everyone knows, the poem sets high value upon personal honor. The Epic of the fall of Troy turns upon the violation of Menelaus's hospitality when Paris abducts Helen.

Man's relationship to god was maintained through ritual, though high value was placed upon obedience to the divine. Only thus could men prosper.[5] "Whosoever obeyeth the gods to him they gladly hearken." Strictly speaking, the Greeks neither then nor later had any consciousness of sin such as we find in the Hebrew penitential Psalms. Pride, insolent pride, was forbidden. Thus Ajax met his death; humility, on the other hand, was unknown. Neither of life nor death was the Greek afraid. Achilles expresses an approved sentiment when over the body of the dead Hector he exclaims: "Lie now dead, but my doom I will accept."

Like the Hebrews, the Greeks had very vague views of the afterlife. When Odysseus meets Achilles in the realm of the dead, the shade of that hero said: "I'd rather be the slave of a poor man and live, than be lord over all the dead."

The religious element in the *Odyssey* is more pronounced than in the *Iliad,* and more mature. The freedom of man's will, an overruling Providence, the presence of deities encouraging men but not often intervening, are threads of gold wrought in the design of an epic poem which has never failed to instruct and interest mankind.

Religion After Homer

Hesiod follows Homer. How much time elapsed between the two we cannot learn. While he employs the dialect and the poetic forms of the Ionian, there is a century of difference in thought. We seem to have crossed the threshold

---

[5] See *Iliad,* Bk. I.

into a different world. Homer, as we have seen, wrote objectively. He saw life sanely and saw it as a whole. It was desirable for men to live, to desire, to achieve. He exulted in their heroic deeds. Homer, the man, is lost; as an artist he lives in the immortal characters which he created and which still stalk across the stage before our enchanted eyes.

Hesiod, on the other hand, is reflective, self-conscious, often complaining. He lives in "the age of iron," born to poverty, victim of misfortune. His birthplace, he tells us, was Ascra "of inglorious summer, winter vile, and bad all the year." He tended the flocks on the slopes of Mount Helicon, where the Muses found him and bade him celebrate them in song. The event which disturbed the tenor of his days was a lawsuit preferred against him by his brother, Perses, an idle, dissolute fellow who succeeded in the suit by bribing the judges. The inheritance was awarded to him, but was soon squandered, and Perses reduced to poverty appealed to his brother for help. All he received was advice.

Whatever Homer's environment, we suspect it was far different from this. He lived in the midst of affluence with men of culture, for whom he sings. It was remarked by the ancients that Homer wrote for princes and Hesiod for peasants. The more praise for Hesiod, a democratic age declares; but not so the age of Pericles, which despised a poet who dedicated his muse to pastoral lays. It is evident that these poets write from a different point of view— Homer of a past which he idealizes, and Hesiod of a present which he scourges. Homer's poetry was sung to the accompaniment of the cythara. Hesiod recited his verses leaning on the staff which the Muses once decked with laurel. Homer, the aristocrat, a kingly man walking in the midst of princes in the most advanced and cultured province of Greece, and Hesiod of backward Boethia, a shepherd inured to the cold of winter and the heat of summer, vexed by the lawsuits, victim of injustice—how could men so differently conditioned write in similar vein? Hesiod is far more like the shepherd of Tekoa,[6] who addressed the inhabi-

---

[6] Amos, see Chap. XXII.

tants of Samaria with cutting words as he pitted the poor against the injustice of the arrogant rich.

Hesiod's chief works are the *Theogony* and *Work and Days*. The first was of great value to the Greeks, for it contained, as Symonds says, "an authorized version of the genealogy of gods and heroes, an inspired dictionary of mythology from which to deviate was hazardous." The second, however, has greater interest for us. It deals with Prometheus's theft of fire from heaven and Zeus's vengeance, who punishes all mankind by giving them Pandora.

The woman is a creation of all the gods, hence the name. Hephaestus mixed earth and water, and infused into the plastic form the human voice and powers. Athena taught the woman household work and weaving. Aphrodite gave her charm, desire, and consuming love; Hermes, the mind of a dog and wily temper. Afterward Athena girded and adorned her. The Graces hung golden chains about her flesh and the Hours crowned her with blossoms. Thus she was sent to mankind in a day when evil was unknown. All the bad things of life were shut up in a great jar. Epimetheus (symbol of mankind) received her with joy, forgetting the warning of his brother, "Receive no gift from Zeus." The rest of the story is familiar. Pandora consumed by curiosity as to what the jar contained opened it, and out flew all the evil that since has beset mankind. Only hope was left shut within the jar, indicating that life is hopeless.

The story of Prometheus is followed by the *Vision of the Four Ages,* of which the first was the age of gold; the second, the age of silver; the third was brass, and the fourth iron. Of the fourth period in which the poet lives, he has only evil to say. Again, we are made to feel the bitterness of his lot.

Then he launches his tirade against injustice, not forgetting the positive gain to that city which exalts justice and multiplies in peace. Here he paints the pastoral picture of felicity which has had its echo in verse and art down through the ages on the part of those who linger lovingly upon a life which, as Symonds says, is neither stirring nor heroic.

He concludes the first part of his work with an eulogy of

labor, in·which sententious maxims abound. This writing is inferior to what has preceded.

The second part is a farmer's almanac in which are directions as to when to sow and reap, lucky days for planting, and scattered throughout moral reflections. What he says about marriage may be briefly considered. A man, according to Hesiod, ought to be thirty and his wife nineteen when he marries. He should be exceedingly careful. The chances are that he will make a bad bargain. But since it is not possible to get along without marriage, if one would leave his inheritance to sons, it is to be preferred to a marriageless existence and ensuing old age. With a good marriage there is trouble enough. In the case of a poor one, there is utter ruin. Such is the evil devised by Zeus.

The moral maxims of Hesiod[7] are of value to us only so far as they reflect the period in which the poet lived. His theology was bad. It undermined whatever belief men had. Better worship no god than a bad one. The society in which Hesiod lived seemed to him to be governed by immoral gods and devoid of justice and good.

SUPPLEMENTARY READING

T. R. Glover, *Progress in Religion,* Chapters III, IV.
Clifford H. Moore, *The Religious Thought of the Greeks,* Chapter I.
Edmund D. Soper, *The Religions of Mankind,* Chapter IV.
J. A Symonds, *Studies of the Greek Poets,* Vol. I, Chapters III, IV, V.
Cambridge Ancient History, Vol. II, Chapter XXII.
The Iliad and *The Odyssey.* Translations in Modern Library are satisfactory.

---

[7] See J. A. Symonds, *The Greek Poets,* Vol. I (Harpers), for a fair estimate of Hesiod.

CHAPTER XXX

THE DEVELOPMENT OF GREEK RELIGION

To the student of religion it seems extraordinary that so little emphasis has been placed upon the religious beliefs and practices of the early Greeks. Much has been written upon the classic beauty of their temples, but we have forgotten to inquire for what purpose the temples were reared. Men have praised without stint Greek plastic art but have failed to note the embodiment of the idea in those lovely forms. It may be that the secular life of the Greeks, their attainment in arts, philosophy, and literature reached such a towering height that it overshadowed everything else.

On the other hand, we may remind ourselves that Greek religion is tied up with Greek art and life in its many phases. The buildings which endured were temples; the statuary we revere represented deities, the Panhellenic games were religious festivals; philosophy which began with the purpose of explaining the myth, the stories of gods, ended by becoming ethical and religious.

Any traveler taking his stand with Saint Paul on the Areopagus in Athens might say with him of the Athenians and of all Greeks, "Sirs, I perceive that in all things you are very religious."

The preceding chapter dealt with the religious ideas common to Homer's time. The poet depicted a society both human and divine. His gods were comparatively few; they dwelt apart but were accessible to men. They had grave faults but were not infrequently idealized and capable of moral development. Had there been in Greece during the centuries following the Homeric epoch a monarchical form of government and a powerful priesthood, the result would have been an effective state religion. But what chiefly impresses one is the reverse of this—a disintegrating process, the rejection of the Homeric myth, the cleavage between the

THE HEBREW HERITAGE

cults Oriental rather than Greek in origin, the increasing
importance of rival shrines. The diverse tendencies in Greek
religion even in early times make the situation complex and
analysis difficult. Any pretense of survey should include
myth and mystery cults, the religion of the poet, and the
reaction of the philosopher.

MYTH AND CULTS

In Greece myth took the place of dogma and was received
with unquestioning faith on the part of the people. It purported to give an account of natural phenomena, the origin
of the earth, the starry sky, the dark underworld. It explained why vegetation dies and later revives, why night follows day and the motions of winds and water. Always the
explanation involved the gods, so the myth was in the nature
of religious instruction.

One of the oldest and best beloved of the Greek myths
concerns the goddess of the harvest, Demeter, and associated
with her Persephone. They seem originally to have been
goddesses of fertility probably having their separate cults,
but Homer knows them as mother and daughter.

The myth has been told in a Homeric hymn. Persephone,
with the deep-bosomed daughters of the Ocean, is playing in
a flowering meadow. Here she sees amid the roses, the
crocus, and the violets, a flower fairer than all the others—
the narcissus, which Zeus has caused to grow as a lure. As
she reaches out her hands to pluck the flower the earth yawns
and the god of the Underworld appears in his chariot to
snatch her away as a bride. The hills gave back her cries,
her deep lament. Demeter hears but knows not whence the
sound nor who has borne her daughter away. When later
she learned that the cloud-wrapt Zeus alone among immortals had caused this, in anger she left Olympus for the
haunts of man.

Demeter in her wanderings came to Eleusis. In the guise
of an aged woman, she sought out the king and queen and
was received of them. They put in her charge their infant
son. Demeter in order to render him immortal fed him

ambrosia and breathed into him her own divine breath. She also sought to purify him by fire, but in the act was discovered by the child's mother who frustrated the purpose. She then revealed herself and commanded that a temple be built in her honor.

Still bereft of her daughter she punished the earth by retarding the increase of the flocks and fruitful harvests. Zeus, implored by mankind to relieve their want, permitted Demeter to find Persephone. It was decreed that the latter should henceforth spend two thirds of the year with her mother while for the remaining months she must abide in the lower world.

Whatever the Eleusinian mysteries may have been, they included for the initiates instruction in the myth and its significance. They were promised bliss after death, and to them Pluto became Plutos, the giver of wealth.

Soper reasons that the rescue of Persephone from the land of the shades was the earnest of the expectation that men too might look for immortality on the other side of the grave.[1] This may have been included in the teaching at Eleusis, but such immortality could only belong to the initiates. In any case, it is one more instance of the germinal ideas resident in the observation of the resuscitation of plant life after winter's death.

Eleusis became a place of pilgrimage, its converts increased, and subsequently the world was conquered by the Eleusinian mysteries.

THE CULT OF DIONYSUS

The second of the mystery religions is the Dionysian. Unlike the Eleusinian cult, which was featured only at Eleusis on the sea, it had no central sanctuary but was related to the festivals held in honor of the god of the vine.

Clifford Moore writes concerning the cult as follows: "The worship of this god was wholly unlike that of the Olympian gods. Under his influence the devotees, mostly women, in divine madness left their homes and daily tasks

---

[1] *The Religions of Mankind*, p. 120. The Abingdon Press. Also to the same effect George F. Moore, *History of Religions*, Vol. I.

to roam the wild mountainside, clad no longer in ordinary dress but wearing the skins of wild beasts, their flowing hair bound with ivy and wild bryony. In their excitement they were unconscious of time and place, unfettered by the normal limitations of human powers and sensibilities. Wild music stimulated their orgiastic dance; in frenzy they tore living creatures limb from limb and devoured the raw dripping flesh, calling meantime on the god by name. This mad revel was continued until the participants fell exhausted to the ground."[2]

Hans Licht commenting upon the Dionysian festivals reminds us that the phallic equipment played a considerable part. "The retinue of Dionysus consisted of ithyphallic spirits, spirits of fruitfulness and vegetation." This is confirmed by a red figured vase from the Acropolis which pictures a frenzied maenad, naked, bearing a phallus aloft as she dances ecstatically in the procession that follows the god; and also by Aristophanes, an authority on the social manners of the Greeks in the fifth century B. C., who has described vividly such a phallic procession.

Among modern painters Rubens better than any other has caught the spirit of the Dionysian cult, as any one can see who remembers his "Triumph of Dionysus" in the National Gallery.

Carl Clemen, writing on the religion of the Greeks, says: "The cult of Dionysus promised its initiates a rank above that of other men and union with the deity through sacrament. By means of orgiastic dances, loud cries, and wild music ecstasy was produced, and in this condition the devotee ate the god, that is, the animal in which the deity was believed to be embodied. The worshiper thus became filled with god and attained the condition of ecstasy or inspiration."[3]

The Dionysian cult met with protest. Its extravagances were thought to have no kinship with Greek religion. In

[2] Clifford H. Moore, *The Religious Thought of the Greeks,* p. 49. Harvard University Press, Cambridge. Used by permission.
[3] *Religions of the World,* p. 190. Reprinted by permission of Harcourt, Brace and Company.

fact, as first practiced, it was Oriental rather than Greek. The devotees were regarded as mad. Gradually the excesses were worn away and the cult was Hellenized and human-ized.

Meanwhile the native rural festivities in honor of the wine god continued to be observed as in the past. They were so different in character from the cult just described that we cannot confuse the two trends. The former was capable of improvement. Some of its elements, the desire to be united with deity, the exaltation akin to inspiration, remained to be given a new significance by later-day followers.

Orphism was an important modification of the Dionysian worship. As the name indicates, it centered in Orpheus, a god of the forests, whose sweet music had power to charm even the wild animals. Orpheus was a priest of Dionysus according to an ancient tradition, but his musical gifts over-shadowed his priestly function. "With the appearance of the myth in the sixth century, we recognize a second wave of Dionysiac religion, now spiritualized and ennobled, in which ceremonial purity became a chief concern."[4] Later Orphism had wide repute, its tenets and practices influencing Christian thought. It organized brotherhoods and stressed asceticism. While its cult did not encourage a numerous following, it was very influential and survived far into the Christian era.

THE RELIGION OF THE POETS

The poets who followed Homer add little to the moral and religious concepts which we find in the Homeric epics. There is a growing tendency to make Zeus supreme, to identify him with the fates, and to stress the belief that all things good or evil come from him. Sententious or moral maxims abound. One is not far from truth in speaking of the poetry of the period as gnomic and lyrical, although any such classification must admit exceptions. By gnomic poetry one means didactic or proverbial, the writer's purpose being

---

[4] Clifford H. Moore, *The Religious Thought of the Greeks*, p. 52. Harvard University Press, Cambridge. Used by permission.

to inculcate good morals. Both Theognis and Solon give us many examples of verse which is chiefly ethical in content. Lyrical poetry, on the other hand, is personal, highly emotional, and its theme the pleasures of love and wine. Apparently, the epic or narrative poem was fast becoming extinct, while meditative or reflective writing took its place.

The verse of Theognis abounds with moral sentiments. A poem addressed to Cyrnus, a youth of whom he was very fond, consists for the most part of rules for good conduct. Sometimes his theme takes the form of protest against prevailing injustice. He wonders that Zeus who rules over all things should permit the wicked and the righteous to have the same lot; or that a man who has had no part in unjust deeds should suffer as if he had.

Solon has left us a prayer which runs as follows: "Bright daughters of Memory and Olympian Zeus, hear my prayer. Grant me wealth from the blessed gods, and from all men a good name. May I be sweet to my friend and bitter to my foe; revered by the one and dreaded by the other. Money I desire, but no ill-begotten gain, for the wealth that the gods give lasts and fleets not away—but the fruits of insolence and crime bring vengeance sure, though slow."

Mimnermus writes in a different vein. He was born and lived among the Ionian Greeks. He was accustomed to luxury and enervated by it. His verses breathe the air of gardens or banquet rooms and are pervaded, as Symonds says, by a tone of lingering regret that he must die and leave all that was so desirable.

"When the flower of youth is past," he writes, "it is best to die at once." The following lines are illustrative of the melancholy sentiments to which he was addicted. They are worth quoting because even in translation they exhibit the delicacy of his touch as well as his frame of mind.

"What life or pleasure wanting Aphrodite?
When to the gold-haired goddess cold am I,
When love and love's soft gifts no more delight me,
Nor stolen dalliance, then I fain would die!
Ah, fair and lovely bloom the flowers of youth;

On men and maids they beautifully smile. . . . Old eyes forlorn
Scarce reck the very sunshine to behold,
Unloved by youths, of every maid the scorn,
So hard a lot God lays upon the old."[5]

The Greeks' Emphasis Upon Sensuous Beauty

Can the love of sensuous beauty prevalent in the literature,
the art, the drama, and the religious festivals of the Greeks
be reconciled with good ethics? Certainly not with Puritan
morality. But the Greek had his own code, and when he lived
according to it, managed to develop culturally and morally
although the pagan spirit which found joy in all life was
foreign to any faith which taught asceticism. He was
religious, but his was a religion without a cross, without the
practice of self-immolation, and without regard for the
future. Perhaps its noblest expression was the frieze on the
Parthenon showing a stately procession of men and girls in
festal array bringing gifts to the gods; its basest were the
phallic processions and the bacchanals of the religious festivals. These were agricultural, celebrating a god of fertility
or harvest, when license to a shocking degree was permitted,
drunkenness rife, and sexual passions unrestrained. But
these orgies were exceptional and no more characteristic of
the Greeks than the excesses of similar festivals in other
lands were of those who suffered them.

Religion and Philosophy

The problem of the philosopher was to find a unifying
principle that would explain the origin and nature of the
world. The myths were of little value. They were unscien-
tific, inexact, often incredible. To a man of moral earnestness they misrepresented the gods. Thus the seeker after
truth, whether in the physical or moral world, had to seek
elsewhere for an explanation.

The Greek, who had a genius for logical and abstract
thought, as truly as for poetry and art, laid the foundations

---

[5] The poem and the preceding quotations are cited from *Studies of
the Greek Poets*, by J. A. Symonds, Vol. I, p. 246. Reprinted by permission of Harper & Bros.

for philosophy in all times. In this he served religion well, for he destroyed superstition. Whatever rubbish there was —and there was a good deal—burned in the fierce fire of his criticism.

The first philosophers were physicists. Their attention was wholly occupied with the external world. They thought there must be some primal substance from which all else is derived. Thales named water, but failed to explain how the world developed from it; Anaximines thought air was the first substance. He had observed the condensation of vapor (which he identified with air) and its opposite, rarefication, or air growing hot. The heat or fire borne aloft gives us the stars, or condensed we have the earth, water, rocks.

Anaximander did not name the primal substance. He thought of it as matter formless and characterless, and infinite in amount, so that it might not be exhausted in the creative process. Heraclitus thought fire was the elementary principle; Democritus thought atoms, and Empedocles, like Zoroaster, reasoned that there were several primal substances. He named air, water, fire, and the earth, all of which he held to be incapable of transformation into anything else, save its own kind. It is needless to say that all such philosophy is materialistic and, properly speaking, not philosophy but physics.

To follow the development of the Eleatic school, we must leave Ionia for a town in southern Italy, Elea, which gave its name to the first true philosophers, as many think. They were distinguished for abstract reasoning, although, unlike the Pythagoreans and others, they sought the abstract not in phenomenal elements but "went straight through language to the notion of pure being."

The chief representatives of the school are Parmenides and Xenophanes. The latter is as interesting to the student of religion as to the philosopher. He was not a native of Elea but undoubtedly visited the town. Much of his life was spent in wanderings in Sicily and southern Italy, completely absorbed in meditation. The starting point of his philosophy was found in theology. Aristotle's contention that "looking up to the universal heaven, Xenophanes proclaimed the unity of God" is probably true. He wrote in poetry, and in the largest fragment of his metaphysical verse he attacks the Homeric conception of polytheism, and the immorality of the gods. The Divine Being to him was an abstraction, one and indivisible, without motion or beginning or ending. He attributes thought and volition to God but does not seem to have connected him with the universe.

Stace regards Xenophanes as a pantheist, but this does not seem to be the case of one who thinks of God as supreme "neither in body nor in mind like mortals"; and of man as derived from earth and water. Deity is an abstraction, the man a finite being material in origin and limited in knowledge, so that he cannot know God. Opinion or conjecture is the only approximation to truth that man can have, and opinion at the best is only a shadow of the truth. This is certainly a dualistic theory leading to agnosticism. He is unable to reconcile the antithesis between true being on the one hand and appearance on the other.[6]

Parmenides, following his teacher, exchanged the theological terms of the latter for a metaphysical phraseology and "pushed to a logical conclusion the fatal insufficiency of Eleatic dualism." To him also God was pure Being, existing but not creating.

There is a striking parallel between the agnosticism to which the Eleatic school was driven by its premises, and that which philosophy faced at the close of the nineteenth century. John Addington Symonds has pretty well summed up the position of his contemporaries when he writes: "Men postulate the identity of the human and the divine mind and end by asserting that thought is the only reality. Their fallacy lies here, that while the mind possesses the faculty of reflecting upon itself, everything which it knows is of necessity expressed in terms of itself, and therefore in pretending to give an account of the universe, it is only giving an account of its own operations. At the end of philosophies one feels tempted to exclaim—

---

[6] Plato (fourth century B. C.) was concerned with the same problem, seeking through the postulate of Ideas to bridge the chasm between man and Xenophanes' unknowable God.

'I heard what was said of the universe,
Heard it and heard it of several thousand years.
It is middling well as far as it goes,—
But is that all?' "[7]

Ontology, or the science of pure being, is doubtless a wornout, discredited method of finding out God, but there are other ways of approach, other modes by which the notion of the Divine Being may be apprehended. The Eleatic school and their modern followers have not brought us to the bankruptcy of faith but only demonstrated the fallacy of their mode of approach to the truth. In this they have rendered a real service to religion.

SUPPLEMENTARY READING

G. W. Botsford, *Hellenic Civilization*, pp. 11-18; 118-130; 185-209.

J. H. Breasted, *Ancient Times*, Chapter XII.

Carl Clemen, *Religions of the World*, pp. 185-191.

Clifford H. Moore, *The Religious Thought of the Greeks*, Chapter II.

W. T. Stace, *Critical History of Greek Philosophy*, Chapters II-IV.

J. A. Symonds, *Studies of the Greek Poets*, Vol. I, Chapters VI-VIII.

Warner Library of Best Literature for examples of the verse of poets of this period.

---

[7] Citation from *Studies of the Greek Poets*, by J. A. Symonds. Vol. I, p. 206. Harper & Bros.

CHAPTER XXXI

THE GREAT FIFTH CENTURY IN GREECE

THE century which concerns us in our present study witnesses the flowering of Greek genius in many fields. Most noteworthy is the rapid development in building, in plastic art, in poetry, drama, and philosophy. It is doubtful if any city ever assembled so many men of genius as Athens in the decades immediately following the Greek defense against Persia. Possibly the ferment of the conquests of Marathon and Salamis gave the necessary stimulus. Athens was self-conscious as never before. She had borne the brunt of the war, and to her chiefly the renown was due. Not merely a few men, but the whole body of citizens were lifted out of the commonplace to a high level of thinking.

Broadly speaking, the fifth century in Athens and elsewhere is distinguished for progress and attainment in art, while the fourth is remarkable for its achievements in philosophy. To generalize concerning Greek civilization is tempting, for it affords any number of instances to support a given thesis, but it must be owned that no satisfactory evaluation can be reached save through the laborious task of reviewing all Greek life and manners in a stated period, while one at the same time scrupulously accounts for the many conflicting ideas and practices. The seriousness of the great tragedians is matched by the ribald laughter and obscenities of the comic writers; the state religion ambitious to build costly temples, with its insistence upon cult and its adherence to myth, is opposed by the Sophists, one of whom could begin his book with the words: "Now, as to the gods, I do not know whether they exist" (Protagoras). The Greek love of family life, the respect paid to wife and mother, is to be measured by the increasing number and influence of the hetaeri. A line drawn between Socrates and his disciples on the one side, and pleasure-loving Greeks on

the other would show the great majority on the side of
pleasure. All this must be conceded. It has been true of
every race and in every age, but moral and religious evalua-
tions are based, not on majority votes, but upon what is valuable and permanent in human life. Socrates is acquitted by
posterity and not by his contemporaries.

The Religious Influence of the Poets

We find Pindar, foremost poet of his age, at the Pythian
games, that is, we find him at Delphi when he is not at
Olympia or attending the Isthmian celebration near Corinth.
That he was essentially a religious poet no one can deny who
has read his verse. Their stately measures remind us of the
procession of Athenian youth on their way to the temple
bearing gifts for their gods. He pays reverence to the past,
and no lover of the Bible can outdo him in his familiarity
with religious tradition. Under his skillful touch the myth
is transformed and refined of its absurdities and immorali-
ties. We have him saying in reference to the shameful deeds
of Tantulus, who offers his son at a banquet of the immortals, that he will not call anyone of the blessed gods a canni-
bal. His own awakened moral sense prevented him from
thinking of deities other than perfect. Moreover, in subject-
ing the myths to the test of reason as well as goodness, he
was doing much to improve the moral welfare of the people
who heard him. His ideas of immortality were doubtless
not different from the Orphics who influenced him. The
soul, he taught, would pass through successive incarnations
until, wholly purified, it attains happiness. He dwells upon
the ultimate destiny of the righteous, who abide "on the
islands of the blest where ocean breezes blow." His imagery
is comparable to the Egyptian description of the future state.

The presence of Pindar at the games, the hymns he wrote
in honor of the victors and dedicated to the gods, remind us
that the Panhellenic games were something more than
athletic contests. Here poets vied with one another, orators
declaimed, religious ceremonies were held with great pomp.
At Delphi the god honored was Apollo, who was thought to
have inspired his priests. At Olympia there was a splendid

temple to Zeus, in whose honor the games were celebrated, while the chief deity at the Isthmian games was Poseidon.

As to the games themselves, there is little to be said. They gradually fell into disrepute, principally on account of the brutality of the boxing and wrestling. We hear Cicero indignantly denying that he had been present at a contest, but they were sufficiently popular to attract visitors from every part of Greece and the colonies, and thus gave a powerful impetus to the Panhellenic movement.

Religion in the Drama

The fifth century witnesses the most remarkable development in dramatic art that the world has ever known. Only one other period, the Elizabethan, is comparable to it. Three names and only three are concerned—Aeschylus, Sophocles, and Euripides. Aeschylus was born in 525 B. C., Sophocles thirty years later, and Euripides fifteen years after Sophocles' birth. Thus the three were contemporaneous for a period, but their highest creative activity comes in sequence. Aeschylus and Sophocles were for a time rivals; later Sophocles contended with Euripides. The three were independent artists, in no sense borrowers of one another, having this in common that they used the same source material, the Homeric myth.

Aeschylus is the most titanic and audacious. His flight is that of the eagle; he dares anything. Sophocles is more finished; he is the greater artist, though falling below Aeschylus in the grandeur of his conceptions. Of him Matthew Arnold wrote: "He saw life steadily and saw it as a whole."

Euripides is the most ingenious. He is the innovator, the technician, the stage director. Invention in plot is subordinate to the inventiveness which he exhibited in staging his plays. His dramas were intended to be acted rather than read.

All three were deeply religious and fundamentally sound in ethics, but not in the sense that they consciously proposed to teach religion or inculcate moral duties. Art was their foremost consideration. If religious or ethical truths were

there, it is because they were an integral part of the fabric
of the artist's mind and uttered because he must, while all
the time he was unconscious of saying something which men
ought to believe or of inculcating a duty to be followed.

The attention of the reader should be called to the remark-
ably short period in which Greek drama flourished, and to
the more important question why it appeared at a particular
time. Aeschylus gained his first prize in 483 B. C., Sophocles
his in 468 B. C., and Euripides produced his greatest play,
Medea, in 431 B. C. This is to say, that fifty-three years
sufficed for the complete development of the great period in
Greek dramatic art. We are reminded by way of comparison that the other great creative epoch, the Elizabethan, lay
between 1590 and 1628, allowing only thirty-eight years for
the production of the plays of Marlowe, Ben Jonson, Shakespeare, Beaumont, Fletcher, Webster, Chapman, and others.[1]

If we seek the causes that lie behind these periods of creative activity, we shall find that there was foremost an intense
activity or excitement, a ferment disturbing men's minds, and
secondly, an audience for the dramatists composed of those
who by experience or by mental quickening were prepared
to accept and appreciate what was offered. Not only had
Aeschylus been a participant in the Greek conflict with Persia,
but many of the spectators also. Sophocles was only fifteen
when the battle of Salamis was fought—too young himself
to take part in the conflict, but not too youthful to lead the
chorus which celebrated the victory, or to fail to be impressed
by the significance of the occasion.

The plays, performed in open-air theaters, where the stage
curtain was the sky and the distant sea, were representations
drawn from well-known myths and must have strongly
affected the sensitive, imaginative mind of the spectator.

GOVERNING IDEAS

Nemesis was the fundamental idea of the plot, and is to
be distinguished from fate.[2] Nemesis is a moral law. It

[1] J. A. Symonds, *Studies of the Greek Poets,* Vol. II, p. 11f. Harper
& Bros.

[2] Cited in part from *Studies of the Greek Poets,* by J. A. Symonds,
Vol. I, p. 386f. Harper & Bros.

expresses the conviction that the world is not ruled by chance
but governed by divine laws. The sequence of wrongdoing
runs as follows: pride in great wealth is followed by insolence and impiety, the powder train that leads to the commission of crime. The tragic results ensuing are traced to
the fourth and fifth generations of the family involved. Punishment may fall upon the innocent, again upon those guilty
of infamous deeds, which they would not have performed had
the doers not been involved in the tragic ruin of their family.
The working out of this inexorable law of destiny gives
unity to the plot. There are no loose threads in the Greek
drama, no surprising endings in the earlier plays. The modern reader concludes with the dramatist that there could be
no other issue.

While we do not know the immediate effect of the play
upon the Greek audience, we can imagine it to have been not
less emotionally stirred than modern spectators wrought to
a stage of excitement by an unexpected dramatic situation or
the artistic rendition of a part. Many single lines have a
perfection and completeness which is Shakespearean. This
can be observed in the following selections from *Agamemnon*
and *Antigone*. The king has returned from the siege of Troy.
He is greeted by the guilty, adulterous wife, Clytaemnestra,
who leads him to the inner room of the palace. What happens there we learn first from the chorus, then from
Clytaemnestra:

CHO.   Oh, state of man! Thy happiness is but
The pencilling of a shadow, misery
With a wet sponge wipes out the picture!

AG.   (Within the Palace) Oh, I am wounded with
A mortal wound!

CHO.   Hush! Who is he that crieth out? Who shrieks
Wounded unto the death?

AG.   Again! O God!

CLYT.   I stand upon my act—yea, where I struck
And I confess it . . .
I struck him the third time and with that strike
Committed him to Zeus, that keeps the dead.

Then he lay still and gasped away his life
And belching forth a stinging blast of blood
Spattered me with a shower of gory dew.
And I was blithe, as with the balm of heaven
The young corn in the birth-time of the ear.

Again we hear her at the close of the drama speaking without bravado:

What's sown is yet to reap
It is a harvest where the corn stands deep
And we must carry home full loads of care.[3]

Antigone's defense for her alleged crime, the burial of her brother's corpse, has been quoted often. Mr. Moore's translation reads:

I heard it not from Zeus, nor came it forth
From Justice, where she reigns in the Underworld.
They too have published to mankind a law.
Nor could I think thine edict of such might
That one who is mortal thus could overrule
The infallible, unwritten laws of Heaven.
Their majesty begins not from today
But from eternity, and none can tell
The hour that saw their birth.[4]

The writings of Euripides are tinged with skepticism. He was evidently affected by the philosophy of his day. We may not be able to subscribe to Doctor Verral's words: "His stories assume that the gods do not exist, and unless we are alive to this, unless we keep it always before us the best of Euripides must be sealed up from us." This seems to me to go further than we are warranted. It is true that we have Euripides' own words: "If gods do wrong, surely no gods they are." But this reflects no more than the belief that the ancient myths should be purified. The sentiments put in the lips of his characters and appropriate to them are not necessarily the conviction of the dramatist. However, I think we must concede that Euripides is without the faith of his

[3] G. M. Cookson, *Aeschylus,* Chapman and Hall, London, pp. 56, 57, 59, 69.
[4] Clifford H. Moore, *Religious Thought of the Greeks,* p. 104. Harvard University Press.

predecessors. But while he has no contribution to make to theology, his ethical views are broad and far more embracing than those expressed by Aeschylus and Sophocles. Professor Murray, in commenting upon the Euripidean play, *Trojan Woman,* writes: "This is the first great expression of the spirit of pity for mankind heard in European literature."

We must beware of reading into Euripides' dramas a purpose which he never intended, but one rises from the reading of *Helen* with the feeling that here we have been told in a masterful way and not without a vein of irony that the woman for whom the Greeks fought was a phantom and that the Trojan war and all war is utterly futile. For pure and unrelieved tragedy the reader is advised to peruse *Medea;* for noble sentiment, *Hippolytus,* the young palladin, the knight of purity. How striking the line in reference to the Cyprian goddess: "No god who hath night-homage pleaseth me"!

Interspersed in his dramas are prayers to the gods, but none were so truly Euripidian as the words found among his remains, which run:

"Omnipotent God, send light unto men, that they may know when their evils come and how they may avoid them."

Philosophy and Religion

It is inevitable that an age characterized by intense mental activity, such as we find in Athens in the fifth century B. C., should produce minds in which eager questionings, doubts, and extreme skepticism would rise to shock the complacency of those who accepted without question the religious beliefs of the past.

We have already referred to Protagoras' doubt as to the existence of the gods, but not to the sequel of his skepticism. His books were burned. He was sent into exile, and on the voyage was shipwrecked and drowned.

Another writer of the same school of thought declared that the gods were powers of nature that man had deified, that is, Zeus is the air, Aphrodite is love, etc. The tendency of philosophic thought for a long time had been toward agnosticism. The Sophists were giving publicity to ideas which had

only been dimly understood or which had failed to be carried
to their logical development. We may suspect that the
heretics were outspoken in their ridicule of established beliefs
and brought upon their heads the punishment that a conservative society meted out. It is to be observed that as conservative a thinker as Aeschylus had been severely rebuked for the
way in which he had handled on the stage the furies in
Eumenides.

But once freedom of thought has entered there is no
banishment of the ideas that are promulgated. It was difficult to defend the ancient myths or make a case for the
Homeric gods. It has been frequently pointed out that there
are three stages in religious thought: in the first common
beliefs or traditions are accepted without dissent; in the
second stage they are critically examined and not infrequently rejected in their entirety; in the third there are dis-
criminations, new interpretations, and a reconstruction of
faith. In the fifth century Greek thought finds itself in the
second stage.

THE GREAT TEACHER

At this time Socrates appeared. We know little of his
early life. He was born in 469 B. C. His father was a
sculptor, his mother a midwife. He had a fair education.
While he was uninterested in politics, he was a good citizen;
twice he served his country in war, distinguishing himself
by acts of bravery. How he earned his living we do not
know, for having adopted, like the Sophists, the profession
of a teacher, unlike them he did not accept pay.[5]

Most of his teaching was done in the market place. He
does not seem to have written anything down, and probably
there was no formal arrangement of his ideas other than
that which we find in the early *Dialogues* of Plato.

He was invariably surrounded by youth, whom he taught
by dialectic, that is, by question and answer. He believed,
contrary to the ideas of the Sophists, that truth was objectively revealed, and could be known because the mind has
the pattern of the heavenly ideas. The knowledge of this

---

[5] Xantippe may have had reason for complaint.

objective or real world could be gained by forming concepts or definitions. One may say in this connection that the Platonic Ideas are an amplification of what Socrates had previously taught.

But Socrates was primarily an ethical teacher. He conceived of himself as a missionary. "I do nothing but go about," he said, "teaching you all not to care for your properties but chiefly for your souls." He believed that virtue and knowledge were identical; that is, to know good was to do good. Perhaps this was true of Socrates but not of most men. As Aristotle has pointedly said, Socrates ignored the irrational elements of the mind.

When Socrates prayed, he asked for neither money nor power. One of his prayers has been preserved in Plato's *Phaedrus:*

"Beloved Pan, and all ye other gods who here abide, grant me beauty of the inner soul and make the outward and the inner man but one."

His arrest and imprisonment are familiar to all. The year was 399, just after the turn of the century, when his Athenian judges condemned him on three counts: 1. That he disbelieved in the gods. 2. That he substituted for the Greek divinities his own. 3. That he corrupted Athenian youth. All the charges were untrue. The second count probably refers to Socrates' daemon, which was not so much a divinity as an inner monitor, a voice of admonishment. The real reasons for his condemnation lay in the many private enemies that he had made by his plain speaking; his opposition to vested interests, that is, to the Athenian aristocracy, and chiefly because of the mistaken idea that he was a Sophist.

His defense has been preserved for us in the Crito, and I quote the greater part of it.[6]

SOCRATES' DEFENSE

"Men of Athens, I respect and love you, but I shall obey the God rather than you, and while I live and am able to continue, I shall never give up philosophy or stop exhorting

---

[6] J. J. Chapman. *Lucian, Plato and Greek Morals,* pp. 156, 157. Reprinted by permission of Houghton Mifflin Co.

you and pointing out the truth to any one of you whom I may meet, saying in my accustomed way: 'Most excellent man, are you who are a citizen of Athens, the greatest of cities and the most famous for wisdom and power, not ashamed to care for the acquisition of wealth and for reputation and honor, when you neither care nor take thought for wisdom and truth and the perfection of your soul?' And if any of you argues the point, and says he does care, I shall not let him go at once, nor shall I go away, but I shall question and examine and cross-examine him; and if I find that he does not possess virtue, but says he does, I shall rebuke him for scorning the things that are of most importance and caring more for what is of less worth. This I shall do to whomever I meet, young and old, foreigner and citizen, but most to the citizens, inasmuch as you are more nearly related to me. For know that the God commands me to do this, and I believe that no greater good ever came to pass in the city than my service to the God. For I go about doing nothing else than urging you, young and old, not to care for your persons or your property more than for the perfection of your souls, or even so much; and I tell you that virtue does not come from money, but from virtue comes money and all other good things to man, both to the individual and to the state. If by saying these things I corrupt the youth, these things must be injurious; but if anyone asserts that I say other things than these, he says what is untrue. Therefore, I say to you, men of Athens, either do as Anytus tells you, or not, and either acquit me, or not, knowing that I shall not change my conduct even if I am to die many times over."

There were many votes for his acquittal, and the president of the tribunal asked Socrates to name his own punishment. This he refused to do because it was tantamount to saying that he was guilty. In his simplicity he said that he should be given a seat at the president's table and honored by the men of Athens, and if to discharge the penalty of the law it was necessary to pay some penalty, he suggested for the amount thirty minae. This made his judges furious, and many in the second vote turned against him. However, he should have been taken seriously. The proposals were not uttered ironically but were the expression of the simple-minded man that he was. The world today would applaud had his judges pronounced a favorable verdict.

Socrates' last days were spent in prison, where he discoursed with his friends upon virtue and the immortality of the soul. On the day of his death he did not defer taking the fatal cup[7] until the sunset hour,[8] lest it be thought that he was attached to life, but drank it sooner. Thus he died, passing with serenity into eternity. The life of the greatest moral teacher of the age had ended.[9]

One is not likely to overestimate the influence of Greek religious and philosophic thought upon subsequent generations, not only in Greek cities but notably in Rome and Alexandria. Its germinating ideas bore fruit in both Jewish and Greek circles. One has only to mention such names as Philo and Justin Martyr to recall the indebtedness of the intellectuals to Hellenic ideas.

Thoughtful men in every age have recognized the moral vitality of the great Greek poets.[10] The sublime death of Socrates, the ethics of Plato, the logic of Aristotle, have commanded universal admiration. Philo, who saw inspiration in the writings of Greek philosophers and who sought to synthetize Platonic and Hebrew thought, spoke for the liberally-minded Jews of every age who felt the impact of Hellenic ideas.

While the diffusion of Greek culture penetrated Asia as well as lands bordering on the Mediterranean, its philosophy was less congenial to the Asiatic temper than to the Occidental. We must reserve for a later chapter a more detailed discussion of the leavening of society through the spread of Greek cult and thought.

SUPPLEMENTARY READING

G. W. Botsford, *Hellenic Civilization,* pp. 31-35.
W. T Stace, *Critical History of Greek Philosophy,* Chapter X.

---

[7] A poison concocted from hemlock bark.
[8] This was permitted.
[9] The year was 399 B. C.
[10] C. F. Lavell, *Biography of the Greek People,* p. 119. Houghton Mifflin Co.

J. A. Symonds, *Studies of the Greek Poets,* Vols. I, II. Chapters
on Pindar, Aeschylus, Sophocles and Euripides.

For English translations of Greek dramas: *Agamemnon,* by
Cookson; *Antigone,* by Way or Whitelaw; *Medea,* by Way or
Murray; also the collection in The Modern Library.

PART V

THE CONQUEST OF IDEAS

CHAPTER XXXII

THE HYMN BOOK OF THE SECOND TEMPLE

WHEN the exiles returned from Babylon, they found their city in ruins. The task of restoring Jerusalem by building homes for themselves and a central sanctuary with protecting walls for their city and Temple was a long and laborious one, frequently interrupted by lack of funds and conflicts with a people who had been residents in the land during the exile. The conflict is described in the book of Nehemiah.

The beginning of the erection of the Temple was in 520 B. C., about eighteen years after Cyrus had published the edict which permitted the exiles to leave Babylon. Inasmuch as their return was gradual, by stages, and the immediate necessity was to find shelter for themselves, they do not seem to have been dilatory in the erection of the Temple, though Haggai and Zechariah, postexilic prophets, appear to think so.

Darius was now the ruler of Persia. He controlled his vast dominions by dividing the territory into provinces and governing them by Persian officials. While the religion of Persia was Zoroastrian, and the Persian governors worshipers of Ahura Mazda, no objection was raised if the people of a particular province desired to keep their own cult and erect for the purpose suitable temples.

The Jews returned to Jerusalem to find that they were no longer a political entity but a church. Such voice as they might exert in state affairs must be through the high priest, a functionary probably unknown in pre-exilic days, but now the established political and ecclesiastical head. Both in the Persian and Greek periods he was the appointee of the ruler and responsible to him for the conduct of his people and the collection of revenue. In course of time he was of great influence in religious matters as the head of the priestly aristocracy.

The new Temple built on the ancient site was laid out in generous proportions. It was designed for liturgical worship and not merely a place for the sacrificial cult. The Temple was the center of Jewish life. One can hardly open the Psalter at random without finding references to the devotion inspired by the sanctuary. It is the dwelling place of the Most High, and to his service the people are summoned not only to bring sacrificial offerings but hymns of praise. The liturgical Temple service which at this time had its greatest period of development doubtless checked the legalism which was fostered by those who stressed as most important the sacrificial cult.

The development of the Temple service, requiring as it did religious songs, led to what was perhaps the earliest collection in the Psalter. The songs in the collection had been written in pre-exilic times, the oldest going back to the time of David. There was much encouragement given to the writing of new songs, and probably many of the psalms in the fourth book of the Psalter belong to the period just following the exile. It is appropriate, therefore, to speak of the Psalter as the hymn book of the second Temple, if we understand by this that it contains also hymns of an earlier and later date.

The Revised Version of the Bible, following an ancient classification, divides the Psalter, or "Praise Book," into five groups, each ending with a doxology, namely, 1-41; 42-72; 73-89; 90-106; 107-150. These groups, or books as they are termed, seem to follow a historical and doctrinal development, though one cannot stress this because of the exceptions to any general classification. One can see that many of the psalms in the first three groups are pre-exilic, that those which show disfavor of sacrificial offerings are pre-exilic and prophetic. The glorification of the law, and the references to the three annual pilgrimages to Jerusalem to observe the feasts, are certainly postexilic.

Inasmuch as the Psalms are for the most part lyric poetry of a high order, it will add to our understanding and pleasure in reading them if we consider the characteristics of Hebrew verse.

ORIGIN AND FORM OF HEBREW POETRY

The Hebrews, like other nations, early expressed themselves in verse. Their poetry was sung or recited long before it was put into writing. Most of it was lost but some was embedded in the early narratives and has survived. These precious examples of the beginning of literary expression reflect, as we might expect, their desert origin. The twin curses of the desert, as we know, are famine and war. Thus the songs celebrate the findings of springs in an arid waste, or victories in war, or threats of vengeance.

The form the early poetry took reminds us of our own early verse in which repetition was the dominant quality:

> "Old King Cole was a merry old soul,
> A merry old soul was he."

But while Western nations very soon secured rhythm through measured lines, and continued to find satisfaction in assonance, the Hebrews kept to their early poetical forms, the chief of which was thought or sense rhythm. This has been called parallelism. It is the most striking and constant feature of their poetry. It is "the art of saying a beautiful thing over and over again." Of course, Hebrew poetry has other characteristics: the use of accented syllables, a changed order of words, occasional rhyme and the use of words which in their sound convey the meaning.

There are four varieties of parallelism, the wise distribution of which saves a poem from monotony. The first is known as synonymous or exact, and is the usual form of Hebrew poetry.

> "Bless the Lord, O my soul,
> And all that is within me bless his holy name" (103. 1).

While the words in the second line are different, the thought is unchanged.

A second kind of parallelism is known as antithetic because a contrast is presented:

> "Weeping may tarry for the night
> But joy cometh in the morning" (30. 5).

Here we have a double contrast between weeping and joy, between night and morning.

There is a third variety of parallelism in which the second line completes the first by stating a comparison, a reason, a motive or a consequence. This is known as the synthetic form or progressive parallelism.

"As the mountains are round about Jerusalem,
So the Lord is round about his people
From this time forth and forever more" (125. 2).

Here the couplet is replaced by a verse of three lines known as the trystich. In the second line we have a comparison, and in the third something added to complete the thought. The verse is also an example of the fourth kind of parallelism, the climactic, for the thought is not completed until we come to the end of the third line.

Hebrew poetry found within the Bible has a limited range. It is almost exclusively lyric and gnomic. Lyric poetry is the expression of emotion, whether joy or sorrow. The poet cares or complains; he hopes or despairs; he exults and repents. He is intensely personal.

Gnomic poetry, on the other hand, deals with the external world. It consists of observations on human life and conduct. It is didactic, aiming to instruct readers about the whole of life. Generally speaking, we may say that the psalms are lyrical, while the wisdom poetry, Proverbs, Ecclesiastes and Job, is gnomic.

A better classification than the artificial group system in the Revised Version would be a division of psalms according to their subject matter. The psalms are most frequently songs of praise and thanksgiving. Occasionally they express care and complaint, penitence and passion. There are psalms bearing upon human conduct, psalms which celebrate great occasions—a victory, a marriage, the return of the exiles, a pilgrimage to Jerusalem. There are other psalms showing God in the sanctuary, in the storm, in human life; the psalmist delights in dwelling upon the goodness of God, his forgiveness, his care. Especially noteworthy are the psalms which show the true sacrifice, a broken and a contrite heart.

The authorship of most of the psalms is anonymous. They are popularly assigned to David, but he probably wrote only two or three at the most.[1] Ewald attributes twelve to him, but Driver and Cheyne think the number is less. The titles of the Psalter do not help us, for they do not belong to the psalm proper but are late additions on the part of an editor or collector.

If we assume that the earliest psalms are Davidic and the last belonging to the Maccabean period, the collection as we now have it covers a period of eight hundred years.

The translations of the psalms have been for the most part excellent. When versified, as in modern versions, they are easily read and memorized. The essential poetical form of Hebrew poetry which, as we have seen, is parallelism, is easily kept in translation, a great asset for a literature designed for world-wide use.[2]

The psalms are of universal interest. Publishers frequently bind the Psalter with the New Testament, thus uniting the devotional literature of the Old Testament with the Gospels and the history of the Christian Church. The experiences common to human life and dear to the individual are depicted in the book of which Heine has well said: "In them we find sunrise and sunset, birth and death, promise and fulfillment, in short, the whole drama of human life."

Above all, the psalms are poetry, not because of the parallelism of lines, or accented syllables, but because they speak the language of the soul. In the psalms we perceive the beating of the nation's heart, the cry of the penitent, the ecstasy of the mystic, and the patriot's passionate desire.

Supplementary Reading

E. C. Baldwin, *Types of Literature in the Old Testament,* Chapter V.

J. A. Bewer, *Literature of the Old Testament,* Chapter XX.

John P. Peters, *The Religion of the Hebrews,* Chapter I, p. 29f.

[1] See Chap. XVI.
[2] Irving Wood, *The Bible as Literature,* p. 160. Abingdon Press.

Laura H. Wild, *Literary Guide to the Bible,* Chapter XXII.
Wood and Grant, *The Bible as Literature,* Chapters XXI, XXII.
Prothero's "Psalms in Human Life," in Everyman's Library,
    illustrates the influence of psalms in the history of the church.
Biblical Selections, Psalms 42, 46, 19, 29, 137, 139.

CHAPTER XXXIII

THE BOOK OF JOB

A Dramatic Poem

TRANSITION. During the postexilic period the literature produced by certain Jewish writers reflected the changed viewpoint of many thoughtful men, who were dissatisfied with the traditional acceptance of ancient beliefs. One of these writings, the book of Job, appeared about 400 B. C., a second, the book of Ecclesiastes, was written two hundred years later. While their contents are greatly dissimilar, they have this in common, that they express the eager, almost passionate inquiry of men who are concerned with the fundamental questions, Why do good men suffer? Does life have any meaning? Will death end all? The traditionalist had an answer, but it failed to satisfy the authors, so we have their books, the nearest approach to rational inquiry which we find in the Old Testament.

One writing, the book of Ecclesiastes, shows traces of Greek influence in diction and thought. Both have affinity with questioning souls of every age and race. Job in his defiance of God is the Hebrew Prometheus.

The book of Job is a poem, a dramatic poem, great not only among the books of the Old Testament but as one of the important pieces of writing in the world's literature. The poem is in the form of a symposium in which one debater finds himself pitted against three. In the construction of the poem we find the chief speaker, Job, answered by his adversaries in turn, Job speaking alternately. The subject of the debate is the eternal question, Why do the righteous suffer?

But before the curtain rises upon the debaters there is a prologue. We can imagine someone coming in front of the curtain and telling a story, a very old story, the scene of which is located in Arabia and the characters non-Jewish.

The recountal is told in prose and is related with naïveté. There are four scenes in the prologue, two located on earth and two in heaven. The chief character, of course, is Job, a rich but righteous man, prosperous in all that he does, having a large family and enjoying the comforts and the peace which we always associate with a well-ordered life.[1]

Now, it happens, so the tale runs, that on a certain day Satan appeared amidst the sons of God, that is, the angels. This is not the Satan of the New Testament but an adversary. According to the partially formulated idea of the personification of evil, Satan is a Mephistopheles, a cynic. The Lord inquires of him where he has been and he answers, "From roaming the earth and from going to and fro therein."

And the Lord said to Satan, "Have you noticed my servant Job, that there is none like him in the earth, a man perfect and upright, who fears God and shuns wickedness?"[2]

Satan replies, "This is true, but if the man had been visited by trouble instead of leading a sheltered life, he, like others, would curse God to his face."[3]

Then the test follows. Job for the time being is given over to the power of Satan, who destroys his property, puts his servants to death, and even accomplishes the death of Job's children, and yet in all this Job preserves his equanimity and sins neither in deed nor in word.[4]

Again the scene changes to heaven and Satan also is numbered among the hosts of God. He owns that he has been defeated in his purpose but says that if Job is attacked in his person, "if the skin beneath the skin is made raw and bleeding, then he will curse you to your face."

And the Lord said to Satan, "Behold, he is in your power; but preserve his life."[5]

Then follows the account of the suffering of Job from a form of leprosy, perhaps elephantiasis. He departs from home and his estate to an ash heap, where he seeks to find some relief from the suffering which torments him. His friends, Eliphaz, Bildad, and Zophar, come from their

[1] 1. 1-5.
[2] 1. 6-8.
[3] 1. 9-11.
[4] 1. 13-22.
[5] 2. 1-6.

Arabian homes to condole with him and to comfort him. For seven days silence reigns and Job remains outwardly calm.[6]

Now, if we had the folklore story alone, we should decide with tradition that Job was the most patient of men,[7] but when the curtain rises upon the drama with the opening stanzas of the poem, Job is anything but a patient man. He curses the day which saw his birth, the night in which his parents conceived him. Moreover, the figure of Satan which appears in the prologue is not named in the debate. He is not once cited as a cause of the sufferings which afflict man.

It is apparent to even casual readers that the prologue serves the purpose of introducing the characters of the drama; that while its premises are carried to no conclusion, they serve as a background to the subject matter of the debate, not without some changes, for these men who debate this question are moderns. They are quite skeptical as to the Jewish orthodoxy of earlier days which purported to teach, do good and you will be happy and prosperous; do wrong and you will be punished. It is obvious that we must use the prologue for the study of the poem but not depend too much upon it, for its preconceptions do not govern in their entirety the group who take part in this debate.

The reader of the poem is impressed by the language employed, particularly the striking and forceful metaphors, also by the construction of the poem which is easily followed except for two or three passages which seem to have been erroneously ascribed to Job, and should be more properly put in the mouth of one of his protagonists. But chiefly are we impressed with the thoroughgoing treatment of one of the most serious problems of human life. If one believes that God is omnipotent and can prevent suffering, if we believe that he is merciful and compassionate and presumably desires to remain so, then why do the innocent suffer?

In their approach to this problem we must not expect Orientals to debate like men of a Western nation. They delight in repetition and their approach is varied. The drama concerns the struggle of a human soul who is torn by con-

---

[6] 2. 7-13.
[7] Compare 1. 21, 22; 2. 9, 10 with 3. 1f.; 6. 1-4, 11.

flict, not knowing which of several courses to follow. Genung has called the poem "The Epic of the Inner Life."

In the first speech of Eliphaz, he advances three arguments to account for Job's suffering. He says, "I have observed that those who plow iniquity and sow trouble reap the same."[8] Again he tells us that suffering is inevitable:

"But man is born unto trouble,
As the sparks fly upward."[9]

And again he speaks of the disciplinary character of suffering:

"Behold, happy is the man whom God correcteth:
Therefore despise not thou the chastening of the Almighty;
For he maketh sore, and bindeth up;
He woundeth, and his hands make whole."[10]

In the other speeches there is very little advance upon these arguments.

It is to be observed that as Job grows more bitter and his misery is enhanced, his so-called friends on their part grow more intense and violent in their denunciation. The suffering which Elihu declared first to be disciplinary he afterwards affirms to be punitive. It seemed to his friends that Job's constant affirmation of his innocence, and his blasphemy of God are proofs of his wickedness.

Job prays for death, not by way of compensation for he has no hope for a future life. We find him, indeed, saying,

"If a man die shall he live again?
All the days of my warfare would I wait
Till my release should come."[11]

In the famous passage of 19. 25, 26 (see marginal reading), there is hope of a Vindicator, someone who in a future day will affirm that Job had been right. It is to be observed that the vindication of posterity ordinarily has been the only comfort which persecuted men have found.

[8] 4. 8.
[9] 5. 7.
[10] 5. 17, 18.
[11] 14. 14.

Does the book offer any solution of the problem? Yes, in part but not altogether. It is as if we had a picture puzzle and in the end had fitted most parts of the puzzle in their proper position but there still remained some pieces for which we could find no place. The contention of his friends that evil is rewarded by evil is probably true of ninety per cent of the sufferings that mankind endures. Much of the evil that men suffer could have been prevented either by themselves or by others, and they need not place the blame at the door of God or of his arch Adversary. It is also true that for the innocent as well as for the evildoer suffering is disciplinary. The writer of the Epistle of the Hebrews informs us that Christ was made perfect through suffering. Most men, looking back over a life varied by pleasure and pain, have regarded the latter as disciplinary, something which they could not very well have done without.

Moreover, it is true that suffering is inevitable, that it is so real a part of human life that no one can escape it. This seems to be the view of many modern writers in which they expound the doctrine of contrast. We find, they affirm, both good and evil in life, and the latter exists only that it may be cast down. John Fiske lays great stress upon the argument that we cannot know good save as we find it contrasted with evil, that a world in which there would not be sin and suffering is unthinkable. So the old Puritan divines argued, finding both in this world and in the future the contrast between evil and good, between light and darkness. This, as the reader will perceive, is ethical dualism.

New Testament writers solve the problem by arguing that the compensations of the future life are sufficient to meet all the ills of this life and more.[12]

But even so, many minds feel that the problem is insoluble, and the best position to assume is that found in the correct understanding of Job, chapters 38 to 41, in which we are taught that a man's attitude toward suffering should be one of faith. "Trust God, see all, nor be afraid."

Did the poem of Job originally close with the concluding

---

[12] 2 Corinthians 4. 17; Romans 8. 18.

verse of chapter 31—"The words of Job are ended"? If
we are to follow Morris Jastrow in believing that the book
terminated at this point, then the speeches of Elihu, chapters 32-37; the voice out of the whirlwind, chapters 38-41;
and the epilogue, chapter 42, are all added, which accentuates
the view that the argument originally was inconclusive and
that the book ended with a question mark.

It is difficult to decide. Apparently, the speeches of Elihu
might be omitted without doing any real harm to the book.
He advances nothing new by way of argument. He does
develop the idea of the disciplinary character of suffering.
But the case is different with "the Voice out of the whirlwind."[13] It seems that we have here a real solution. The
mystery of pain is a part of the larger mystery of life. One
loses the thought of his own suffering in the contemplation
of nature which often consoles and heals. It will be recalled
that David Copperfield after the death of his young wife
found comfort from his grief in the mountains of Switzer-
land. He lost sight of his own sufferings in the contemplation of the universe. Most English poets, like Wordsworth,
for example, have emphasized this view.

The epilogue is a conclusion not of the poem but of the
prologue.[14] Both the prologue and the epilogue must be
taken together and regarded as a setting for the poem itself.
Doubtless the author, if we can assign the artistry of the
whole to one person, left the folklore story largely as he
found it. It was enough that it should be a setting for the
jewel, the dramatic poem, to which the book of Job owes its
chief interest.

ANALYSIS OF THE BOOK OF JOB

Chapters 1-2   The Prologue in Four Scenes prefaced by
an account of Job's wealth. (a) The Prosperity
of Job.
(b) Satan challenges God to deprive Job of his
wealth.

---
[13] 38. 1f.
[14] 42. 7-17.

(c) Job remains unmoved by misfortune.
(d) Satan again challenges God, this time urging physical misfortune.
(e) Job still patient in his affliction.

The Structure of the Poem
Chapters 3-31   The Debate

Chapter

3 Introductory—Job speaks.
4-14 Eliphaz begins and Job ends the first cycle.
15-21 Eliphaz begins and Job ends the second cycle.
22-31 Eliphaz begins and Job ends the third cycle. Zophar's speech is missed in the third round. May not some words attributed to Job be Zophar's?
32-37 Added speeches of Elihu.
38-41 The Voice out of the Whirlwind—A Nature Poem.
42 Conclusion 1-6 Job's repentance.
7-17 Epilogue.

SUPPLEMENTARY READING

E. C. Baldwin, *Types of Literature in the Old Testament,* Chapter IX.
J. A. Bewer, *Literature of the Old Testament,* pp. 316ff.
T. K. Cheyne, *Job and Solomon.*
Morris Jastrow, Jr., *The Book of Job.*
John P. Peters, *The Religion of the Hebrews,* Chapter XXII.
Henry P. Smith, *Religion of Israel,* Chapter XVI.
Wood and Grant, *The Bible as Literature,* Chapter XXIV.

CHAPTER XXXIV

A SKEPTIC DISCUSSES THE MEANING OF LIFE

THE FASCINATION OF THE BOOK

THE book of Ecclesiastes is the most fascinating writing in the Old Testament. Its interest lies in its veiled meanings and in its unusual character. It follows no model. It is not written in biblical Hebrew, nor are its ideas those of other Old-Testament writers. It resembles the essay and has been classified as such. It is the only book in the Bible where we find a downright denial of immortality. It is unique in its insistence upon present pleasure as legitimate good. It is the only book in either the Old or New Testament to deny the belief that life has meaning and purpose.

In spite of its unorthodox character, or because of it, the book has had a multitude of readers. Its phraseology is so frequently employed by writers that one suspects it to be the Bible of literary men. A modern writer publishes a novel under the title, *The Sun Also Rises*,[1] and Thackeray's *Vanity Fair* owes its suggestive name to an episode in *Pilgrim's Progress,* inspired no doubt by the language of Ecclesiastes.[2]

The book is very quotable. On the south wall of a well-known college building is an inscription, "Whatsoever thy hand findeth to do, do it with thy might."[3] Who has not felt the mockery of "Vanity of vanities; all is vanity"? or the futility expressed in "There is nothing new under the sun"?[4] Or heard of the publisher's lament, "Of making many books there is no end," or the student's complaint, "Much study is weariness of the flesh";[5] or the proverb, "The race is not to the swift, nor the battle to the strong;"[6] or the solemn word uttered at the grave, "The dust returneth

---

[1] I. 5.
[2] 12. 7.
[3] 9. 10.

[4] I. 9.
[5] 12. 12.
[6] 9. 11.

to the earth as it was, and the spirit returneth to God who gave it"?[7]

THE AUTHOR

The writer is unknown. To be sure, he speaks of himself in chapters one and two as "The son of David, king of Jerusalem," but no one is misled. The author is not Solomon, but someone using a *nom de plume,* which is permissible, if it serves his purpose. He proposes to dramatically present the varied experiences of life, and he can best do this under the character of one whom tradition depicted as having great wealth and unlimited means of enjoyment. But after the second chapter, he drops his mask and speaks of himself as "The Preacher," or, if the word is left untranslated, as Koheleth.

There are other grounds for assuming a non-Solomonic authorship. It is in decadent Hebrew, which a scholar would no more confuse with the language of Solomon's day, than we would confuse the verse of Kipling with the poetry of Chaucer. "To say that the Hebrew of the book of Ecclesiastes was written in the tenth century is to deny that the Hebrew language has a history." Moreover, the allusions to rulers[8] and contemporaneous events, the decidedly Greek flavor of the book places it in the third century before Christ or the beginning of the second. This is more important than it seems, for the correct dating of the book gives us a clue to its interpretation.

It was a time of political unrest. Palestine was an apple of discord, equally desired by the Greek rulers of Syria and Egypt. The Ptolemaic rule had been on the whole benevolent. Now a change of masters was imminent. They were taxed to the limit of their endurance. Is it strange that a work produced in such a period should be tinged with pessimism?

Greek ideas were widely diffused. Three schools of philosophic thought had their adherents in Jerusalem—the Stoics, who said, "No pleasure"; the Hedonists, who urged,

[7] 12. 7.
[8] 4. 13; 9. 13-15; 10. 7, 16-20.

"All the pleasure you want"; and the Epicureans, who tempered pleasure with moderation. It is not difficult to see which school the author prefers. There is a vein of Epicureanism running through his book.

It was a questioning age. However much the three schools, which are referred to, differed in particulars, they were of one mind in denying immortality. The early Hebrew writers had been vague on this point, like the early Greeks and the Babylonians. They believed in survival after death, but the soul merely exists. Their concept did not include the idea of punishment and rewards.

There was probably at that time in Jerusalem a small party which had been influenced by the doctrines of Zoroaster or the mystery cults of Greece.[9] Their tenets included a belief in judgment and a future life of punishment or bliss. It was to these that Koheleth directed his remarks in the famous passage which runs: "Who knoweth the spirit of man whether it goeth upward, and the spirit of the beast, whether it goeth downward to the earth?" "All go unto one place. All are of the dust, and all turn to dust again."[10] "For there is no work, nor device, nor knowledge, nor wisdom in the grave whither thou goest."[11] "But the dead know not anything, neither have they any more a reward."[12] If we are inclined to blame the author overmuch for his skepticism concerning the future, we should remember that he was denying what no early Hebrew had asserted. Nor should we expect in Koheleth the faith of those to whom Christ brought "light and immortality through the gospel."

We may regard the author of our book as a man somewhat past the prime of life, viewing from the vantage point of age and varied experience the facts of contemporary life. Considering the troubled age in which he lived, the prevailing skepticism, and experiences through which he had passed, we must grant him a view of life somewhat tinged with cynicism. On the other hand, he is not a satirist like Lucian nor does he display the cynicism of Heine nor the unbelief of Voltaire. His use of the name of God twenty-seven times

[9] Or by Egyptian thought.
[10] 3. 20, 21.
[11] 9. 10.
[12] 9. 5.

in the brief limits of his book should teach us something. If he is a cynic, he is what Morris Jastrow has called him, "a gentle cynic."

His philosophy of life challenges the reader at three points —his complete denial of a future life, his insistence upon pleasure as a present good, and his reiterated statement that life has no meaning nor purpose. It seems clear that Koheleth thought the second and third affirmations were corollaries of the first.

In his denial of immortality he is too dogmatic. Less than a century later a Hebrew writer explicitly affirmed what Koheleth had flatly denied.[13] Another hundred years and the author of the Wisdom of Solomon leaves nothing unsaid in his clear, unequivocal affirmation of life after death.[14]

Koheleth, because of his disbelief in immortality, insists upon pleasure as a present good. Too soon the curtain of oblivion like night shall fall. Therefore, enjoy life. "I know that there is nothing better for men than to rejoice and to do good so long as they live." "Go thy way, eat thy bread with joy, and drink thy wine with a merry heart. . . ."[15] "Rejoice, O young man, in thy youth, and let thy heart cheer thee."[16] It should be noted that the writer is not speaking of sensual joys, "the madness and folly" to which he alludes in the second chapter as being a phase of some early experience.[17] The pleasures he has in mind are innocent enough, they are joys common in human life, but it is his insistence upon their importance that makes one feel something to be wanting in a philosophy which makes pleasure its central idea.

His second corollary, that life so far as man can understand it has no meaning nor purpose, seems to grow out of his idea that death ends all. Such reasoning will be vigorously challenged by many moderns, but it is to be remembered that this is commonly the way men have argued. Impressed by the brevity of life, humans seem to them to be bubbles floating on the stream of time. They reason,

---

[13] Daniel 12. 3.
[14] Wisdom of Solomon, Chap. 3.
[15] 3. 12; 9. 7.
[16] 11. 9.
[17] 2. 12.

because the individual life seldom enjoys fulfillment, that no meaning can be attached to it. There is no plan. "Time and chance happeneth to all alike," writes Koheleth.[18]

It is not his only approach to the oft-repeated assertion that life is meaningless. He looks about him, and in nature sees only tiresome repetition. "One generation goeth and another generation cometh. . . . The sun also ariseth and the sun goeth down. . . . All the rivers run into the sea, yet the sea is not full; unto the place whither the rivers go, thither they go again. Is there anything of which men can say, 'This is new'? There is nothing new under the sun."[19] That is to say, there is no progress. Nature presents only a merry-go-round. Everything returns to the place from which it started.

Here Koheleth is confuting his own philosophy. Unwittingly he has criticized the law of uniformity in nature, always a stabilizing force. That the sun will certainly rise tomorrow impresses us not as a wearisome repetition but as a ground for renewed confidence.

Positive Values in Koheleth

Now, it will be asked, if these adverse criticisms of the philosophy of the writer are justified, what contribution has he made to give his book its reputation of excellence? Why do modern writers generally approve the action of a Jewish council in Palestine which ended three centuries of stormy debate by including Koheleth in the fellowship of Old-Testament writers?

There are positive moral values in the writing, and chief among them the author's recognition of the beautiful. How sweeping his generalization. "Everything is beautiful in its season," although in keeping with his pessimism he adds, "But God has so veiled man's vision that he cannot understand the purpose and meaning of life!"[20] Does that matter? Suppose we cannot understand the meaning of this kaleido-

---

[18] 9. 2, 11.
[19] I. 4-10.
[20] 3. 11. Author's translation. Cf. T. K. Cheyne, *Job and Solomon*, p. 210, footnote.

scopic, topsy-turvy world or embrace in one view the whole design, we can perceive beauty in its several parts. Perhaps this, after all, is what Koheleth means to say: Everything is beautiful in its season, although God has limited man's vision so that he cannot see the meaning and purpose of it all.

BEAUTY IN LIFE

Of one thing we are certain—that there is beauty in the design. So Koheleth in his day. So we in ours. Here skeptic and believer agree; here the modern and the ancient clasp hands. Of what is he thinking—the procession of the seasons, the pomp and glory of midsummer, the gorgeous coloring of autumn, the piled-up snows of winter, the vernal beauty to follow? Surely, "He hath made everything beautiful in its season."

Is he thinking of the beauty of the world about us? So varied, so intricate, so complete, that it defies description? Of that he could not have been unaware.

WORK

A second positive value in Koheleth is the emphasis he places upon work. He seems, like Carlyle and a good many others, to have hit upon the cure of despondency. The Englishman writes: "Blessed is the man who has found his work! Let him seek no other blessedness."[21] To Koheleth work is both an end in itself and a means of enjoyment. This is what he tells us!

"Go thy way, eat thy bread with joy and drink with merry heart thy wine, for already God hath accepted thy works [labors]. Let thy garments be always white and let not thy head lack oil. Live joyfully with the wife whom thou lovest all the days of thy life of vanity, . . . for that is thy portion in life, and in thy labor wherein thou laborest under the sun. Whatsoever thy hand findeth to do, do it with thy might; for there is no work nor device nor knowledge nor wisdom in Sheol whither thou goest."[22]

Evidently, Koheleth does not believe in deferred dividends.

---

[21] See *Sartor Resartus*, Bk. II, Chap. X.
[22] 9. 7-10.

Enjoyment is due now, and is the profit of labor. His cheerful counsel is continued in chapter eleven, where one is advised to invest widely with a view to the future, though immediate gain cannot be had. The investor is not to put all his eggs in one basket, at least that seems to be the meaning of 11. 2, while verse 6, "In the morning sow thy seed, and in the evening withhold not thy hand, for thou knowest not which shall prosper, whether this or that, or both alike shall prove good," has had universal acceptance.

Koheleth has performed an important service in exploding the shams that were prevalent in his day. Apparently, he does not share the favored nation idea which we meet so frequently in Old-Testament writings. By not so much as one word does he indicate sympathy with the intense nationalistic spirit common to Jews in every age. There is a universalism in his book which is like a breath of fresh air.

He is cynical when he comments upon the wisdom writers whose dictum was, Be good and you will be rewarded. According to Koheleth's observations the fate accorded to a wicked man extolled beyond the grave should have been the lot of the righteous.[23] Again we hear him say, almost bitterly, "The wise man dieth as the fool. . . . As it happeneth to the fool, so will it happen even to me."[24]

The pretenses of philosophy seem to him quite hollow. Undoubtedly in Koheleth's day Greek learning was at a low ebb. He would have subscribed with grim humor to the Persian poet's quatrain:

> "Myself when young did eagerly frequent
> Doctor and Saint, and heard great argument
> About it and about: but evermore
> Came out by the same door as in I went."[25]

He takes a fling at the pretenses of religion. He hated sham and hypocrisy wherever he found it, but especially in the Temple. He speaks of the sacrifices of fools; and says that it is better to hear (as one does in the synagogue) than

[23] 8. 10.
[24] 2. 15, 16.
[25] *Rubaiyat,* stanza 27.

to offer vain sacrifice in the Temple. He reverences God "who is in heaven," and counsels those that would approach him to let their words be few. He does not object to vows but feels that it is better never to have vowed than to vow and break. In all this he is constructive in so far as he can persuade men to adopt a true way of life.

Ecclesiastes Accepted

The history of the book has been rather remarkable. It was not at first regarded as canonical; that is, it was not numbered among the collection of Old-Testament books, probably because of its unorthodox character. But in 90 A. D. the Jewish council in Jamnia accepted the writing and placed upon it their seal of approval. It is extremely doubtful whether our Lord and his disciples even knew the book. Certainly, they would not accept its philosophy nor a teaching which denied the future life. The council undoubtedly was influenced by its supposed Solomonic authorship and the emendations of the text made by editors, who had been careful to correct as far as possible the heterodox statements. Moreover, the Jewish tendency to allegorize which was copied later by the Christian Church made the book acceptable in those parts which otherwise interpreted would have led to its rejection. In the sixteenth century we find Luther denying its Solomonic authorship—a view which was confirmed by Grotius in the seventeenth century and most modern scholars. The rejection of its early date paved the way for an interpretation of the book which has been as fruitful as it has been illuminating.

Supplementary Reading

Lyman Abbott, *Life and Literature of the Ancient Hebrews,* pp. 292-293.
E. C. Baldwin, *Types of Literature in the Old Testament,* Chapter VIII.
J. A. Bewer, *Literature of the Old Testament,* pp. 330-339.
T. K. Cheyne, *Job and Solomon,* p. 179ff.
Morris Jastrow, Jr., *The Gentle Cynic.*
Wood and Grant, *The Bible as Literature,* Chapter XXV.
Encyclopedia Britannica, article on "Ecclesiastes."

CHAPTER XXXV

HELLENISM AND THE MACCABEAN UPRISING

TRANSITION. The fourth century in Greece was quite as remarkable as the great fifth century had been. Not so many names were added to the lists of the immortals, but it left three which shone with undimmed luster long after the men who bore them had passed away—Plato, Aristotle, and Alexander.

Each was a pioneer, Plato, introducing men to the new world of Ideas; Aristotle, discovering for them the secrets of the universe, so far as the tangible and the real could be known; and Alexander, penetrating a vast continent with a conquest which was not only military but political and social.

Plato, it will be recalled, was the teacher of Aristotle and bequeathed to him the latter's eager interest in ethics and government. Alexander, who had the rare good fortune to be the pupil of Aristotle, never lost his interest in scientific inquiry. Thus a tradition was furthered, making us conscious of the bond that united the three, their spiritual kinship in fact.

It does not fall within the compass of the present work to discuss their philosophy or the impact of their personality upon their own time and subsequent generations. It can hardly be overestimated. The philosophy of Plato, which brought to fruition the germinating ideas of the noblest Greek thought; Aristotle's matter-of-fact, realistic attitude toward the universe, coupled with an admirable scientific technique; the wise statesmanship which characterized the Asiatic career of the youthful Alexander, each affords a field of inquiry which has not been exhausted after twenty-three centuries.

THE HELLENISTIC AGE

With the death of Alexander the Hellenic period came to an end, and the Hellenistic age was ushered in. The transition was gradual. The historian is unable to arbitrarily assign limits to the period, but finds it convenient to regard it as lying between Alexander's conquest of Asia and the establishment of the Roman Empire.[1]

"The word 'Hellenistic,' " writes Tarn, "is a convenient label for the civilization of three centuries during which Greek culture radiated far from the homeland." In important respects, it is a continuation of Hellenic culture, but greatly modified by new conditions.

"The Hellenistic age has been treated as a wayside inn, where the historical student on his way from Athens or Sparta to Rome is obliged to halt for a few tedious hours."[2] On the contrary, the period was extraordinarily interesting and vital. Even Rome was Hellenized to a great extent. Alexander the Great wrought the miracle of changing the course of history, at least of breaking its continuity.

It was an age of achievement. In scientific discovery,[3] in literature,[4] in government,[5] notable advance was made. Philosophy flourished in schools which had been transferred from Athens to Alexandria. Stoicism exercised a restraining influence in conduct, and there was much in its metaphysics to commend it to the minds of thoughtful men. The Alexandrian philosophers long before Philo might have boasted, "We have Plato with us."

Its architecture was flamboyant but expressed itself in new and lovely forms. Every Greek city had its temples and monuments which recalled the Athens of Pericles. A certain decline in taste was compensated for by the prodigality and opulence of this age of builders.

---

[1] The genius of certain phenomena of Hellenism begins to appear before Alexander. Hellenism continues after Augustus, but we may appropriately place the limits as Alexander's death, 323 B. C., and Augustus' establishment of the Roman Empire in 31 B. C. W. W. Tarn, *Hellenistic Civilization,* pp. 1, 2. Edw. Arnold & Co.

[2] Quoted from J. B. Bury, *Hellenistic Age,* p. 1. Cambridge University Press.

[3] Aristarchus of Samos (290-260 B. C.) hit upon the truth of the solar system. Perhaps he was not the first. "To establish priority in discovery is as difficult as it was for the lame man to get into the pool of Bethesda" (J. B. Bury, *Hellenistic Age,* Essay 1, p. 16). Cambridge University Press.

[4] Meleager, Lucian, Timon, Theocritus.

[5] Namely, city-states.

Sculpture, measured by the severe classic standards of the great fifth century in Athens, had deteriorated, but we are not to forget the Venus de Milo, or other lovely creations which belong to the Hellenistic age. It was not a period of decay but of growth. A certain rankness would, of course, be exhibited in the teeming opulent productiveness of life at this time.

Much has been said concerning the decay of morals. But how far is this true? Cannot one see with equal clarity of view the emergence of religious instincts and emotions which balance the erotic element in its literature? No sweeping generalization can be made of the times. There were too many cross currents and eddies in the stream of social life to speak definitely of decadence.

ALEXANDER'S INFLUENCE

In our appraisal of Alexander's career, it must be conceded that his dream of a great empire was unfulfilled. Asia was too vast, too loosely knit together, its various peoples too alien to Greek thought to form a political entity. His aim to marry the West and the East also proved abortive. He took as his wife Roxana, an Asiatic princess, his generals and captains took the daughters of nobility, and his common soldiers, women of their class, but nothing permanent came of these unions. A child was born to Roxana and Alexander, but we hear little about him save that he bears his father's name.

However, there is another side of the picture. Alexander gave a powerful impetus to Hellenism. He carried Greek civilization to every country he visited—he built roads, established the Greek form of government, spread the knowledge of Greek language, of Greek customs and religion. After him was named a Mediterranean port, Alexandria, important even in our day.

Alexander was no military adventurer. He was not actuated by lust of conquest. If he seems inordinately ambitious, it is in order to carry Greek culture to a world without it. One should contrast the dream of Alexander with Napoleon's

avarice for France, who plundered every European capital
for the enrichment of his own, while the Macedonian gave
the world the riches which Greece had to offer. It should
be remarked in this connection that Zeno (301 B. C.) dreamed
of world unity, to which he gave the term "cosmopolitanism."
After Alexander's death, the empire he had founded fell to
his generals. A popular report had it, that when the commander upon his death bed was asked to designate his successor, he said, "The empire goes to the best man." The
incident is probably legendary, but one feels that Alexander
might have said it.

Ptolemy chose Egypt. It was a wise selection, for the
territory was relatively small, readily defended, and im-
mensely productive. Concerning the disposition of the remaining territory there was violent dispute during the following twenty years, terminating in a settlement which gave
Antigonus Macedonia and the quasi government of Greece,
while Seleucis took Syria and other Asiatic countries, an area
extending to the Indus. Such an unwieldy state could be
governed only with the greatest difficulty. Seleucis chose,
therefore, several capitals—Sardis for Asia Minor, Antioch
for Syria, Babylon, which he renamed Seleucia, for the East,
finding it necessary to live for a time in each.

In 301 Palestine fell to Ptolemy. Its importance to Egypt
lay in the fact that trade routes from the Nile country to the
east traversed this narrow strip of country on the Mediterranean coast. On the other hand, Palestine adjoined Syria
and its natural boundaries made it one with the Seleucid
territory. While Seleucis I, who owed his life and kingdom
to Ptolemy, could offer no objection to the latter's claim, there
is no doubt as to the hostile feeling of his successors. But
it fell out that Palestine continued an Egyptian dependency
through the third century.[6] In 198 B. C. a decisive battle
between the Ptolemaic and Seleucid armies gave the victory
to Antiochus III.[7] It would seem that the Jews welcomed
a change of masters. The writer of Ecclesiastes speaks of

[6] W. W. Tarn, *Hellenistic Civilization*, p. 167; Bevan, *Jerusalem Under the High Priests*, pp. 28-29.
[7] Died in the spring of 183 B. C., and was succeeded by Seleucis IV.

him as the "high-born king," but Polybius states that the common people favored Egypt.

ESTIMATE OF ANTIOCHUS

In 175 B. C. Antiochus IV, surnamed Epiphanes, came to the throne. In many respects he was an able ruler. He had learned statecraft in Rome, where he was detained as a hostage. He was an Athenian citizen, passionately devoted to all things Greek. In his character he exhibited the qualities of the age in which he lived. He was versatile, passionate, good-humored when things pleased him, swift to act, astute and far-seeing under a dissembling which misled his critics. He was uniformly successful in his military campaigns. His interference with the affairs of Egypt reveal this at least, that he was inordinately ambitious. Here he was checked by Rome. It is said that the envoy who brought him word that the Senate would not tolerate his presence in Egypt drew in the sand a circle and told him to make his decision before he stepped outside of it. Antiochus prudently withdrew, and concentrated his efforts upon the consolidation of Syria and Palestine. This is sufficient reason for his aggressive Hellenistic program in the last-named country.

He does not seem to have stirred up resentment for the first seven years of his reign. It was about 167 when he undertook measures which fanned a revolt. Antiochus had taken the title of Epiphanes, meaning "illustrious." In common with kings before him and afterward, he believed in the divine prerogative of monarchs. He regarded as treasonable the Jewish opposition to measures by which he sought to unify the state, and we need feel no surprise that he dealt promptly and energetically with those who opposed his choice of Menelaus as high priest. There does not seem to be evidence of corruption in the appointment. Menelaus was of priestly lineage. As a Hellenistic Jew he would carry out his measures.

That Antiochus was cruel, unwise, and intolerant in demanding tolerance there is no doubt. He was perhaps fanatical, but he was not mad. Those who derided his pretensions or felt the whip of his scorn would change his name from Epiphanes to Epimanes, or madman. But one should not take too seriously a play upon words. Bevan thinks there may have been in a nature so highly emotional as that of Antiochus a strain of insanity, but his caprices can be accounted for on other grounds.

The common view of Antiochus is based on Jewish records. The book of Daniel in the canonical writings and First and Second Maccabees in the Apocrypha have nothing to say in his favor. Nor should we expect it from such sources. But a modern writer must estimate dispassionately the character and activities of Epiphanes.

THE MACCABEAN UPRISING

From the writer of First and Second Maccabees we gather that the Syrian king, frustrated in his plans for capturing Egypt, through the opposition of Rome, vented his wrath upon the Jews. What he had been unable to gain by persuasion he meant to accomplish by compulsion. He forbade worship on the Sabbath and mothers to circumcise their sons. The frequent sacrifice of unclean animals, like the pig on an altar of Zeus, awakened and intensified resentment. The height of Antiochus' folly was reached when he entered the Temple in Jerusalem and thus profaned it. The feeling of hostility long pent up had its first outbreak at Modein, a little village sixteen miles northwest of Jerusalem. A priest, Mattathias, angry with a Syrian official and the Jew who assisted him in offering an offensive sacrifice, slew both, destroyed the altar, and then with his sons fled to the mountains. The country in the vicinity of Jerusalem afforded plenty of opportunity for hiding and for the guerrilla warfare which they pursued. They were joined by many Jews who felt as they, and when finally they met the Syrian army they were, though greatly outnumbered, a formidable foe. Judas Maccabeus, the son who succeeded his father, was in command at this battle, fought near Emmaus. He thoroughly routed the Syrian force, followed up the advantage gained by other victories and triumphantly entered Jerusalem December 25, 165 B. C. It was a day long remembered, for then Judas purified the Temple and rededicated it.

There were setbacks after these first successes. Demetrius had seized the Syrian throne following the death of Antiochus IV, and put a large force into the field to contest Judas. The Jews were frightened at the size of the army and deserted in considerable numbers. Only a handful of faithful followers remained loyal to the end and with Judas perished.

Whether Judas Maccabeus deserves the laudation he has received is doubtful. That he was an excellent soldier, courageous, devout, one can well believe. But the tradition that he appealed to Rome for its interference in the affairs of Palestine is not to his credit. Moreover, it is hard to understand the defection of the Chasidim, who were lukewarm even to the extent of deserting his cause, unless Judas had forfeited their regard.[8] One thing is certain—he threw himself wholeheartedly and heroically into the task of liberating an oppressed people. His death after nine years of incessant struggle was the fitting crown for what men hold most dear.

He was succeeded by Jonathan, surnamed "the diplomat," who secured through negotiation what he most desired, and who was not averse to supporting any claimant to the Syrian throne who would promote his interests. We find him intriguing with Alexander Balas, a low pretender, against Demetrius. Later he is on the side of Demetrius II, but when the promises made to him do not materialize, he passes swiftly over to the side of Antiochus, the son of Alexander Balas. In the end he became the civil and ecclesiastical head of the enlarged Judean state. However, Tryphon, prime minister to Antiochus, thought he was a dangerous man to have around, and treacherously murdered him.[9]

Simon distinguished himself by his fair administration, the expulsion of the Syrians from the citadel, and the

---

[8] See remarks of Edwyn Robert Bevan, *Jerusalem Under the High Priests.* Edw. Arnold & Co.
[9] 1 Maccabees 13. 23.

rebuilding of the fortifications. By a popular vote he was made high priest forever, that is, the office was to be a hereditary right, "until a trustworthy prophet shall arise."[10]

His one surviving son, John Hyrcanus, took office upon Simon's death. As to the unscrupulousness of his character and the infamy of many of his official acts there can be no question. It was he who ordered the burning of the Samaritan temple on Mount Gerizim; who after he had conquered the Idumeans forcibly circumcized them. When we remember that from these Idumeans came the detested ruler Herod, we perceive the irony in this summary act, by which a people not Jews were compelled to become such. Had John Hyrcanus lived a few years longer, he would have seen his chickens coming home to roost. He died in 104 B. C., leaving the administration of his affairs to his wife and giving his oldest son, Aristobulus, the office of high priest. This did not satisfy the latter, who promptly shut up his mother in prison and left her there to starve to death while he kept his three brothers in bonds, finally killing one of them. During his brief reign he arrogated to himself the title of king.

The details of the reigns of his successors need not detain us. It is sufficient to say that the government of the Maccabees had sunk to the depth of a common Oriental despotism, eventually leading to the interference of Rome in the person of Pompey. Once more the Jews changed masters and entered upon the closing period of their national life. But the change was political merely, not social nor religious.

Supplementary Reading

Edwyn Robert Bevan, *Jerusalem Under the High Priests*.
Carl Clemen, *Religions of the World*, pp. 207-216.
W. O. E. Oesterley, *History of Israel*, Vol. II, Chapter XIII.
Henry P. Smith, *Old Testament History*, Chapter XIX.
W. W. Tarn, *Hellenistic Civilization*, Chapter VI.
Apocrypha, 1 and 2 Maccabees.
Hellenistic Age, essays by Bury, Bevan, Barber.

[10] A Messianic reference.

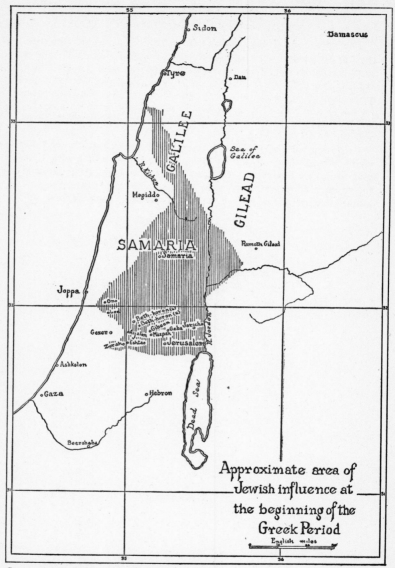

Approximate area of
Jewish influence at
the beginning of the
Greek Period

English miles

Courtesy of the Oxford University Press

ADDITIONAL NOTE TO CHAPTER XXXV

The spread of Greek culture commenced long before the Hellenistic age, when the Greeks settled in western Asia, Sicily, and southern Italy. It could never have been difficult for mariners from either the east or west coast to reach opposite shores. On quiet days in summer one can row across the Aegean from one island to another. No doubt the *Iliad* was a historical episode, and reflects the early colonization of the country around Troy and the resistance encountered.

Professor Sukenik, of the University of Jerusalem, showed the writer Greek inscriptions of the sixth century B. C., which he had found in Palestine. Commenting upon them, he expressed the opinion that the invasion of Asia by Alexander was the culmination of a period which had its beginning long before.

CHAPTER XXXVI

THE FINAL PHASE

TRANSITION. We have seen that the Jews were unable to govern themselves. In seeking religious independence under Judas Maccabeus they gain our sympathy, for it was incredible folly on the part of Antiochus to violate their Temple and trample under what the Jew regarded most sacred. However, we view less sympathetically their aim to establish and maintain a political entity in the midst of warring states. Had they concentrated on the aim of preserving religious freedom, had the religious leaders accepted in general the benefits which accrued from Hellenistic culture, had they cultivated a tolerant spirit, the course of their history might have been far different. As it turned out, their country was wasted by long and ruinous wars; they were miserably governed by their Maccabean rulers, Simon excepted; they were torn by factions. Eventually, there came recovery, but the party divisions remained. We have Hellenists, who hate the orthodox for their narrow, exclusive spirit, and the Chasidim upbraiding the Hellenized for their backsliding, not hesitating to call them renegade Jews. The strife began in pre-Maccabean times, but later was intensified.[1]

THE SPREAD OF GREEK CULTURE

Judas Maccabeus, having secured the religious freedom of the nation, had won for his people all that they as a state governed by a foreign power could reasonably expect. This was perceived by the Chasidim,[2] who soon became lukewarm in their support of the ambitious, politically-minded members of the Maccabean family.

Palestine was girdled with towns, either newly built for Greek occupancy or transformed into Greek centers and

---

[1] Cf. W. O. E. Oesterley, *History of Israel,* Vol. II, p. 315. Oxford Press.
[2] The "Pious."

renamed.[3] There was no reason why all elements in the population should not have been benefited through the spread of Hellenism. Cities were connected by excellent roads, promoting domestic commerce, and arterial highways to ports and neighboring countries advanced foreign trade. The Greek language was the ordinary medium of intercourse and facilitated through literature and public speaking the culture of which the Hellenes were justly proud. Even when the Jews had regained under the Maccabees their political independence, they were unable to vanquish a mode of living which pleased and profited the majority of the people.

THE RISING TIDE OF HELLENISM

The question now arises as to the real extent of Hellenistic influence upon Jewish thought and practice. Could the Jews, living in a world where revolutionary changes, political, social and religious, were taking place, remain so aloof as to be untouched by Hellenism? We have seen that the Jews of the second century in the time of Antiochus IV passionately resisted the encroachments of the Hellenists. But the conflict was restricted to the Judean area and lasted for a relatively short time. Moreover, the Jews of Palestine were of divided opinion, many of them looking favorably upon Greek culture and benefiting themselves by it. These and other factors must be taken into account before we venture upon an answer. Any survey of the Hellenistic age in its bearing upon the Jew must review the policy of the governing power, the social changes, and the evidence in Jewish literature of Greek influence.

THE POLITICAL STATUS

Following close upon Alexander's death, we note the rise of Greek towns in Syria and Palestine. Ancient cities were newly named; others were rebuilt and essentially new. The government was locally administered. The problem which confronted first the Greek and later the Roman power was to conciliate Oriental peoples accustomed to autonomous

---

[3] Particularly in Galilee and to the east of the province, where there were ten Greek towns known collectively as Decapolis.

government with one of central authority. Much had to be conceded to the subject people. Through the medium of the city-state this was effected.

The towns were peopled by colonists from both the west and the east. Macedonian soldiers and Orientals mingled. Jews living in Persia during the beginning of the Greek period moved to Syria and Palestine, occupying the newly built towns and engaged in a flourishing and lucrative commerce.

Social Changes

Both Syria and Palestine were prosperous in the third century, and again in the first. The Ptolemaic rule in Palestine was beneficent, and one has only to read a book like Sirach's, which reflects the social life of 200 B. C. to realize the material prosperity of the period which continued until the Maccabean wars. Nor were conditions different in the revival of trade which occurred in the first century B. C. A hundred years before Christ, Posodonius, a Syrian writer, gives a highly colored picture of the times. "The people of these cities are relieved by the fertility of the soil from a laborious struggle for existence. Life is a continuous series of social festivities. Their gymnasiums they use as baths, where they anoint themselves with costly oils and myrrhs."[4]

Every Greek city had its gymnasium, baths, stadium, and theater. We know that Jewish youth favored the recreations that the Greeks introduced. In the gymnasium the Jew caught the Hellenic enthusiasm for physical beauty. Guilds of youth known as *Epheboi* found the center of their social life here. They participated in the festal processions, wearing the fashionable riding dress of the day—a broad-brimmed hat and the chlamys, an upper garment described as an oblong mantle fastened by a clamp at the front or over the shoulder.

The performances in the theater were not of high order as a rule. The popular taste ran to the *mime,* which were

---

[4] Edwyn Robert Bevan, *Jerusalem Under the High Priests*, p. 41. Edw. Arnold & Co., London.

either spoken or sung. But occasionally, as Shakespeare with us, the plays of the great Greek dramatists were put on.

Hellenism, as Bevan remarks, had its defects.[5] It could and did take on forms which were far from lovely. The religious festivals fostered by the Greeks celebrated their myths, and there is reason to believe that in Syria Hellenism took on baser forms than elsewhere. As to the gymnasia, the hippodromes and theaters, however innocent the ideas connected with their inception, it is quite understandable that degrading exhibitions would take place, revolting alike to noble minds whether Jew or Greek.

The Chasidim could not be expected to condone the amusements which distracted their youth, nor stand as idle spectators while the festal processions which celebrated the Greek gods passed by. But their opposition was an ineffective barrier against the tide of Hellenism. It is difficult to generalize when one writes of a period of three hundred years' duration, marked by many changes. Doubtless, the party of protest and their followers stood more than once irresolute and dismayed. But they continued to be regarded as a stabilizing moral force in the nation. With them were the oracles of God, the race traditions which the Hebrew prized. "If the ideals of the Greek and the Jew conflicted," writes Tarn, "the world needed both."[6]

JEWS OUTSIDE OF JUDEA

We saw that in Jeremiah's day Jewish colonists settled in Egypt.[7] From time to time there were fresh migrations, until the Jews were sufficiently strong to build and maintain a temple at Elephantine on the upper Nile. Subsequently, under Ptolemy I, who favored them, we find them an important element in the population of Alexandria. Here they have the same treatment as that accorded to Macedonians. They did not participate in the government of the city, for that would have involved the recognition of foreign gods.

---

[5] Ibid.
[6] W. W. Tarn, Hellenistic Civilization, p. 181. Edw. Arnold & Co., London.
[7] See Chap. XXV.

Philo tells us that in his day, 30 to 40 A. D., there were a million Jews in Egypt. In Alexandria there was no ghetto, but they congregated in two of the five districts. There was probably a scattering of Jews in the other three. They had their own law courts and seem to have been exempt from Greek jurisdiction. The Greek language was in common use, and so few of the Alexandrian Jews could read the Scriptures in the original language that a demand was made for a translation of the Old Testament into Greek. While there were some orthodox among the Jews of the Dispersion, their guiding, restraining hand was not felt, especially in a cosmopolitan city like Alexandria, where the Hebrew rubbed elbows with men of many nationalities.

Alexandria, because of its favorable location, attracted merchants of many nationalities. It was the center of a flourishing grain trade and the price of its wheat determined the markets of Athens and Rome. But it owes its pre-eminence to culture rather than commerce. Its pride was a library, said to be the finest in the ancient world, and to contain every known Greek writing. Its schools of philo-sophic thought flourished. So did science, mathematics, astronomy.

Greeks and Jews were living and developing culturally in the same world, even as in our day. "There was a body of thought in the air," remarks Tarn, "call it the spirit of the age or what you will, which unconsciously affected men."[8]

Not only the Jew of the Dispersion felt the powerful impulse of the Hellenistic age, but the Jew of Palestine as well. Fresh springs of impulse, the revival of learning, epochal discoveries, engaging pastimes, stimulated and stirred the imagination of men, who felt themselves part of a new or improved society. According to the creed of Hel-lenism all barriers were down. There was to be no race hatred. True, there were blots—slavery, the terrible condi-tions which prevailed in the mines, the rise of tyrants—but on the whole the three centuries of the Hellenistic age made the world a better place in which to live.

---

[8] W. W. Tarn, *Hellenistic Civilization*, p. 185. Edw. Arnold & Co., London.

GREEK INFLUENCE IN LITERATURE

Conditions in Alexandria fostered the growth of literature. It was natural that Jews who were unable to read the Old Testament in the original language should wish to have it translated. This led to the making of the Septuagint, the earliest version of the Jewish Scriptures. In time other Greek translations followed, but the Septuagint was most widely influential. It was this version which our Lord and his disciples read, and from which most New-Testament quotations were taken.

As fast as the Apocryphal books became known, they were translated into Greek, most of them having been written in Hebrew. But not all had a Palestinian origin. Reference has already been made to First and Second Maccabees and to the proverbial wisdom of Ben Sira.[9] The first two are decidedly anti-Hellenistic, the last moderate in tone. The books included in the Apocrypha are Hebraic in style and content. Some show a Pharisaic tendency[10] and others exhibit a leaning toward Hellenism.[11] But when we turn to the Pseudepigraphia, we find ourselves in a different world of thought. Two books in this collection may be cited as influenced by Hellenism, the Fourth Book of Maccabees and the Sibylline Oracles. In each the style and mode of reasoning is Greek. The author of Fourth Maccabees extols the cardinal virtues of the Stoics, reason, courage, temperance and justice;[12] while the writer of the Sibylline Oracles delights in Greek phrasing and diction.[13] Both are classified as apocalyptic writings.

BELIEFS CONCERNING THE FUTURE LIFE

When the Chasidim and their followers felt that their hope of an early restoration of the nation to its former place of power was destined to fail, so far as the expectation rested upon a member of the Maccabean family, they turned

---

[9] Known as Ecclesiasticus.
[10] Judith and Tobit.
[11] Ecclesiasticus and Wisdom.
[12] Fourth Maccabees 1. 18.
[13] Sibylline Oracles, Bk. III, line 121, "the garland-loving Aphrodite."

to another source of help, the direct intervention of God at an indefinite future date. In the establishment of the kingdom of God and the coming Messiah, they hoped to realize all that the prophets had promised. There were undoubtedly stages in the development of this belief which it does not fall within the scope of this chapter to discuss. That the hope was deferred, that it lingered until apostolic times and was shared by the early church is well known.[14] Its immediate result was the diffusion of certain books which might be called "tracts for the times," but which history knows as the apocalyptic writings. Like the last book of the New Testament, to which they bear a close resemblance,[15] they are designed to reveal future events.[16]

Their dogma of the resurrection of the body was Jewish, not Hellenic, for the Greeks believed only in the immortality of the spirit. Some writers[17] question even this, but the mystery cults, the direct statements of Socrates, the implied teaching of Plato, and even Homer, constitute weighty evidence against the view that to the Greek immortality was only a remembrance.

A Jew of Alexandria whose name is unknown wrote during the first century B. C. a book called the Wisdom of Solomon, in which he sets forth current ideas on immortality. The writing has a decided Greek flavor and the author was undoubtedly a Hellenistic Jew, perhaps a Sadducee who mediated between two groups holding very different views. While he says nothing concerning the resurrection of the body, he is strongly of the opinion that the soul survives death, as the following quotation indicates (2. 1-3. 9):

CONTRASTED VIEWS OF LIFE

For they said within themselves, reasoning not aright,
Short and sorrowful is our life;
And there is no healing when a man cometh to his end,
And none was ever known that gave release from Hades.

---

[14] See Acts 1. 11; 3. 18-21.
[15] The Revelation or Apocalypse of John.
[16] Consult translations in R. H. Charles, *Apocrypha and Pseudepigraphia*. Oxford Press.
[17] W. W. Tarn, *Hellenistic Civilization*.

Because by mere chance were we born.
And hereafter we shall be as though we had never been:
Because the breath in our nostrils is smoke,
And while our heart beateth reason is a spark,
Which being extinguished, the body shall be turned into ashes,
And the spirit shall be dispersed as thin air;
And our name shall be forgotten in time; . . .
Come, therefore, and let us enjoy the good things that *now* are;
And let us use the creation with all our soul as youth's *possession*.
Let us fill ourselves with costly wine and perfumes;
And let no flower of spring pass us by:
Let us crown ourselves with rosebuds, before they be withered:
Let none of us go without his share in our proud revelry:

.   .   .   .

Thus reasoned they, and were led astray;
Nor did they judge that *there is* a prize for blameless souls,[18]
Because God created man for incorruption,
And made him an image of his own proper being;
But the souls of the righteous are in the hand of God,
And no torment shall touch them.
In the eyes of the foolish they seemed to have died;
And their departure was accounted *to be their* hurt,
And their journeying away from us *to be their* ruin:
But they are in peace.
For even if in the sight of men they be punished,
Their hope is full of immortality;
And having borne a little chastening, they shall receive great
    good;
Because God made trial of them, and found them worthy of
    himself.
As gold in the furnace he proved them,
And as a whole burnt offering he accepted them.

The reader will observe that the reward of the righteous,
"the prize for blameless souls," is incorruption or immortality
for which God has created man. The tenses are in the present and the reward immediate. The end of the journey is
peace. Evidently, he is as far from the teaching of the
eschatologists as he is from the doctrine of those Hellenists
who said that death ended all.

---

[18] Note the present tense throughout.

The parallelism of the verse, the sentence constructions, the phrasing, and ordinarily the diction is Hebraic. Even in the translation one cannot miss the Old-Testament sound. On the other hand, the phrase, "Reason is a spark," and the imagery employed in describing those who would use life as a means of enjoyment is Greek.[19] The author may be regarded as one who holds the Platonic view of immortality, but pours the thought into a Semitic mold. Between two groups, one influenced by Zoroastrianism in their speculations about the future, the other denying the soul's survival, he steers the straight course of noble minds in every generation.

POPULAR RELIGION

Stoicism was widely influential in the Hellenistic age. Its lofty code of morals, its concept of God as spirit, and personal according to the common view, was congenial to many educated Jews. Attempts were made by writers like Philo to read into the Old Testament a popular amalgam of Platonism, Neo-Pythagoreanism and Stoicism.[20] The effort was futile, but furnishes evidence of Jewish interest in Greek philosophy. The writer of the fourth Gospel, as the terminology in the first chapter suggests, was not unaffected by the Greek concept of wisdom. Finally, there were ideas which were "in the air," not specifically Stoic or Platonic, but a fusion of both. These gave a content to popular religion.[21]

TWO TYPES OF MIND

While the Jews during the Hellenistic age produced a mass of literature, only a few books had exceptional merit. There was as much difference between the highest and lowest among the Jews as among Greeks. In the later Hellenistic age the east flooded the west with a stream of astrology

---

[19] W. O. E. Oesterley quotes Goodrick's "sober estimate" that the writer of the Book of Wisdom has the philosophy of the market place or that of the lecture room. He adds that what he knew of Aristotle came through the Stoics. *History of Israel*, Vol. II, Chap. XIII, p. 182. Oxford Press.

[20] Edwyn Robert Bevan, *Later Greek Religion*, Introduction, p. 31. E. P. Dutton & Co.

[21] *Ibid.*, p. 27.

and magic. The books which Paul caused to be burned at Ephesus[22] were the property of Jewish exorcists. "It seems strange," remarks Tarn, "that the Jew would reject Greek thought and accept oriental mysticism and magic."

Those to whom the historian refers, citing the reference in Acts, were neither strict Jews nor Hellenists, but a group who sought financial gain by imposing upon the credulity of the populace. Other New-Testament allusions[23] of similar import indicate that magical rites were common, and that the Jews were not exempt from the fascination they exercised. But among educated classes in Jewish populations, broadly speaking, we discern two types of mind, the Pharisaic, which excluded all that was not Jewish, and the Hellenistic, which was broadly tolerant to all creeds. The difference, of course, was more fundamental than that. It concerned creeds and conduct. The meticulous care with which the Pharisees observed the law tended to make them self-righteous and arrogant. So they became in fact as well as name the "separatist" class. Neither Hellenism nor Christianity appealed to them, although they were not indifferent to the material benefits which accrued from the former.

The high-priest party in Jerusalm were Sadducees. Their attitude toward Hellenism, which they favored, brought them into conflict with the Pharisaic group. Too often they were political adventurers, opportunists, and corrupt. This was unfortunate and tended to disparage the movement toward Greek culture. But the advance continued, and in the first century of the Christian era there were many Hellenists among the Jews of Judea, as well as among those of the *Diaspora*. From such, Christianity recruited its Jewish converts, while from the Pharisees it met its chief opposition. It does not, of course, follow that hostility toward Christianity meant antagonism to Greek civilization. Many Sadducees were opposed to the tenets of the Christian faith, and, as we have seen, even the Pharisaic group were affected by the externals of Greek culture. But Hellenism produced the type of mind that could tolerantly, even sympathetically, view

---

[22] Acts 19. 13-19.
[23] Acts 8. 9; 13. 6; 16. 16.

an alien faith, and thus prepared the way for the Christian advance.

SUPPLEMENTARY READING

Edwyn Robert Bevan, *Jerusalem Under the High Priests,* Chapter II.

W. O. E. Oesterley, *History of Israel,* Vol. II, Chapters XIII, XXI.

Henry P. Smith, *Old Testament History,* Chapter XX.

W. W. Tarn, *Hellenistic Civilization,* especially Chapter VI, on "Hellenism and the Jews."

Apocrypha: *Book of Wisdom;* Pseudepigraphia: *Fourth Maccabees,* and *Sibylline Oracles,* R. H. Charles' translation.

Hellenistic Age, essays, Bury, Barber, Bevan, Tarn.

RETROSPECT

MANY factors contributed to the religious and cultural advance of Israel. Those which appear to be of chief importance we have noted in the preceding pages.

We have perceived that the nomadic experience was formative and lasting. Its echoes were heard long after the voice which caused them had died away. Something rich and precious there must have been in this heritage, or it would have been ignored. What was it? In a word, the awareness from the beginning of the supernatural, redeeming life from its dullness and adding to its dignity; a certain fierce independence which the desert had bred in them and every oppression had nourished; a sentiment of the solidarity of the family group which had always been the unit of their communal life.

The Hebrew occupancy of Canaan did not prove to be an unmixed blessing. From their neighbors they learned agriculture and city ways. They were apt pupils and eagerly assimilated both evil and good. But this must be conceded as significant, that the transition changed them from wandering tribesmen to a settled and somewhat stabilized social group, paving the way for national greatness.

The suzerainty of Egypt, the trade relations with that country, and intimate social contacts influenced the Hebrews far more than is generally recognized. There are allusions to this influence in the Scriptures, some clear, some veiled; but if they are to be otherwise interpreted, it is to be remembered that the archaeologist's spade has uncovered in Palestine abundant evidence of objects of Egyptian manufacture, temples erected after the Egyptian manner, and the images of gods whose early home had been the Nile Valley. The evidence is incontrovertible which shows that the Hebrews valued what the oldest civilization of the world had to offer them.

There can be no question about the importance of the

353

Babylonian contact. Their laws governed the civic life of Canaan, their legendary lore, refined of its impurities, enriched the Jewish Scriptures, and their cultic practices modified to suit the race experience of the Hebrews were embodied in Hebraic ritual.

It is not easy to generalize on Greek influence, even in the Hellenistic age when the Jews were in constant contact with it. There are too many eddies and cross-currents in the stream to mislead the investigator. More than once he has seen the chip which he tossed into the river borne by an adverse wind in contrary direction to the flow of the stream. But speaking generally of three centuries of Hellenism, and of all groups, the Jews were benefited culturally in things external and very many gained through Greek contact an enlarged outlook upon life.

However, the Jews are not to be regarded as mere recipients of favors. They borrowed but they also gave. When in the tenth century an Egyptian Pharaoh with his army invaded Palestine, he took from a weak and intimidated king the three hundred golden shields which hung in the armory of Jerusalem. On this same visit the Egyptian left a memorial of himself, a stele of victory, which he hung on the walls of a Megiddo building. The latter, a mutilated fragment, the prized possession of an American university, is significant. It confirms the biblical record of Sheshonk, the invader, who attached Rehoboam's kingdom to his own. It is a symbol of invading, conquering civilizations leaving behind them a writing which we have sought to decipher. But, like the Pharaoh, these civilizations have carried away something priceless, the golden shields of a noble moral code, a sublime faith, and a priceless literature—Israel's bestowment upon mankind.

BIBLIOGRAPHY[1]

Abbott, Lyman, *Life and Literature of the Ancient Hebrews.* Houghton Mifflin Co., 1901.

Bade, W. F., *Old Testament in the Light of Today.* Houghton Mifflin Co., 1915.

Baedeker, Karl, *Egypt and the Sudan.* Scribners, 1929 (Leipzig). *Palestine and Syria.* Scribners, 1912 (Leipzig).

Baldwin, E. C., *Types of Literature in the Old Testament.* Thos. Nelson & Co., 1929. *The Prophets.* Nelson, 1927.

Baikie, James, *History of Egypt,* Vols. I and II. Macmillan, 1929.

Bertholet, Alfred, *A History of Hebrew Civilization.* George G. Harrap & Co., London, 1926.

Bevan, Edwyn Robert, *Jerusalem Under the High Priests,* Arnold (London). *Later Greek Religion,* E. P. Dutton Co., 1927. *The Hellenistic Age,* Cambridge University Press.

Bewer, J. A., *Literature of the Old Testament.* Columbia Press, 1924, 1933.

Botsford, G. W., *Hellenic Civilization.* Columbia Press, 1915.

Breasted, J. H., *Ancient Times.* Ginn & Co., 1916. *Conquest of Civilization,* a library edition of the above. Harpers, 1926. *Development of Religion and Thought,* Scribners, 1912. *Dawn of Conscience.* Scribners, 1933.

Bury, J. B., *Hellenistic Age.* Cambridge University Press, 1925.

Carter, George William, *Zoroastrianism and Judaism.* Richard G. Badger, Publisher, 1918.

Chapman, John Jay, *Lucian, Plato and Greek Morals,* Houghton Mifflin Co.

Charles, R. H., *Apocrypha and Pseudepigraphia,* Vols. I, II. Clarendon Press, 1913.

Cheyne, T. K., *Job and Solomon.* Trench & Co., London, 1887.

Clemen, Carl, *Religions of the World.* Harcourt, Brace & Co., 1931.

Cook, Stanley A., *The Religion of Ancient Palestine.* Oxford, 1925.

Cookson, G. M., *Agamemnon.* Chapman & Hall, Ltd.

---

[1] Only books referred to in the text are listed.

Driver, S. R., *Introduction to the Literature of the Old Testament.* Scribners, 1891.

Erman, Adolf, *Handbook of Egyptian Religion.* Archibald Constable & Co., London, 1912.

Fisher, Clarence S., O.I.C., No. 4, *The Excavation of Armageddon.* University of Chicago Press.

Fleure, H. J., *Corridors of Time.* Yale Press, 1927 (Oxford University Press).

Fowler, H. T., *Origin and Growth of Hebrew Religion.* University of Chicago Press, 1916.

Frazer, Sir John, *The Golden Bough,* Macmillan. *Folklore in the Old Testament.* Macmillan.

Garstang, John, *Joshua and Judges.* Constable (London), 1931.

Gadd, C. H., *History and Monuments of Ur.* Chatto and Windus, London, 1929.

Glanville, S. R. K., *The Egyptians.* A. C. Black, London, 1933.

Glover, T. R., *Progress in Religion.* London Student Christian Movement, 1922.

Grant, Elihu, *People of Palestine.* Lippincott, 1929. *The Bible as Literature,* The Abingdon Press, 1914.

Guy, P. L. O., O.I.C., No. 9, *New Light From Armageddon.* University of Chicago Press.

Hall, H. R., *Ancient History of the Near East.* Methuen & Co., 1927.

Harper, William R., I.C.C., *Amos and Hosea.* Scribners, 1905.

Hooke, S. H., *Myth and Ritual.* Oxford, 1933.

Jackson, A. V. W., *Zoroastrian Studies.* Columbia Press, 1928.

Jastrow, Morris, Jr., *Hebrew and Babylonian Traditions.* Scribners, 1914. *Civilization of Babylonia and Assyria.* Lippincott, 1916. *The Gentle Cynic.* Lippincott, 1921.

Kent, Charles F., *Heroes and Crises.* Scribners, 1908.

Knight, G. A. F., *Nile and Jordan.* James Clarke & Co. (London).

Lavell, C. F., *Biography of the Greek People.* Houghton Mifflin Co., 1934.

Macalister, R. A. S., *History of Civilization in Palestine.* Macmillan, 1912.

Marett, R. R., *The Threshold of Religion.* Macmillan, 1914.

Moore, Clifford H., *The Religious Thought of the Greeks.* Harvard Press, 1916.

Moore, George F., *History of Religions,* Vol. I. Scribners, 1928.

Moulton, James Hope, *Treasure of the Magi.* Oxford Press, 1917.

Olmstead, A. T., *History of Palestine and Syria.* Scribners, 1931.

Oesterley, W. O. E., *History of Israel,* Vols. I, II. Oxford, 1932. *Myth and Ritual,* Essay 6. Oxford University Press, 1933.

Osborn, H. F., *Men of the Old Stone Age.* Scribners, 1916.

Peake, J. H. E., *Corridors of Time.* Yale Press, 1927. (Oxford University Press.)

Peritz, I. J., *Old Testament History.* The Abingdon Press, 1915.

Peters, John P., *The Religion of the Hebrews.* Harvard University Press.

Petrie, William Flinders, *Social Life in Ancient Egypt.* Constable (London), 1923.

Reinach, Solomon, *Orpheus.* Putnam, 1909.

Robinson, T. H., *History of Israel,* Vols. I, II. Oxford University Press, 1932.

Rogers, Robert W., *History of Babylonia and Assyria,* Vols. I, II. The Abingdon Press, 1915.

Sanford, K. S., *First Report of the Prehistoric Expedition,* O.I.C., No. 3. University of Chicago Press.

Shorter, Allan W., *Everyday Life in Ancient Egypt,* Sampson. Low, Marston & Co. (London), 1933. *Introduction to Egyptian Religion.* Macmillan, 1933.

Smith, George Adams, *Historical Geography of the Holy Land.* Harpers. *Jeremiah.* Harpers, 1923. *Book of the Twelve.* Harpers, 1898-99.

Smith, Henry P., *History of Israel.* Scribners, 1914. *Old Testament History.* Scribners, 1903.

Smith, J. M. P., *The Prophets and Their Times.* University of Chicago Press, 1925. *The Old Testament—An American Translation.* University of Chicago Press, 1927.

Smith, William Robertson, *Religion of the Semites* (New Edition). A. C. Black, 1927.

Soares, T. G., *Social Institutions.* The Abingdon Press, 1915.

Soper, Edmund D., *The Religions of Mankind.* The Abingdon Press, 1921.

Sprengling, Martin, O.I.C., No. 12, *The Alphabet, Rise and Development.* University of Chicago Press.

Stace, W. T., *Critical History of Greek Philosophy.* Macmillan, 1920.

Symonds, J. A., *Studies of the Greek Poets,* Vols. I, II. A. C. Black (London), 1902. (Harper & Brothers.)

Tarn, W. W., *Hellenistic Civilization.* Arnold (London), 1927, 1930.

Thomson, J. Arthur, *The Outline of Science.* G. P. Putnam's Sons.

Wallis, Louis, *Sociological Study of the Bible.* University of Chicago Press, 1912.

Weigall, Arthur, *History of the Pharaohs,* two vols. E. P. Dutton & Co.

Wild, Laura H., *Literary Guide to the Bible.* Harpers, 1922.

Wood, Irving F., *The Bible as Literature.* The Abingdon Press, 1914.

Woolley, Sir C. Leonard, *The Sumerians.* Oxford University Press, 1928. *Ur of the Chaldees.* Scribners, 1930. *Ur Excavations,* Vols. I, II. *The Royal Cemetery.* Joint publication of University of Pennsylvania Museum and the British Museum.

GENERAL WORKS

Cambridge Ancient History, Vols. I, II.
Encyclopedia Britannica.
Hastings' Dictionary of the Bible.
Hastings' Encyclopedia of Religion and Ethics.
The Mishnah, tr. by Herbert Dandy. Oxford Press.

PUBLICATIONS

Illustrated London News, Issues for February 8, 1930; November 29, 1930; May 12, 1934.
Oriental Institute Communications, Nos. 3, 4, 9, 12.

INDEX

INDEX

Abraham, 47f., 60, 85, 123
Acheulean, 36
Adonijah, 214
Adonis, Gardens of, 153 (ft. 4)*
Adultery, 70
Aeschylus, 299, 300, 301-303
Ahijah of Shiloh, 214
Ahura Mazda, 271, 311
Akkad, 61, 63, 67
Alexander the Great, 332, 333-335, 343
Alphabet, Canaanites adopt, 155
  diffusion of, 157, 158
  origin of, 157
  Ras Shamra, 158
Al-Ubaid, excavations of, 63
Amenemhet, tomb of, 102
Amenemope, proverbs of, 139
Amenhotep III, 112f.
  his achievements, 113
  his policy, 113
Amenhotep IV (see *Ikhnaton*)
Amon-Ra, displaced by Aton, 115
  incarnate in Pharaoh, 108
  sacred marriage, 100, 101
  same characteristics as Min, 116
  temple of, at Karnak, 100
Amorite, 67, 147, 151
Amos, 217f.
  book of, 221f.
  familiar with nature, 218
  herdsman of Tekoa, 217
  ideal of social justice, 221
  keen insight of, 218
  knowledge of social conditions, 217, 219, 220
  literary ability of, 217, 221
  opposed ritual, 218, 221, 222
  visions of, 221, 222
Anaximander, 294
Anaximines, 294

* ft.—footnote.

Ancestor worship, 51
Animism, 50
Anthropoid apes, 37
Antiochus IV (Epiphanes), 336
  character of, 336f.
  measures of hostility against Jews, 337
Antum, queen of heaven, 69, 246
Anu, Babylonian god of sky, 69
Aphrodite, 281, 292, 303
Apocalypse, 348
Apocalyptic ideas, 274, 348, 349
Apocryphal, 347, 348, 349
Arab (s), 45, 46, 47, 48, 147
  hospitality of, 60
Arabia, 45, 46, 157, 317
Aralu, abode of the dead, 80
Aramaean(s), 47, 123, 147
Aristophanes, 290
Ark, 135f.
  center of Israelite worship, 136
  placed by David in Jerusalem, 173
Artists, in Paleolithic period, 38, 41, 42
Ashera, 48, 153, 155 (ft. 7)
Ashtoreth (see Ashera)
Ashurbanipal, 73, 75, 76, 77
Assyria
  attack Israel, 217, 220, 235f.
  colonists of, 163
  cuneiform writing in, 73-76
  excavations in, 71f.
  library of Ashurbanipal, 73, 75
Assyrians, 217, 218, 219, 220, 230, 233, 234, 238, 243
Astarte, 153, 155, 181, 182
Astrology, 211
Aton
  hymns to, 119, 120
  Sun-god, 115f.
Atonism, 117
Aurignacian, 36, 40, 41

361

INDEX

363

Dionysus, 289, 290, 291
Divination, 210
Dramatists, Greek
Aeschylus, 299, 300, 301-303
Aristophanes, 290
Euripides, 299, 300, 302f.
Sophocles, 299, 300, 301-303
Dreams, 211-212

Ecclesiastes, 324f.
acceptance of, 331
author of, 325
contains Greek ideas, 326
denies immortality, 324, 326, 327
denies life has purpose, 327f.
frequently quoted, 324
late composition, 325
positive values in
beauty in life, 329
work, 329f.
confutes hypocrisy, 330
condemns religious pretense, 330
Ecstatics, 213f., 215
Egypt
climate, earliest time, 86, 87
irrigation, 88
predynastic period, 88-90
topography, 87f.
Egyptians
environment influenced, 91-93
ethical standards of, 103, 104
origin, 90f.
prehistoric, 88-91
Egyptian religion
abode of the dead, 102, 103
belief in immortality, 95, 102, 103
early religious ideas, 91-93, 96, 97
immortality maintained, 103
judgment after death, 103
ka and *ba*, 103
magical ceremonies, 95, 100, 102
multiple gods, 97
myth and ritual, 98-101
symbolism in, 96, 97

tendency toward monotheism, 97, 116
weakness of, 97
Elephantine, temple, 345
Eleusis, 288, 289
Eleusinian mysteries, 289
Elhanan, kills Goliath, 171
Elihu, 320, 322, 323
Elijah, 203, 213, 214, 215
Eliphaz, 318, 320, 323
Elisha, 203, 213, 214, 215
Elohist, 199, 200, 201
Enlil, 64, 69
Epheboi, 343
Ereshigal, goddess of the dead, 80
Euphrates, 61, 84, 85, 123, 147
Euripides, 299, 300, 302f.
Exile(s), 245, 246, 248, 258, 263, 311
postexilic period, 312, 317
Exodus, date of, 124-126
Ezekiel, 248f.
emphasizes ritual, 252f.
inaugural vision, 248
narrowly exclusive, 255
nature of visions, 248, 249
social position of, 248
vision of Temple, 250; of Dry Bones, 251; of Jerusalem restored, 251f.

Fayum basin, 90
Feast of Tents, 165
Fertile Crescent, 46, 47, 145
Fertility cult(s), 155, 166, 223, 224f., 250
Festivals
associated with fertility cults, 166
barley harvest (Passover), 165
Canaanitish and Hebrew, 154, 164f.
feast of tents, 165
feast of weeks, 165
productive of good, 166
Food-gatherers and food-producers, 43

Date Due

MAR 14 '78			
APR 13 '78			
MAY 2 '79			
APR 4 '79			
MAY 15 '79			
MAR 25 '80			
APR 22 '80			
NOV 12 '80			
DEC 10 '80			
APR 1 '81			
APR 22 '81			
MAY 6 '81			
FEB 24 '82			
APR 14 '82			
DEC 16 '87			